Hitler

A *Study in Personality and Politics*

William Carr

S oratory

68 — uses Calic book uncritically
69 purge of civil service — stats
70 exposure Nürnberg 3 laws
71 Kristallnacht figures

Edward Arnold

© William Carr 1978

First published in Great Britain 1978 by
Edward Arnold (Publishers) Ltd, 41 Bedford Square, London WC18 3DQ

Edward Arnold (Australia) Pty Ltd, 80 Waverley Road, Caulfield East, Victoria 3145,
Australia

Edward Arnold, 3 East Read Street, Baltimore, Maryland 21202, USA

First published in paperback, with corrections and minor changes, 1986
Reprinted 1987

British Library Cataloguing in Publication Data

Carr, William, *1921–*
  Hitler: a study in personality and politics.
  1. Hitler, Adolf
  I. Title
  943.086′092′4   DD247.H5

  ISBN 0-7131-6462-X

Printed and bound at The Bath Press, Avon

Contents

The German catastrophe was not only caused by what Hitler made of us, but by what we made of Hitler. Hitler did not come from outside; he was not, as many see him today, a demoniacal beast who seized power by himself. He was the man the German people wanted and the man we made master of our own destiny by our unrestrained glorification of him. For a Hitler only appears in a people which has the desire and the will to have a Hitler. It is a collective failing in us Germans that we give honour to men of extraordinary talents—and no one can deny that Hitler had these talents—and arouse in them the feeling that they are infallible supermen.

Baldur von Schirach, *Ich glaubte an Hitler.*

But it is a horrible and ghastly sight when a great people emasculates itself in favour of a 'great man'; when ideals count for nothing compared with the iron foot on their necks . . . . But one would think there was a very simple and efficacious remedy against this particular form of spiritual debasement: the experience, confirmed on every page of history, that peoples have always to pay very dearly for the actions of the 'great man' . . . . For it is a permanent characteristic of the 'great men' that when the infallible spirit leaves them, they reach out in sheer delight for the more infallible [weapon of] force.

F. Mehring, *Gesammelte Schriften.*

To my daughter Mary Louise

Preface

Another book about Hitler? The question is a very natural one likely to occur to anyone who has watched with growing apprehension the never-ending stream of literature on Hitler pouring forth from the presses in several lands. Hardly a month goes by without some work on Nazi Germany appearing, whether it be a biography of Hitler or some other Nazi leader, a collection of documents or a learned monograph on some aspect of the Third Reich, to say nothing of films and television plays about this period.

It is therefore incumbent upon a writer who persists in entering this highly competitive field, despite the warning notices, to state at the outset what his intentions are. Even though my book ranges pretty widely over Hitler's life from his childhood to his death and touches upon most aspects of his career, let me say at once that it is not intended to be a biographical study. Rather I prefer to describe it as a contribution to the continuing debate about the historical role of Hitler in the National Socialist era.

Broadly speaking, there are two schools of thought on the subject of personality in history. There are those who believe in what might be termed 'the primacy of personality'. For them history is primarily the history of great men and their deeds and the economic and social dimension is never of more than marginal significance in the historical process. Though the traumatic effect of the Second World War and the growth of the social sciences have made serious inroads into this traditionalist position, some of the new Hitler biographies still lay what appears to me to be undue emphasis on the personality of one man in explaining the Nazi phenomenon. Those psychohistorians who have concentrated almost exclusively in their researches on the minutiae of Hitler's idiosyncrasies and on his alleged physical defect also belong in the traditionalist camp—which is not to deny the importance of this new branch of historical study now that it is moving away from its preoccupation with individual pathology and turning more and more to the study of collective phenomena.

Diametrically opposed to the traditionalists are the Marxist historians who believe in what might be termed 'the primacy of impersonal forces'. In their writing Hitler is depicted as a shadowy figure, the helpless puppet of monopoly capitalism, jobbed into power by reactionary forces out to destroy parliamentary democracy and the free trade union movement and prepare Germany for wars of aggression in the interest of the possessing classes. True, there is an element of inconsistency here for, while these historians completely reject the traditionalist explanation of German fascism in terms of the personal power of a malevolent individual who seduced the German people from the paths of righteousness, they are perfectly willing to attribute the fascist phenomenon in large measure to the sinister machinations of a handful of politically-motivated industrialists and landowners. Admittedly, there is an element of distortion in my description of both schools of thought. The most successful biographers have never neglected to place their subjects firmly in the context of their times. And the unhistorical Marxism, which has been reluctant to give proper recognition to the crucial role fascist leaders—like any other group of leaders—play as the executants of the historical process, shows signs of dissolving in the thaw which is moving East and West away from the worst excesses of the Cold War. It may not be too long now before we have at last a biography of Hitler written from a Marxist standpoint.

In this book I have attempted to present Hitler in the light of modern historical science which embraces the totality of historical experience—political, social, economic and cultural history, the investigation of individual pathology and, what is more significant for the historian, the study of the collective psychology of peoples. My concern, in a sentence, is with the interrelationship between the personality of Hitler and those social forces which made National Socialism possible. To the objection that this is not, after all, so far removed from the practice of the best biographers, I would reply that what is implicit in their work is explicit in mine by virtue of the fact that I have concentrated on the specific problem of personality and politics to the exclusion of much that must perforce be included in a biography.

At times it has been difficult not to resist the feeling that I had embarked on a voyage uncertain of my destination and, worse still, in a leaking craft with a faulty compass to guide me and constantly in peril of running aground. This basically for two reasons. In the first place, as this work progressed I have become increasingly conscious of the need for an up-to-date definition of personality. Psychologists have, of course, their (several) definitions. But historians urgently require a definition which will enable them to relate historical personalities in a meaningful fashion to the totality of historical experience in industrialized societies, where the techniques of modern communications and the demands of mass democracy have transformed the functional relationship between leaders and led.[1] Secondly, my terms of reference have obliged me to interest myself in virtually every aspect of life in the Third Reich. And since no one can hope to master the published material or the massive archival deposits in their entirety, I write in the sure and certain knowledge that my book can be no more than a contribution to the continuing debate about Hitler's role in the events of the second quarter of our century.

A word about the structure of the chapters. I commence my examination of Hitler's personality with an analysis of his oratorical gifts, and hopefully set the pattern for the rest of the book by relating his messianic oratory to a specific historical and psychological situation. Later in the first chapter I assess the extent to which other personal qualities helped or hindered his rise to power by studying specific points in his career between 1919 and 1933. In the second chapter, instead of a chronological treatment of Hitler in power, I prefer to concentrate on foreign policy (1933 to 1939), economic policy and the fate of the Jews as three areas for close analysis, in the hope of establishing Hitler's influence on events and, equally important, the extent to which factors external to the man moulded the contours of Nazi policies.

If the first two chapters emphasize on the whole (with significant qualifications in the case of foreign policy) the importance of external factors in shaping the policies of the Third Reich, in the third chapter on Hitler the military leader it may be that I lean too far in the opposite direction. If so, the fault is mine for not stressing strongly enough the political and economic restraints on a supreme commander in wartime. However, I would still defend my view that, within these limits, Hitler did exert major influence on the course of the war. No doubt the Nazi 'new order' would have shared the fate of all tyrannies in the fullness of time. What Hitler did by his personal intervention in the conduct of the war—notably when he resolved to attack Russia before defeating Britain—was hasten the inevitable collapse of the Third Reich.

In chapter 4 Hitler's philosophy of life, his religious opinions and his interest in architecture and Wagner are examined systematically both in order to clarify the concepts and to try to ascertain the relationship between his ideas and his political practice. That the chapter ends with many questions and supplies few answers is a healthy sign in the present state of research and infinitely preferable to the reverse situation. Nor does the final chapter on Hitler's health pretend to solve the riddle. Clarification of his physical and mental state is a major objective in this chapter. But towards the end I am again concerned to emphasize what is for me the crucial point in this book—namely, that the individual pathology of the Führer must be related to the collective psychology of the German people if sense is to be made of the Nazi phenomenon. That this kind of investigation has a wider significance and more immediate relevancy is suggested by the persistence of neo-fascist movements since the last war, slight though their chances of political power may seem to be at this point in time.[2]

Finally, it is a great pleasure to acknowledge my indebtedness to many colleagues who have helped me with this book. I am especially grateful to Dr Wolfgang Michalka of the Historisches Seminar at the Johann Wolfgang Goethe University of Frankfurt who read the book in manuscript form and discussed it with me at great length. The final draft has benefited enormously from his constructive criticism and stimulating comments. I am also indebted to Professor David Milner, Head of the Department of Paediatrics at the University of Sheffield, Emeritus Professor John Pemberton, formerly Head of the Deparment of Social and Preventive Medicine at the Queen's University of Belfast, and Professor Helm Stierlin, Head of the Abteilung für psycho-analytische Grundlagenforschung und Familientherapie at the University of Heidelberg, all of whom read the chapter on Hitler's health and by their comments saved me from several blunders; and to Dr Terry Rick of the Department of Psychology at the University of Sheffield for his expert assistance in identifying several of the many drugs Hitler took. I would like, too, to express my gratitude to Herr Albert Speer who, at short notice, gave generously of his time to discuss Hitler's personality with me.

A word of sincere thanks is due to the many archivists who assisted me over the years: at the Bundesarchiv, Koblenz; the Bundesarchiv-Militärarchiv, Freiburg; the Militärgeschichtliches Forschungsamt, Freiburg; the Haupt-staatsarchiv, Geheimes Staatsarchiv and the Stadtarchiv Munich; the Institut für Zeitgeschichte, Munich; the National Archives, Washington; and the University of Pennsylvania Library, Philadelphia. And a special word of thanks to Mrs G. Johnson, Miss J. Langmaid and Mrs C. Wichmann who presided so graciously over the reading room at the Wiener Library, London, where I spent many hours working on this unique collection of material on the Nazi period. The patience of the publishers in waiting for the manuscript should not go unmentioned either. I am also pleased to acknowledge my thanks to the Research Fund of the University of Sheffield for several grants, to the *Deutscher Akademischer Austauschdienst* for a research scholarship in 1973, and to the British Academy for one grant in 1975. And most of all, I wish to record my deep sense of gratitude to my wife for the unfailing patience and tolerance she has displayed during the long periods when I have neglected her for this book. Without her constant support it would have taken much longer to write and its completion would have given me immeasurably less satisfaction.

Preface to the paperback edition

Since this book was written in the mid-1970s research into National Socialism has continued unabated casting still more light on the dark recesses of the Third Reich. Although I have not modified the main thrust of my argument about Hitler's role in the history of that period, I have here and there in this edition modified my views on particular points. This is most noticeably the case in respect of the origins of the Holocaust where I am now much less persuaded by Martin Broszat's argument in favour of a date in the late autumn of 1941. The balance of the evidence, such as it is, does seem to me to point to an earlier date as Christopher Browning argues convincingly in *The Final Solution and the German Foreign Office* (New York, 1978).[1] Also, I have toned down somewhat the argument I advanced for a non-ideological explanation of German expansionism in the late 1930s and early 1940s as readers of my *Poland to Pearl Harbor: The Making of the Second World War* (1985) will already be aware. My views on Ribbentrop as the advocate of an alternative strategy in 1940 owe much to the doctoral thesis of Wolfgang Michalka now teaching at the Technische Hochschule in Darmstadt. This has now appeared as *Ribbentrop und die deutsche Weltpolitik 1933–1940. Aussenpolitische Konzeptionen und Entscheidungsprozesse im Dritten Reich* (München, 1980). Several works from which I could have profited had they then been in print deserve special mention. On the Second World War in general four volumes of *Das Deutsche Reich und der Zweite Weltkrieg*, an authoritative ten-volume history, written by the historians at the Militärgeschichtliches Forschungsamt in Freiburg, have appeared. Their high quality, and admirable integration of military history with the political and economic background of the period, leave no doubt that this will be an indispensable work of reference. On economic development, Richard Overy has made a significant contribution with *Goering: The 'Iron Man'* (1984). Dr Overy criticizes the whole concept of the limited war or Blitzkrieg as a military–economic strategy and argues strongly that Hitler was, in fact, preparing all along for a long war. Finally, a book full of insight which all students of National Socialism can read with profit is Professor Ian Kershaw's *The Nazi Dictatorship*.

1 See 'A reply to Martain Broszat regarding the origins of the Final Solution', *Simon Wiesenthal Center Annual* 1 1980.

1

The politician, 1919–33

More than thirty years after Adolf Hitler's death in the Berlin bunker, historians still find difficulty in writing dispassionately about a man whose deeds were written in blood across the face of wartime Europe from the Atlantic coastline to the Russian steppes. The crimes for which he and his associates were rightly held responsible still deserve dishonourable mention today in a world grown daily more accustomed to violence and untimely death. No sane person would seek to minimize the enormity of these crimes against humanity, much less deny that Hitler was the prime instigator of the mass murders at the death camps in Eastern Poland despite recent attempts at his rehabilitation.[1] Nevertheless many of those who lived through the tumultuous 1930s will also remember him as the populist orator and firebrand who—so it seemed to the outside world—cast a spell over millions of Germans seeking reassurance at a time of unprecedented crisis, a spell which for many of them was not broken until enemy forces swept into Hitler's Reich in 1945.

By any objective standard Hitler must rank as one of the great orators of history, perhaps the greatest in the twentieth century. Others have surpassed him by the brilliance of their verbal dialectics, many by the originality of their arguments, and nearly all by the broad humanity of their message. Yet surely no one ever mastered the art of public speaking so thoroughly or exploited the shifting moods of audiences with greater skill than Hitler. As this was, perhaps, the most obvious manifestation of the Hitler phenomenon, it would seem an appropriate point at which to commence an examination of his personality.

At the very outset we are confronted by a dense thicket of mythology which has grown up around the person of Adolf Hitler. The popular image familiar to millions through the media of the cinema and television is of a ranting mob orator, a demoniacal figure carried away by the elemental power of his own oratory and utterly incapable of controlling his own emotions. Film extracts from the 1930s have contributed to this false picture by showing Hitler—invariably for a few seconds only—shouting at the top of his voice, gesticulating, head thrown back, eyes raised to heaven, features distorted, sweat pouring down his face and back, his raucous tones reverberating round the hall while a brown-shirted rally responds ecstatically to his unrestrained outpourings. From this picture one is left to infer either that Germans are peculiarly vulnerable to hysterical oratory, or else that Hitler was an unsophisticated rabble-rouser who relied on unusually strong lungs to captivate an audience—or possibly a combination of both.

Almost exactly the reverse is the truth. Sophistication in the use of the techniques of public speaking and care in the preparation of speeches were the hallmarks of his oratory. No one worked harder or in a more calculating manner to win the hearts of an audience. In public he spoke always by design and rarely by accident. His speeches, like those of his great antagonist, Winston Churchill, were always well-structured and thought out in considerable detail. But unlike the generality of German politicians before and after the Third Reich, Hitler did not read out his speeches word for word, or at any rate not in the early years. He was far too astute a psychologist not to appreciate the debilitating effect written perorations have on the rapport between speaker and audience. Having an exceptionally retentive memory, he could convey an impression of spontaneity and freshness however long he spoke, and with no more than a few notes on the rostrum containing key phrases to remind him of the sequence of his argument.

One should remember, too, that Hitler's earliest oratorical triumphs were achieved with a minimum of pageantry. In the early days when he was struggling for recognition, a table top in a beer hall was his only platform, his dress not the ill-fitting brown uniform, ungainly jack boots and unflattering peak cap of later years but the modest nondescript garb of the man in the street—dark suit, white shirt and black tie. In the rough-and-tumble atmosphere of the rowdy Munich beer kellers he proved his mettle as an orator without the pomp and circumstance of later years. He did not rant and rave all the time—a physical impossibility for a man who spoke normally two hours and more—but addressed his audiences in quiet tones at first, even hesitantly, developing his chosen theme with occasional shafts of humour and invariably with lucidity and skill. Unlike many public speakers of those days he could deal expertly with hecklers. During the discussion periods—which in the early days invariably followed his speech—he stood with folded arms listening to opponents before dispatching them with a few well-chosen and sometimes humorous words.[2] Only later did the Brown shirts save him the trouble, though from the start Hitler's audiences were never particularly tolerant and often shouted opponents down.

Hitler took immense pains over the minutiae of his oratory. Take, for example, the extravagant and theatrical gestures at which he excelled—the clenched fists, the admonitory forefinger pointing now at the audience, now heavenwards, and the outstretched arms. Histrionic gestures of this kind were something of a novelty for German audiences; political speakers either did not gesticulate or, if they did, gave little or no thought to the effect of awkward gestures on their audiences. Hitler went to endless trouble over such details. He is said to have studied the technique of Ferdl Weiss, a popular Munich comedian, for capturing the attention of noisy beer-hall crowds before commencing his act. According to Heiden, an early biographer of Hitler, he practised his gestures diligently in front of a mirror in his shabby room in

Munich's Thierschstrasse.[3] He also had the party photographer, Heinrich Hoffmann, snap him in action so that he could study each gesture minutely. Only those passing the most severe scrutiny were employed on public platforms. It was equally characteristic that he studied in great detail the acoustics of the major beer halls in Munich and adjusted the pitch of his voice to suit each one. Once the party grew in size and Hitler was firmly established as leader, he paid much attention to the external trappings of meetings as part of a calculated attempt to heighten the emotional experience and to lower the mental resistance of the audience.

A typical example of the changing style of Hitler's oratory was the Zirkus Krone meeting in March 1927, where he addressed his first public gathering since the removal of the ban on public speaking imposed on him in 1923.[4] As usual he was billed to speak at 8 o'clock in the evening. It was never his practice to appear punctually. Instead he remained in his room pacing up and down going over his speech (usually composed a few hours before). By telephone he kept in touch with the meeting, ringing at frequent intervals to ascertain the size and political complexion of the crowd. By 8.00 the Zirkus Krone was half-full. On the swastika-draped platform a military band was playing the old familiar tunes setting the feet tapping while a sprinkling of uniformed Brownshirts chatted to friends in the audience. At 8.30 Hitler strode in, having delayed long enough to arouse expectancy but not long enough to arouse hostility towards the unpunctual speaker. Greeted with rapturous applause by a crowd of some 8,000, he walked briskly to the platform surrounded by his henchmen. A trumpet sounded and a hush fell on the crowd. Through the hall marched the Brown shirts, preceded by two rows of drummers and by the 'blood flag'—the banner carried in the march to Munich's Feldherrnhalle during the abortive putsch of 1923 and stained with the blood of fallen comrades. The audience greeted the flag with shouts of *Heil* while Hitler stood arm outstretched (a salute he picked up from the Italian fascists) at the rostrum until all were seated. The stage was set; the audience, reassured by the parade of party strength, their emotions aroused by the banners and uniforms, listened to the Führer full of expectancy. With the party firmly established, if only on a local base, Hitler avoided anything likely to fracture the rapport between perspiring orator and ecstatic audience. Discussion time had gone for good, partly because of the intrinsic difficulty of organizing discussion at a mass meeting, but primarily because the Hitler of the late 1920s was consciously cultivating a different public image—that of the Führer rallying the faithful for the long haul ahead, not the agitator goading the masses into rebellion. At the end of the speech, which usually ended in a great emotional crescendo, Hitler strode out theatrically into the night to the thunderous applause of the audience brought to its feet as the band struck up the *Deutschlandlied*.

Once the Nazis were in power the pageantry grew more impressive and ostentatious, culminating in the great party rallies at Nuremberg, the old imperial city and home of Dürer and the Meistersinger. For eight days each year the high drama of the party rally was enacted against the magnificent setting of a medieval town with all the sophisticated paraphernelia of mass propaganda at the organizers' disposal. The meeting of the *Gauleiter* or regional party leaders in the middle of rally week was an excellent example of brilliant staging. Tens of thousands of party members gathered in the evening in the Zeppelinwiese to await the Führer. To the roar of applause and illuminated by a circle of one hundred hidden searchlights, the Führer entered the vast arena. At the head of a procession of high party officials he walked slowly down the steps and up to the tribune to the accompaniment of thunderous applause. When silence fell at last on the arena, thousands of Nazi banners moved forward through the serried ranks while searchlights picked out the golden eagles on the red standards, a superbly impressive setting for the speech that followed.

Yet, when all is said and done, oratory has a gossamer-like magic about it that defies precise analysis. Skilful techniques and a receptive audience are essential ingredients of success but the indispensable element is the personal magnetism of the speaker. Though Hitler clearly experienced great difficulty with ordinary human relationships, was rarely completely at ease outside the immediate circle of party cronies and established few if any intimate relationships, on public occasions and in front of an audience private inhibitions rolled away and he became literally a man transformed. A Hitler speech was superb theatre—at any rate for those who liked old-fashioned melodrama. Hitler was his own script writer, choreographer and actor-manager rolled into one. With uncanny skill he exploited the whole register of human emotions. Contrary to popular belief he did not lack a certain sense of humour either in public or in private; some of the speeches in the late 1920s and early 1930s attacking republican politicians still make entertaining reading provided that one does not lose patience with a speaker whose mordant wit was always at the expense of opponents and never at his own.[5] And however preposterous his premises seem to rational men, it has to be admitted that he could argue a case cleverly and on occasions persuasively.

It would, however, be grossly misleading to suppose that Hitler's speeches were designed primarily to appeal to the intelligence or good humour of his audiences. Nothing could be further from the truth. Hitler's aim in the early years was quite simply to arouse and mobilize the emotions of his audience—the noble and the ignoble alike—as a means of bringing the Nazi Party to power.[6] Whether or not he ever read Gustav Le Bon, there is no doubt that he had a firm grasp of the principles of mass psychology.[7] More than most politicians he was acutely aware that civilization is only skin deep, that primitive emotions lie very close to the surface of ordinary people, and that these instincts can be most effectively manipulated at mass meetings held in the evening when mental resistance is low. As he remarked with revealing candour in a well-known passage in *Mein Kampf*:

> When from his little workshop or big factory in which he [the individual] feels very small, he steps for the first time into a mass meeting and has thousands and thousands of people of the same opinion around him . . . he

is swept away by three or four thousand others into the mighty effect of suggestive intoxication and enthusiasm, when the visible success and agreement of thousands confirm to him the rightness of the new doctrine and for the first time arouse doubt in the truth of his previous conviction—then he himself has succumbed to the magic influence of mass . . . suggestion. The will, the longing, and also the power of thousands are accumulated in every individual. The man who enters such a meeting doubting and wavering leaves it inwardly reinforced: he has become a link in the community.[8]

Hitler's blend of dogmatic assertion, repetition, biting sarcasm and emotional appeal usually did the trick. By the time he reached the end of the two hours' speech, the audience was applauding frequently. Applause, as a contemporary recalled, seemed to inspire a veritable torrent of words in him and his voice rose to a crescendo.[9] Yet always he remained 'ice cold', never carried away by the enthusiasm he engendered. He waved applause down and continued quietly never losing his place, continuing to build up his arguments pyramid-like before the eyes of his audience as his voice moved from *pianissimo* through *fortissimo* to *furioso*. To that extent his speeches were always contrived and never spontaneous. But what really counted was his remarkable ability to persuade an audience that he was in deadly earnest. So when the spellbinder released them, the people streamed homewards—or occasionally marched shoulder to shoulder into the centre of Munich singing patriotic songs and shouting anti-semitic slogans—their prejudices confirmed, their hopes rekindled by a man who identified himself with their fears and aspirations and in masterful fashion promised to realize their deepest desires. As Otto Strasser said of him: 'His words go like an arrow to their target, he touches each private wound on the raw, liberating the unconscious, exposing its innermost aspirations, telling it what it most wants to hear.'[10]

It is surely no accident that Hitler's meetings bore at least a superficial resemblance to revivalist gatherings of the old-fashioned bible-thumping variety, full of fire and brimstone, immortalized in Sinclair Lewis's *Elmer Gantry*. There was the same infectious enthusiasm, the same electrically charged atmosphere, the same extraordinary credulity and the same intensity of feeling welding speaker and audience together in a mystical union.[11] There is much force in the contention that Nazism is only properly intelligible in terms of a pseudo-religion.[12] In an age when faith in transcendental religion was faltering, political creeds were able to mobilize the religious sentiment in man for purely secular goals. In this way nineteenth-century nationalists often made a religion out of their love of the fatherland. In the twentieth century fascists were able to do the same with the concepts of race and war. The elaborate ritual of the Nazi movement, the love of pageantry, the cult of fallen heroes, and the emphasis on the virtue of sacrifice were evidence of the pseudo-religious strain in Nazism which its organizers consciously exploited.[13] When Hitler's speeches are seen in this light, much of what at first seems empty gibberish assumes a new significance. Hitler did not demand of his followers intellectual assent to his propositions but quite simply blind faith in the Führer and readiness to follow him to the bitter end, much as the leader of a chiliastic sect guarantees final victory to all who believe in him regardless of the overwhelming odds against them. Thus, writing of the uphill task facing the party in 1922, Hitler observed: 'If it is impossible then we will attempt it and be defeated; but if it is essential and true then we must believe that it is possible and this faith we do have.'[14] A clearer statement of the belief that faith can move mountains one could not hope for. And this mentality lay at the very heart of Hitler's doctrine. What he invited his audiences to do was reject the reality of the external world, disregard the proof of their own eyes and immerse themselves totally in a dream world which would one day become reality through their faith in him and their own will to victory.[15] For Hitler politics, like Wagnerian opera, was essentially a systematization of illusion to capture the total allegiance of the audience.

What kind of people did Hitler's messianic politics appeal to? Detailed investigation of the composition of the party in the early days is difficult as few membership lists have survived. Such evidence as we possess is somewhat inconclusive and much depends on the social classification one applies. According to the most reliable analysis—based on a fragment of the 1923 membership list—31 per cent of a total of 4,800 members were lower middle class; 13·6 per cent were small businessmen and shopkeepers; 11·1 per cent were clerks; and 6·2 per cent were minor officials. Another 25 per cent might be classified as skilled working class; in this group, craftsmen (*Handwerker*) formed 20 per cent and specialist workers 8·5 per cent Only 9·5 per cent were unskilled working class.[16] And as yet the party had only a limited appeal for the farming community. Clearly the centre of gravity of the Nazi Party on the eve of the 1923 putsch lay fairly and squarely in the lower middle and upper working classes.

These classes are often regarded as the 'natural standard bearers of fascism'. It is argued that after the First World War small businessmen, craftsmen and white-collar workers all over Europe were fearful for their economic future and social status. Poised precariously between proletariat on the one hand and affluent upper middle class on the other, they were in imminent danger—or so they believed—of being ground out of existence between powerful unions and massive industrial combines. Recent research has, however, emphasized the continuing importance of these classes in the 1920s and 1930s in defiance of all Marxist prophecies of their imminent extinction.[17] In 1933 there were still over three million small businessmen in Germany each employing under fifty men and representing a total working force of nine millions. These people, with their economic grievances and their nostalgia for the golden age of prosperity at home and greatness abroad in the days of William II, were potentially a reservoir of support for fascism. Hitler, the son of a minor official sprung from farming stock in Upper Austria, was well placed to articulate the hopes and fears of the lower middle class. That a significant proportion of party activists, among them Goebbels, Himmler, Koch and Bormann, came from this social milieu seems to lend further credence to this argument.

However, one should probably treat with reserve any explanation of fascism which tries to pin down Hitler's followers like butterflies easily identifiable by their bright social and economic markings. For one thing, the vast majority of lower middle-class voters did not support the Nazis but the more respectable right-wing German Nationalists and smaller middle-of-the-road parties throughout the 1920s. Only the Depression made Nazism an attractive proposition for these people. The true complexity of the situation is revealed in Peter Merkl's recent analysis of party attitudes.[18] The sober fact is that a wide spectrum of discontent and frustration—of which economic grievance formed only a relatively small part—attracted people to the party. The lower middle class was not a sharply defined social group whose members reacted uniformly to the same external stimuli but a collection of individuals in a state of social flux. Civil servants and military types, members of the old middle class, white-collar workers and urban craftsmen, each had their own reasons for joining the party. Whether a man was moving up or down the social ladder was another important variable modifying attitudes. Merkl's poineering analysis is significant in another respect. It reveals that only a minority of the original sample of party members was attracted to the party by Hitler's personal charisma, and that only one third of them joined after attending a party meeting—a timely warning, of which more later, that one should not exaggerate the personal influence of Hitler in explaining the growth of the party.[19]

An exception would have to be made here in respect of the influx of young men into the party in the early 1920s. Some were ex-soldiers embittered by defeat and resentful of a world they could not—or would not—understand. Many found temporary employment in the Free Corps fighting the Russians and the Poles but as the situation stabilized found themselves once more at a loose end. Other new members were too young to have fought in the war. But they had been militarized through youth movements during the war, and hoped to find in street brawling the excitement they supposed they had missed in the mud and blood of Flanders.[20] It was Hitler, and also Captain Ernst Roehm, both typical examples of the disoriented ex-soldier, who attracted many of these young men to the Nazi Party where they quickly outnumbered the older members and gave it a youthful profile, bringing the average age down to twenty-eight. As these men were 'used to removing obstacles with hand grenades and pistols',[21] they soon changed the party's image; by 1922 hooliganism and physical attacks on opponents became the distinctive feature of the party with the whole-hearted approval of the leader.[22] These emotionally insecure and paranoid young men were more vulnerable than most to Hitler's personal magnetism and his reckless oratory—expecially that not inconsiderable group which had no front-line experience at all. Hitler offered these people a naively simple explanation of their discontents, a spiritual haven in a hostile world and every encouragement to vent their frustration on Jews,

Marxists, 'November traitors' and other enemies of the fatherland. In innumerable cases these young men repaid him with dog-like devotion for the next twenty years.

It is more difficult to generalize about the audiences Hitler attracted in the early 1930s when the party broke through into national politics. Much work has still to be done on electoral behaviour, and generalizations must remain tentative until we possess a more sensitive picture of regional variations.[23] Still, the broad pattern is clear enough. At no time before or after 1930 did the Nazis make any appreciable inroads into the working-class electorate.[24] Once economic conditions began to deteriorate, the party gained support not in the great cities, generally speaking, but in the countryside and in the small towns. What in the early 1920s had been essentially a cry for help from a small group of frustrated and *déraciné* people on the fringes of the middle class, unable to adjust to military defeat and political change, suddenly became a mass movement as a result of the near collapse of the capitalist system. It is not going too far to say that the farming community and the urban middle class were in the throes of an identity crisis in the early 1930s. Heavy tax burdens, an inability to meet mortgage repayments on farms, shops and small businesses, and the plight of their children no longer able to slip easily into comfortable bourgeois occupations, brought the crisis to flash-point. Economic grievances, though obviously important, were only the ostensible cause of middle-class alienation from the republic. At a deeper level economic grumbles merely sharpened middle-class awareness of the decline in their status since 1914, deepened their resentment at working-class gains since 1918, and made them turn away impatiently from the middle-of-the-road parties and, to a lesser degree, from the German Nationalists, all of whom—as they saw matters—had failed to protect the middle classes. Instead, they threw themselves into the arms of the Nazis who, with their eye on the main chance, were promising to stop the rot and restore the 'backbone of the nation'.[25]

What was it that drew middle-class audiences to Hitler? Certainly not the content of his speeches, full of vague and woolly phraseology and markedly deficient in detailed, let alone credible, policies. Denunciation of the Versailles treaty, rhetorical talk about Germany's future glory, promises of tax reductions and measures to promote agricultural self-sufficiency—all this was commonplace stuff at any right-wing meeting. Hitler made no attempt to explain how an unarmed Germany could achieve any more than Stresemann had already achieved as foreign minister. Hitler's audiences could hear from other right-wing speakers the same vituperation against parliamentary democracy and the same bombastic appeal for a revival of the spirit of 1914, when all classes allegedly closed ranks and became a truly united nation. What was compelling about Hitler and what distinguished his party from other right-wing parties were not only the external trappings—the feverish activity, the endless marching, the mass rallies and the ceaseless propaganda drives—important though these were in gathering in the votes, but above all the ruthless will to victory and the fanatical sense of commitment emanating from the Führer and his followers. When Hitler promised to sweep out 'the old gang' he carried conviction. The old established middle class, frightened by the radicalization of working-class politics implied in the mounting Communist vote, felt instinctively that this man meant what he said: he would destroy Marxism and restore the old values on which the greatness of the pre-war middle class had rested and, in the case of the lower middle and new white-collar middle class, he would confer on them the assured status they had never enjoyed under the republic.

While it would be absurd to suppose that the whole of the German middle class was 'waiting for Godot', nevertheless many of those who thronged to hear Hitler, and other top speakers, were, like many of the Führer's early followers, looking for a faith to sustain them in their hour of crisis. Some at least found in Hitler what they were looking for—a man in whom they could believe. In his presence they could suspend all rational judgment, and wallow in the ecstasy of complete dependence on a messianic figure.[26] Their personal frustrations and fears were suddenly lifted right out of the political arena and acquired cosmic significance as part of the eternal struggle between good and evil, in which man has been involved since the dawn of history. Present suffering and sacrifices for the cause (if they were party members) could be endured as the pledge of future glory in the never-never land of the *Volksgemeinschaft*, or people's state, where national solidarity would prevail over class conflicts. When victory came, the good would be rewarded while the evil ones—principally the Marxists by this time—would be cast out into exterior darkness. Hitler's audiences were not greatly interested in the details of the new Jerusalem where all were promised economic gains, but rather in the assurance of the Führer that victory, when it came, would be final and absolute. Only at this deeper psychological level can one fully comprehend the potential power of Hitler's rhetoric in the 1930s. As a contemporary shrewdly observed: 'Hitler never really made a political speech, only philosophical ones.'[27]

However, to suppose that the German middle classes capitulated to Nazism through one man's diabolical genius or because many of them longed for a father figure, would be a totally inadequate explanation of a complex historical phenomenon. The question that remains, after due weight has been given to the above considerations, is why did the middle classes succumb to fascism only in Germany and not in other advanced industrial countries? The old Marxist contention that it was the general crisis of capitalism which led to the establishment of a National Socialist dictatorship in Germany is, at best, a half-truth. In Britain and in the United States, despite severe economic difficulties, the capitalist system survived intact without recourse to fascism. Are we, then, to conclude that abnormal socio-political conditions in the Anglo-Saxon countries aborted the normal historical process? Or is it not more likely that the German experience was exceptional? For it is undeniable that only in partially-industrialized Italy and in backward eastern and southeastern European countries did fascist-style movements ever come to power, from which one might well conclude, provisionally at any rate, that pre-industrial societies were much more vulnerable to the fascist virus than advanced ones.[28] In the present state of knowledge about the relationship between fascism and capitalism, general theories can offer only limited insights into the National Socialist phenomenon. For more precise guide lines one must look to Germany's past history.

Seen in its historical perspective, Nazism was no temporary aberration, an unforeseen 'factory accident', as some German historians have called it, which distorted the historical process. Equally, it would be a futile exercise to try to force Hitler into a putative line of continuity stretching from Luther through Hegel to William II, in the style of allied wartime propagandists. Continuity carried to these absurd lengths reduces history to a meaningless jumble of events torn out of context, 'a tale of sound and fury signifying nothing'. If, however, we narrow the focus to the history of the last two hundred years, then a case could certainly be made for taking 1848–49 as a turning-point in modern German history, and possibly even for 1789. In fact, many German historians today favour the period between 1871 and 1945 as a meaningful time-scale within which one can comprehend the true historical significance of the National Socialist phenomenon.

Broadly, these historians argue that agrarian-feudal forces, politically on the decline in other lands, remained deeply entrenched in the social and political structure of Bismarck's and William II's Germany because of their dominant role in the unification process. These forces were powerful enough to offer tenacious and effective resistance to pressures for democratization arising out of the rapid industrialization of Germany in the 1880s and 1890s. A state of latent crisis was the result, with anachronistic talk of *coup d'états* to put the clock back running like a red thread throughout this period from Bismarck to Papen. To maintain the balance of power in their hands, as the political struggle deepened with the rise of a Marxist-oriented working-class movement, the agrarian-industrial forces resorted to one expedient after another. Thus Bismarck's campaigns against socialism and Catholicism, the search for overseas possessions, the high seas fleet created by Emperor William II and Admiral von Tirpitz, are seen as examples of 'national concentration' policies, designed to rally middle-class support round the charismatic figure of the emperor in a bid to prevent a pre-revolutionary polarization between middle class and proletariat on the one hand and the agrarian-industrial complex on the other. While it is, to say the least, questionable whether one can interpret the war of 1914 primarily as a last desperate expedient on the part of the German ruling class to escape from an insoluble internal crisis, it cannot be denied that the German people was united in the summer of 1914 to an unprecedented degree. The yawning chasm opening up between ruling class and people was bridged over once German armies started to roll westwards. National solidarity had been achieved temporarily under the shadow of *Blitzkrieg* or 'lightning war'.

In a Germany defeated and humiliated by the Versailles treaty, where the conflict between property-privilege and mass democracy was radicalized first by inflation and then by deflation, it is not surprising that a middle class with little faith in the democratic system should once again demonstrate a preference for a lethal combination of national unity and *Blitzkrieg*. It is surely no coincidence that a Führer cult was emerging in middle-class circles during the First World War, that is quite independently of Hitler—an aspect of the period which would, incidentally, repay closer examination.[29] The charismatic leader who spoke the authentic language of 1914 and propounded a more radical mixture of anti-Marxism, anti-semitism and expansionism to rally the middle class against the enemies of property-privilege represented 'the culmination of all the political aims, economic demands and ideological views existing in Germany since 1866–71'.[30]

There is much one could disagree with in this reinterpretation of German history; some of the assumptions are questionable and many of the generalizations difficult to substantiate.[31] For all that, it is sufficiently plausible to serve as a useful working hypothesis, which will anchor Hitler down firmly to a specific historical epoch and ensure that discussion of his personality does not take place in a historical vacuum but is related to the socio-economic problems peculiar to that stage of historical development.

When Hitler came across the German Workers' Party in September 1919 it was little more than an obscure discussion club, run by a handful of eccentrics meeting in a back street tavern in Munich, and he was only a lowly corporal in the defeated German army. Eighteen months later Hitler had worked himself up to become leader of the newly-formed National Socialist German Workers' Party. After the disastrous putsch of 1923, he returned to the fray, re-formed the party, presided over its breakthrough into national politics in 1930 and led it to final victory three years later, a veritable *tour de force* for a man of obscure origins who entered politics at the age of thirty without previous experience of public life.

Is it legitimate to conclude from the bare facts of this unknown soldier's rise to fame that he was, in the words of the well-worn cliché, 'a born leader of men'? Did he possess in an extraordinary degree qualities which would have enabled him to make a name for himself in any historical epoch? That was by no means the case. Personality has been defined as 'the habitual mode of bringing into harmony the tasks precribed by internal demands and by the external world',[32] a useful enough formula so long as one realizes that 'habitual modes' can change in response to alterations in the nature of the internal demands and external pressures. Personality is a dynamic not a static concept. Burckhardt's celebrated dictum about 'acquiescing, struggling and acting man as he is, and always was, and will be' is unhelpful to the historian precisely because it does not take into account the interdependence of psychological development and socio-economic phenomena.

Hitler's fanaticism is a case in point. His burning sense of mission, unwavering belief in his own star and the uncompromising arrogance with which he habitually expounded his opinions does not add up to a universal recipe for political success. In a stable, relaxed, democratic society, where tolerance and compromise are the hallmarks of the political system, and where passion is harnessed to 'the pursuit of limited objectives,' fanaticism may well be a decided hindrance to a would-be political leader. Everything depends on the ethos of the times. The fact is that Hitler's fanatical and messianic brand of politics stood a greater chance of success in a disturbed country where many were lukewarm in their commitment to democracy than it would in our own age where, until comparatively recently, economic and political problems were widely believed to be manageable by governments, and still are to a degree inconceivable fifty years ago.

Similarly, in respect of Hitler's personal charisma. Not everyone he encountered fell under his spell. Many took an instant dislike to him. But there is no doubt that Hitler did arouse genuine enthusiasm and dog-like devotion in a sufficiently large number of people (not all young by any means) to justify the description 'charismatic leader'. Admittedly, democratic societies throw up charismatic political figures from time to time. But the chances of success for such leaders are proportionately much greater where a sizable minority is looking for a father figure to satisfy emotional lacunae in their own lives. And particularly so when the charismatic leader is a recurring theme in a country's history. Bismarck, William II, Ludendorff and Hitler all represented the factor of 'social integration', each in his own way seeking, with the assistance of bonapartist-plebiscitary methods at home coupled with expansion abroad, to overcome the stagnation and tension in a system deadlocked by antagonistic interests. Because conflict was endemic in the modern German political system, the charismatic leader, the man on the white horse, was always lurking in the wings waiting for 'the bugle call of history'. Thus in 1933 when the Marxists were unable to overthrow the system and the middle class was no longer able to operate it effectively, the demagogue Hitler was allowed to restore the equilibrium by abolishing the system, an outcome which in other advanced countries would probably have led to civil war.

Much the same can be said of Hitler's extraordinary instinct for propaganda. Few men have understood the art of propaganda as well as Hitler or have ever employed it on so massive a scale and with such skill and unscrupulousness. Indeed, it was as a propagandist, the *Trommler zur Deutschheit* or 'drummer to Germanism', that Hitler made his reputation in the party, not as a 'leader of men'. And in the re-formed party of 1925 he continued to exert a major influence over the style and content of propaganda. As a shrewd contemporary once observed: 'Hitler's contribution to the intellectual ingredients of his movement is slight—what he gave it was temperament, the full-blooded devotion of the agitator and its style of propaganda.'[33] What is also apparent is that this type of political evangelism can only be exploited effectively in a society where there are many people incapable of coming to terms with reality, who prefer the incredible myth to the sober truth in their own personal lives as well as in their political fantasies.

Only Hitler's remarkable acumen can really be said to possess any universal validity for the aspiring politician. He was a thoroughly political animal, cunning as a fox, a wily intriguer of Machiavellian proportions, extraordinarily adept at weaving and threading his way through political labyrinths, skilled at delaying difficult decisions and playing for time until his sensitive political antennae detected the chinks in an opponent's armour or until he discovered the appropriate formula for avoiding unwelcome confrontation. All political leaders require these gifts in some measure if they are to survive in the corridors of power. And had Hitler not possessed a delicate political touch, the fissiparous Nazi Party might have fallen apart on more than one occasion. That is not meant to imply that Hitler was never guilty of politically unwise conduct: the putsch of 1923 and his stubborn and unrelenting intransigence at the end of 1932 are only two examples that spring to mind in this context.

Biographers of Hitler have tended at times to overlook those defects in his personality which militated against success in politics. Those who knew him well were aware that the idol of the Munich crowds was in private life a paranoically suspicious, cantankerous and choleric individual extremely sensitive to the slightest criticism. 'Idiot', 'dolt' and 'imbecile' were epithets that fell easily from his lips whenever anyone dared to question the wisdom of his tactics. And associates unwise enough to oppose him consistently soon found themselves the target of utterly unscrupulous campaigns of denigration. Only by completely subordinating their wills to his, could associates in close contact with Hitler survive in the long run. Such behaviour was hardly likely to win for Hitler a wide circle of political friends. And in fact his querulous style was deeply resented by many party comrades in the early days.

The truth is that Hitler had much of the artist in his temperament. His dislike of and avoidance of routine work, his unpunctuality and his reluctance on many occasions to make decisions—unless completely cornered—were infuriating characteristics which drove party officials to distraction. Also his habit of delivering long repetitive monologues (even on social occasions) wearied those unfortunate enough to be trapped into listening to him. Some of the older members were offended by Hitler's partiality for the company of women and by the constant efforts of the 'king of Munich' to ingratiate himself with the social élite of the city. Many were critical of the power exercised by the private entourage Hitler had gathered round himself in the style of an Italian *condottieri* chieftain. Men such as the American-educated art dealer, Putzi Hanfstaengl, the ex-beer hall bouncer, Christian Weber, and the unsavoury ex-Socialist Hermann Esser built a 'chinese wall' round Hitler, flattering him shamelessly, boosting his ego and making him virtually inaccessible for the rank-and-file members.[34] To be sure, a leader's remoteness from the rank and file is the inevitable consequence of a party's expansion. Nevertheless, the belief that Hitler's byzantine court was corrupting him and giving him delusions of grandeur was shared by many in Munich. Although the most fanatical and devoted followers might tolerate this side of Hitler's personality, less committed supporters were bound to see in these character defects an insuperable obstacle to Hitler's political advancement.

In what follows some attempt will be made to examine the development of Hitler's personality with reference to selected points in his career between 1919 and 1933. The points chosen for closer scrutiny are his appointment as virtual dictator of the party in 1921; the abortive putsch of 1923; the re-formation of the Nazi Party in 1925; the leadership crisis of 1925–6 culminating in the Bamberg conference and its aftermath; the referendum on the Young Plan in 1929; and, finally, Hitler's intransigent political line during the second half of 1932 ending in the Strasser crisis.

For convenience, a serious consideration of the contribution made by psychoanalysts towards an understanding of the Hitler phenomenon has been relegated to the final chapter. That does not necessarily mean that the insights psychiatry and social psychology have to offer are of only marginal importance. On the other hand, readers will not find there a Pandora's box full of new perspectives that can solve the riddle once and for all. However exciting these insights are, it would be utterly misleading to pretend that one can, at the end of the day, evaluate the role of personality in historical situations with any pretence at accuracy. Historians do not possess sensitive instruments capable of quantifying the human element and disentangling it from the 'objective' reality of social, economic, political and cultural factors which mould and fashion behavioural patterns. Indeed, it might well be argued that any attempt at quantification, however sophisticated, is bound to distort historical reality by destroying the delicate relationship between the individual and the society of which he is an integral part. Still, imperfect as the tools at our disposal are, there may be some merit in making tentative suggestions about the possible balance between personality and the totality of the historical situation at specific moments in time. It is, at any rate, with this hope in mind that the present writer approaches his task.

Mein Kampf, a revealing record for those interested in Hitler's personal pathology, is grossly misleading as a guide to the rise of National Socialism. Throughout the book Hitler speaks of the early days as a period of unremitting struggle against overwhelming odds. That was largely fabrication. The fact was that exceptionally favourable conditions existed in post-war Bavaria for his inflammatory politics. The people in this Catholic, conservative and particularist corner of Germany had been shocked to the core by events since the armistice. On 7 November 1918 the followers of the Independent Socialist, Kurt Eisner, seized power in Munich, set up workers' and soldiers' councils, deposed the Wittelsbach ruler of Bavaria and proclaimed the republic. Though left-wing Socialists were overwhelmingly defeated in the January 1919 elections, unrest continued after the murder of Eisner by a right-wing extremist in February. Emboldened by the setting up of a soviet republic in Hungary in March, left-wing extremists set up a soviet republic in Munich. Within a few days it was ruthlessly suppressed by army units and Free Corps men led by Colonel Franz Xaver Ritter von Epp. Munich never forgot these experiences. Nothing was ever done by the state authorities to check the mushroom growth of paramilitary bands formed by extremists flocking in to counter-revolutionary Bavaria. The government and Munich army command saw positive advantages in having them around, not to defend Munich against a non-existent 'red threat' but as a reservoir of support for the eagerly-awaited confrontation between 'national' Bavaria and what conservatives regarded as the 'Marxist' government in Berlin. For these reasons revolver-butt politics were allowed to flourish in Munich to an extent quite inconceivable in any other *Land*.[35]

Nor was Hitler fighting a lone battle in the party as he implies. Very soon he gathered round himself a 'kitchen cabinet' of devoted men who contributed much to the growth of his power base in the party. The group included Dietrich Eckart, poet and *bon vivant*, author of the scurrilous periodical *Auf gut deutsch*, who educated Hitler in the social graces and introduced him to influential political circles; Max Erwin von Scheubner-Richter, a well-connected Baltic German and talented fund raiser who brought Hitler into contact with Russian émigrés; Julius Streicher, paranoid anti-semite who led Nuremberg's right-wing hooligans into Hitler's camp; Hermann Esser, the ablest speaker and propagandist in the party second only to Hitler; and most influential of all—though never under Hitler's spell—Ernst Roehm, chief of staff at the Munich military command, a soldier of fortune with a finger in every right-wing intrigue in Bavaria, a manipulator of great ability who kept Hitler in touch with the Reichswehr, or army, supplied the party with funds and introduced many ex-Free Corps men to it. Collectively, these men contributed at least as much if not more than Hitler to the growth of the party.

In the past it has been assumed far too readily that from the moment Hitler joined the German Workers' Party he was consumed with a burning ambition to become dictator of Germany. In a study of major importance Albrecht Tyrell argues that it is a great mistake to attach too much importance to Hitler's post-facto rationalization of his early political career.[36] Is it very likely that a disputatious individual who experienced grave difficulties with personal relationships (as opposed to people in the mass), a chronic procrastinator who had not even sought promotion in the army (or been considered worthy of it) would see himself as the natural leader of a political party much less as the future ruler of Germany? If, on the face of it, this does seem improbable, one must look for a quite different explanation of Hitler's conduct in July 1921.

For several months the party had, reasonably enough, been discussing a merger with other *völkisch* groups, a proposal strongly opposed by Hitler probably because one of the groups—the equally minute German Socialist Party—wanted to take part in local elections. Finally, when the party executive resumed negotiations with these groups during a temporary absence of Hitler's in Berlin and without informing him, he resigned from the party more in a fit of pique than as a carefully-prepared manoeuvre in the power game. Faced with the loss of an illustrious member whose departure would probably split the party asunder, the executive eventually capitulated to his demands. It is interesting to notice in passing that the executive referred to 'his immense knowledge, his services to the growth of the movement carried out with extraordinary self-sacrifice . . . and his extraordinary talent as a speaker' and not specifically to his leadership potential, as the reasons why they considered Hitler indispensable to the party.[37] True, as the price of his return to the fold, Hitler insisted on dictatorial powers to reconstruct the party. Tyrell maintains that this was basically a negative reaction on Hitler's part motivated solely by a wish to prevent the party moving in a direction of which he disapproved. Characteristically, after months of vacillation on this issue, Hitler made his mind up only under the pressure of events. In other words, Hitler became first chairman of the party armed with dictatorial powers as a last resort in order to safeguard his position as 'drummer-in-chief' to the broad nationalist movement and not, as so often alleged, to satisfy an insatiable lust for power. Of course, it may be objected that the distinction between *Trommler* and future Führer was never as clear-cut as Tyrell implies. Nevertheless, this important reinterpretation of Hitler's career in the early 1920s offers a more credible explanation of his motives than we have had before precisely because it pays due regard to the weaknesses as well as the strengths in Hitler's personality.

In the two years between Hitler's appointment as party leader in 1921 and the abortive Beer-Hall putsch of 1923, local, national and international developments contributed much to the rapid growth of the party, probably, on balance, much more than all the rhetoric and propaganda of the new leader. Locally, the continuing indulgence of the authorities enabled the party to conduct a campaign of organized violence against political opponents as the prelude to the 'National Revolution', that is the violent overthrow of the 'Marxist' government in Berlin and its replacement by a nationalist regime, which was the common objective of all right-wing extremists in Bavaria. The difference between the Nazis and other right-wing groups lay not in the final goal but in the superior organization of the Nazis and in the exceptional degree of violence, verbal and physical, they employed against opponents. In August 1921 Hitler chose exactly the right moment to found the party's first paramilitary unit, which at once attracted disgruntled Free Corps men at a loose end since the allied governments had just insisted on the disbandment of the Einwohnerwehr, or citizens' militia, a middle-class body formed in 1919 to preserve public order. The new recruits wielded rubber truncheons and revolver-butts so expertly that by the end of 1921 the brown-shirted storm troopers or SA (Sturmabteilung) were masters of the Munich streets. By 1922 they had extended their disruptive activities into the surrounding countryside going out on weekend maurauding expeditions in the style of the Italian *fascisti*. Open violence against opponents, a feature of Nazism which drew many hooligans into the SA, would simply not have been tolerated without the connivance of the Munich police. In the police president, Ernst Pöhner, and in the head of the political police, Wilhelm Frick, Hitler had the good fortune to find influential middle-class sympathizers ready to turn a blind eye to lawlessness and inflammatory propaganda out of a misguided sense of 'patriotism'.

Nationally, the republic entered a period of unprecedented crisis in 1923. In

January French and Belgian troops occupied the Ruhr to force the Germans to face up to their reparations responsibilities; the German government retaliated with passive resistance; in the west separatism threatened the unity of Bismarck's Reich; and a disastrous hyper-inflation swept through the land driving thousands of desperate men in and around Munich into the Nazi party in the vain hope that a spectacular gesture such as a march on Berlin would, in some unspecified way, alleviate their misery. Internationally, there were signs that 'the strong men of history' were on the march, especially in Italy. In October 1922 the Italian government capitulated to Mussolini after his spectacular but contrived *Marcia a Roma,* an event which deeply impressed Hitler, an admirer of the Italian fascist leader, and encouraged him to believe that his own hour was at hand.

Much of the difficulty in understanding Hitler's behaviour in the summer and autumn of 1923 arises out of the sharp dichotomy between his reckless platform manner and the caution of his political tactics. Shortfall between promise and performance is not uncommon in oratorically-gifted politicians. In Hitler's case the dichotomy reflected very clearly the tension in his own psyche between the man of resolution he wanted to be and the man of indecision he often showed himself to be, a point which will be discussed later on in this book.

It cannot be denied that the qualities which make a successful *Trommler* are not necessarily those needed by a successful putschist. However, to say as General Otto von Lossow, commander of the Bavarian Reichswehr, did at the trial following the putsch, that Hitler lacked a sense of reality and the ability to see what was possible and practical, while not wholly untrue, is somewhat harsh and reveals more about Lossow's guilt complex than Hitler's personality.[38] Nor was Hitler, to quote a recent historian of the putsch, 'a fool who did not know when he was beaten'.[39] Hitler was far too intelligent a politician not to appreciate all along that the success of a march on Berlin depended on the fullest cooperation of all right-wing organizations in Bavaria and above all on the wholehearted support of the civilian and military authorities.

It should be remembered that when the authorities stood up to the Nazis on 1 May 1923 Hitler drew the the correct inferences at once. On that day Nazis and other extremists planned to disrupt the traditional May Day demonstration. Despite ominous signs that police and army would not tolerate any disturbances, Hitler went ahead.[40] Two thousand men from paramilitary bands, 1,300 of them Nazi, gathered on the Oberwiesenfeld armed with weapons Roehm had procured by subterfuge from the barracks, while a belligerent steel-helmeted Hitler strode up and down vowing vengeance on the 'Reds'. For once the authorities stood firm. Roehm was sharply reprimanded by Lossow and ordered to collect in the arms at once. This he did having first thrown a cordon of soldiers and police around the Oberwiesenfeld. When Hitler decided to surrender the weapons it can hardly be denied that he displayed a much firmer grasp of power realities than either Colonel Hermann Kriebel, the military commander of the assembled extremist band, or Gregor

Strasser, both of whom advocated resistance. Only a madman or a complete fool would have resisted, on the dubious assumption that the local Reichswehr might be stampeded into siding with the Nazis if the latter made it clear that they only wanted a free hand to beat up the 'Reds'. And Hitler was neither madman nor complete fool.

Still, this was a humiliating defeat. Though he had avoided senseless bloodshed, Hitler had miscalculated and his deflated followers were scarcely mollified by an inflammatory speech in the Zirkus Krone on the evening of the Oberwiesenfeld débâcle. Faced with the first serious crisis since he had become the Nazi leader, Hitler seemed to lose confidence in himself. He made no attempt to fight back but retired to Berchtesgaden for the rest of the summer, making occasional speeches and visiting Munich once or twice accompanied by his niece, Geli Raubal. Whether he contracted out of politics because of gnawing self-doubt or through lethargy or possibly because a sixth sense told him that if he waited patiently the steadily deteriorating situation would save him from the consequences of his mistake, it is quite impossible to say. But certainly one cannot regard his conduct as a piece of firm leadership in a moment of crisis. Rather it goes to confirm the view that he was basically a *Trommler* momentarily thrown off balance by a setback, and not a Führer capable of rallying his followers when they lost heart. In fact, the downward spiral of the national crisis rescued Hitler from his personal crisis and from the political eclipse so confidently predicted for him in the opposition press. By August 1923 inflation was completely out of contol. In early September Stresemann ended passive resistance and opened negotiations with the French to the accompaniment of howls of rage from the right wing. Extremism was suddenly given a new lease of life.

The Nazis joined forces with other right-wing organizations in the Kampfbund, an association pledged to overthrow the 'Marxist' regime in Berlin. Hitler was chosen as its political leader though it is a measure of his diminished stature that Roehm had great difficulty in persuading other organizations to accept him. In October the smouldering dispute between Berlin and Munich burst into flame when the newly-appointed state commissioner general, Gustav von Kahr, who had proclaimed a state of emergency in Bavaria the month before, now defied orders to suppress the Nazi Party weekly, the *Völkischer Beobachter*. Instead he ostentatiously reinstated Lossow after Berlin dismissed him for insubordination. Naturally Hitler's spirits rose as the breach with Berlin widened. However, early in November Kahr, Lossow and Colonel Hans von Seisser, commander of the Bavarian police, began to suspect that the Berlin government had weathered the worst of the crisis and that the moment for marching on Berlin had passed. Accordingly they warned the Kampfbund leaders that a premature putsch would be promptly suppressed. Whereupon the Kampfbund, fearing that the march on Berlin had been abandoned, decided to take the initiative and start the 'National Revolution'.

Hitler's Beer-Hall putsch has been universally condemned as a mad gamble by a crazy fanatic with little or no purchase on reality. While no one would deny that Hitler was a fanatic, nor that the putsch failed ignominiously, to understand why he acted as he did, it is important to realize that he had virtually no choice but was impaled on the horns of a cruel dilemma. If he wished to survive politically, he had to live up to the expectations his reckless propaganda had aroused. Had he not made a bid for power, his restless followers, many of them recent recruits suffering genuine economic hardship, would very likely have deserted him. No room for manoeuvre existed. After the sharp reverse on 1 May, he dare not restrain his men even had he wished to do so—for one must not forget that leaders remain in command only if they respond to the wishes of the group they claim to be leading. In that sense Hitler was truly 'a desperate man with a cliff at his back'.[41] There were other considerations. If Kahr stole a march on him by restoring the Wittelsbach dynasty—and Hitler seems to have thought that Kahr might announce this at the Bürgerbräukeller meeting on 8 November—then Hitler's chances of exerting political influence in a new national Germany would be extinguished. Unless he acted now, the great 'National Revolution' to save the German soul would degenerate into a squalid monarchist *coup d'état* with no place in it for Adolf Hitler. If, on the other hand, he struck now, was it not likely that those reluctant conspirators Kahr, Lossow and Seisser, would be carried along on a tidal wave of patriotic feeling—which he confidently expected would sweep through the fatherland once he, Adolf Hitler, had given the signal—and would be compelled to march on Berlin this time under Hitler's leadership? What Mussolini had achieved in Italy and Kemal Pasha in Turkey could surely be achieved in the German fatherland. Most certainly a dangerous enterprise resting on dubious assumptions but not perhaps quite the hopelessly crazy gamble it is often made out to be.[42]

Up to the spring of 1923 the evidence suggests that Hitler did not think of himself as anything more than a *Trommler*.[43] By the autumn his views were changing. An officer at Munich army command recalled that in the spring Hitler was still talking of his mission as being to arouse the working class to a sense of national consciousness. By early October he had developed unmistakably Napoleonic and messianic airs: now he talked of being called to save Germany, a task which would undoubtedly fall to his lot 'if not at once, then certainly later'.[44] Was this, as Tyrell maintains, another example of Hitler the *Trommler* being catapulted into a new role by fears that Kahr, Lossow and Seisser were about to betray the 'National Revolution'? This seems highly likely. As he was taking the initiative, not unnaturally he expected a share of power in the nationalist regime. Other evidence suggests, however, that he still did not see himself as the dominant figure in a new nationalist Germany.[45] All he felt moved to do was start off the revolution when others had reneged on it. That he supposed a *Trommler* would be equal to the task, reveals only too plainly that Hitler never evolved any strategy of revolution in which the respective roles of the party, the state and the masses were defined with precision. In his muddled way he believed that the power of the spoken work would be sufficient to mobilize the masses in support of the actions of the determined minority which, in his reading of history, had always played the major role in great events. One may conclude, tentatively, that Hitler had reached an intermediate position in his political evolution. He was certainly more than a 'drummer' but had not yet reached the point where he was absolutely sure of himself as Germany's strong man of the future.

As a revolutionary Hitler cut a far from impressive figure on 8–9 November. The theatrical behaviour at the Bürgerbräukeller beer hall, where he jumped on a table, fired a shot in the ceiling and proclaimed the 'National Revolution', did not impress the audience.[46] Worse still, he failed to persuade Kahr, Lossow and Seisser to join him after haranguing them at gun point in a side room. It was General Erich Ludendorff, hurriedly summoned from his home by Scheubner-Richter, who saved the putschists from disaster in the first hour. For Ludendorff, Hindenburg's right-hand man in the second half of the First World War, was a figure of national stature prominent in *völkisch* circles, who succeeded where Hitler had failed. It is true that Ludendorff persuaded the triumvirate to join in a national government headed by Hitler but, like the 1933 cabinet, respectable conservatives hemmed in the demagogue on all sides—Ludendorff in charge of the army, Lossow as minister of defence, Seisser as minister of the interior, and Kahr as regent of Bavaria. Bursting with childlike pride, Hitler paraded his new allies in front of the beer-hall crowd, confident that victory was assured.

The euphoria was shortlived. During a brief absence of Hitler's, Ludendorff, a romantic who believed that a gentleman's word was his bond, allowed the triumvirate to depart. Once outside Nazi reach, Kahr, Lossow and Seisser took the necessary steps to put down the rising. Early on 9 November, as time passed without a sign from his 'allies', Hitler had his first premonition of disaster. He has been accused of losing his nerve at this point.[47] Yet what could he do once the Bavarian establishment turned against him? Very little. Military resistance was impossible. There was no proper plan for taking over in Munich because the putschists assumed the authorities would side with them. And if it came to fighting, many of the youngsters in the Kampfbund were little more than boys, incapable in some instances of maintaining their rifles and machine-guns in proper working order. Throughout the night Hitler alternated between wild hope and black despair. At one moment he was so despondent that he handed over the organization of the next day's proceedings to Streicher.[48] Later he tried to persuade himself that he could still rally the people of Munich at a series of mass meetings the next day and save the putsch. It is difficult to believe that he had much hope of success. It is significant that at 7.30 a.m. he sent an officer to request Crown Prince Rupprecht, heir to the Bavarian throne, to intervene and prevent nationalists shooting at nationalists, an eventuality which he foresaw. In fact, the emissary turned up far too late at the home of the crown prince; finding no motor vehicle to hand, he waited in true comic opera tradition for the next train to Berchtesgaden. While Hitler waited, trapped in a hopeless situation, Ludendorff proposed the fatal march, whether to arouse patriotic fervour or to relieve Roehm—besieged in the war ministry—remains obscure. Hitler fell in with the scheme but played a fairly inconspicuous role in what followed. On the Marienplatz, Streicher, not Hitler, harangued the crowds.[49] Minutes later on the Odeonsplatz the inevitable occurred when columns of marchers singing O, *Deutschland hoch in Ehren* encountered the police. Shots were exchanged. Sixteen demonstrators and three policemen died, and the putsch was over.

Hitler's precipitate flight from the Odeonsplatz has often been contrasted unfavourably with Ludendorff's calm and impassive walk through the police cordon to surrender to the officer in charge. It is a matter of taste. One could just as easily argue that Ludendorff behaved in a foolhardy manner, exposing himself to unnecessary risks when bullets were flying whereas Hitler, the seasoned front-line soldier, obeyed the dictates of common prudence and took cover.[50] Actually, he was thrown to the ground by the shot that killed Scheubner-Richter (with whom he had linked arms) and dislocated his shoulder. Coward Hitler was not, as his war record proves. But to stay behind with the smell of defeat in the air would have been a romantic gesture out of keeping with his sense of political realism. The 'whiff of grapeshot' was the final incontrovertible proof that the forces of law and order were not on his side and that he could not, therefore, succeed.

Hitler had once again misread the signs. His party had been dissolved. And he and his associates faced prison sentences—at first Hitler feared summary execution. On the face of it, one might have supposed that the political career of this thirty-four year old fanatic was over and would rate at most a footnote in the history books. So it might have been, had it not been for his trial in February 1924.

The twenty-four day trial at the Munich infantry school was one of Hitler's greatest political successes. As usual, he had more than his fair share of good luck. The prosecution, anxious to spare Ludendorff as much as possible, depicted Hitler as the prime mover in the putsch. This distortion of the facts coupled with the extraordinary indulgence of the presiding judge and the lay assessors (for which Hitler could thank Franz Gürtner, pro-Nazi minister of the interior) gave him a unique opportunity to snatch victory out of defeat. Encouraged by the sympathetic attitude of the court, Hitler quickly turned the dock into a political platform. Boldly claiming full responsibility for the putsch and defending it as a patriotic act not to be compared with the vile 'treason' of the revolutionaries of 1918, he drove the prosecution onto the defensive. It was not Hitler but Kahr, Lossow and Seisser, appearing as prosecution witnesses, who emerged with tarnished reputations as men who ought to have marched with Hitler but instead betrayed him. So the trial ended on a note of triumph for Hitler. Finally, thanks to the leniency of the authorities, he spent only nine months of the absurdly light five-year sentence in prison.

The ten months between the trial and Hitler's release from Landsberg prison in December 1924 were of crucial importance in the development of his personality. The mood of black despair before the trial when Hitler, filled with remorse, talked of starving himself to death, was transformed into supreme self-confidence while he was in prison. Secure in the knowledge that he had a considerable public awaiting him outside the walls, and flattered by sycophantic admirers inside the prison—including some of the prison staff—he started to plan his return to politics.

One of Hitler's least endearing characteristics was a readiness to blame others for his personal misfortunes. It did not take him long to reach the conclusion that dependence on the broad *völkisch* movement and not his own miscalculations had been the cause of the débâcle. The lesson was plain: he must create a new party strong enough to carry through the 'National Revolution' unaided. And this carried with it the implication that if the Nazis ever came to power on their own, their leader would *ipso facto* become ruler of Germany. In short, the roles of *Trommler* and Führer were beginning to converge in the post-Landsberg Hitler.

One should not, however, ante-date this metamorphosis. At the end of 1924, before his release from prison, Hitler still believed his historical role would be restricted to 'loosening the soil around the post'; to get the post out of the ground would be a task for 'another greater one still to come'.[51] Even in 1926 speaking to Hans Grimm, author of the bestseller *Volk ohne Raum*, about the need to awaken the masses to an awareness of the defeatism of the bourgeois world, Hitler remarked that, 'a leader is certainly needed for this and that he was not. He was only the one who was attempting to do it until the leader comes; he was simply doing the preparatory work. What he himself lacked, he knew.'[52] In the absence of any detailed analysis of this political metamorphosis, all one can safely say is that between 1925 and 1929 the role of Führer was superimposed upon that of the *Trommler* so that the Hitler of 1930 was probably convinced that he was Germany's man of destiny certain of office in the not-too-distant future.

Immediate post-war conditions probably did more to put Hitler on the political map than his oratorical skill and charismatic appeal. For this period it would be true to say that Hitler 'arose more out of the possibilities of the situation than out of the capabilities in himself . . . a historical situation did not exactly produce him but it made him possible.[53]' The reverse was the case for the years between 1925 and 1929. The return of political stability and a dramatic improvement in economic conditions caused extremism to decline sharply. Secondly, the Bavarian establishment lost interest in their blue-eyed boy. Only with difficulty and through the good offices of Franz Gürtner could Hitler even persuade the new minister-president, Heinrich Held, to lift the ban on the party and the *Völkischer Beobachter*. And after his first appearance at the Bürgerbräukeller Hitler was promptly banned from public speaking for two years. It is a measure of the power of his personality that he was, nevertheless, able to create what was virtually a new party in February 1925 and over the next few years to turn it into a highly centralized machine responsive to his will.

With extremism on the decline, one would have supposed that a leader with an eye on political power even at local level would have sought a broad accommodation with all right-wing extremist groups so that the new party might command maximum support for the long haul that lay ahead. Not so. With complete indifference to contemporary political realities, Hitler set about his task in the uncompromising mood of a minor prophet founding a religious sect. While still in prison, he obstinately opposed all attempts by the right wing to cooperate on a broad front, such as the meeting of *völkisch* politicians at Weimar in the summer of 1924. And by refusing to intervene in inter-party disputes he quite deliberately allowed the party to fall apart, an interesting example of the way he turned his congenital vacillation to positive political advantage. For by maximizing chaos in the party, he minimized the danger of pretenders emerging for the vacant throne. Outside the prison walls his unyielding attitude soon fragmented the fissiparous extremist camp still further. At his first meeting with the *völkisch* deputies in the Bavarian *Landtag* his insufferable arrogance alienated most of them. Very soon he had quarrelled with the *völkisch* politicians in North Germany acidly informing them that he intended in future to be a *Trommler* for Germany, not for them. He took an early opportunity of breaking with Ludendorff, recognizing in him a potential rival who had overshadowed him during the putsch. Even Roehm was dropped in April 1925 when he opposed Hitler's decision to make the new SA a political organization completely subordinate to the party, instead of allowing it to become one more paramilitary band associated with similar groups in the newly-formed Frontbann or association of front-line fighters. All the same, at the Bürgerbräukeller meeting on 25 February 1925 to re-found the party, the leaders of the warring factions were sufficiently moved by his oratory to make up their quarrels in public and submit to his arrogant demand for dictatorial power over them. By no stretch of the imagination can his behaviour since his release from prison be regarded as politically imaginative and attuned to the realities of the mid-1920s. Only in terms of his personal pathology did it make sense. Being a completely self-centred but basically insecure individual, he craved esteem and recognition and found the emotional satisfaction he needed in lording it over a small group of followers regardless of the cost to the broad *völkisch* movement.

Exactly what this style of leadership amounted to is illustrated by the first serious crisis in the party in 1926. While Hitler's hands were tied by the new ban on public speaking, the party was making some progress, led by the Strasser brothers, in the Rhineland, Saxony and Prussia. New members in these industrial area, while accepting Hitler as leader, felt no special veneration for him. On tactics Eberfeld—where the headquarters of the new-style Nazis were situated—differed from 'petty bourgeois' Munich. It toyed with national Bolshevism and sought to win over urban workers by emphasizing the 'socialist' elements in the party programme such as nationalization of heavy industry and expropriation of large estates.

While the crisis deepened, Hitler's interest in politics seems to have been minimal. After a burst of energy early in 1925, he virtually contracted out of politics again. Most of his time in the summer and autumn of 1925 was spent at Haus Wachenfeld, a small country house on the Obersalzberg which the party had just rented for him. Here he was busy at work on the second volume of *Mein Kampf* (it appeared at the end of 1926) and was seen only occasionally in Munich with Geli Raubal.

A combination of factors forced him out of his bucolic retreat. First, there was the decision of the North German Nazis to support the left-wing line of expropriation on the burning issue of the disposal of the property of the former princely houses. Hitler instinctively disliked attacks on private property and, now that he was begining to make systematic overtures to big business, the North German line was especially unwelcome. Secondly, as he had already made a pronouncement on the question, the decision of the Strasser faction was a challenge to his authority. Another threat was the so-called Hanover programme, which the North Germans hoped to substitute for the party's twenty-five points proclamed by Hitler in February 1920 when the party was first founded. Thirdly, his leadership style may have been criticized at a faction meeting in Hanover: Gauleiter Bernhard Rust allegedly declared that National Socialists were free and democratic men who needed 'no pope who can claim infallibility'.[54] Finally, Hitler was probably displeased with Gregor Strasser's call to the party in January 1926 to employ all means including violence to come to power—a policy completely at variance with Hitler's tactical repudiation of putschism.

How did he meet the challenge? His solution was to hold a special conference of top leaders at Bamberg in February 1926 to discuss party policy. In the course of a five-hour speech he ranged over the entire field of domestic and foreign policy. He insisted that the party oppose the expropriation of the princes; he rejected the Hanover programme; he declared the twenty-five points inviolable; and he condemned all deviationism as treason to the philosophy of the party—which he incorporated in his own person—and to the men who fell at the Feldherrnhalle. As if by magic the opposition crumbled away. All Hitler's demands were tamely accepted. The Strasser faction soon withdrew the offending programme. Having won a sweeping victory, Hitler carefully avoided a purge of the dissidents in the Russian style. Instead, he offered his chief antagonist, Gregor Strasser, the post of propaganda chief in Munich—where he could also keep an eye on him. A little later Josef Goebbels, Strasser's most gifted henchman, was appointed *Gauleiter* of Berlin. Hitler's behaviour in 1925–6 reveals plainly enough that he was still an indolent individual, a chronic procrastinator who allowed crises to creep up on him, then relied heavily on personal magnetism and native cunning to wriggle out of them. In most German parties a leader who worked in fits and starts, as Hitler did, could scarcely have survived very long. That he did survive was largely because these personal idiosyncrasies were perfectly compatible both with the structure of the Nazi Party and with conditions in Germany. Up to a point—an important qualification—one might almost say that Hitler's idiosyncrasies were a positive advantage to him and this basically for two reasons.

The strength of the party lay not in ideological posturing but in the personal commitment of the members to the Führer. The faith of the rank and file in Hitler was the rock on which the party-church was founded. Ideological wrangling, the life blood of most parties especially those on the left, was a matter of indifference to the leader. As long as members remained loyal to him, it was positively advantageous for a leader to be a remote and aloof figure uninvolved in petty disputes. Only when the leadership principle was challenged, as in 1926, was he obliged to intervene. Then, precisely because loyalty to the charismatic leader was the fundamental precept of the movement, Hitler's rulings were invariably accepted without dissent.

Secondly, circumstances forced the Nazis to turn their backs on simple putschism and seek power by the infinitely more complex processes of democracy. In practice the political dinosaurs in the Nazi Party found it difficult to learn new tricks. What held them together, apart from personal commitment to the Führer, was a thin amalgam of frustration, nostalgia for a mythical past and romantic expectations only realizable through some cataclysmic upheaval inimical to the workings of the democratic system. Hitler probably made no irrevocable choice between putschism and constitutionalism in 1924. Until at least 1926, if not later, he seems to have hovered uneasily in the middle ground.[55] On the one hand, he fully appreciated the dangers of out-and-out putschism. At the same time, he was too astute not to realize that the mores of an activist party can easily be corrupted once it is caught up in the parliamentary machine. To have to concentrate on bread-and-butter issues, and to work out a detailed programme articulating the party's vague and woolly philosophy would inevitably polarize it into left and right on economic issues. This would destroy the 'classless' nationalistic élan of the party and blunt its cutting edge as an instrument for carrying the Nazis to power.[56] Deep down Hitler must have sensed that final victory, if it ever came in his lifetime, would depend on the return of chaos and crisis. In an interim situation a leader who followed the line of least resistance on tactical issues, holding the reins loosely, was more likely to preserve party unity. One is reminded of a lazy old crocodile, lying motionless in the mud sunning himself, until the imminence of danger or the prospect of prey galvanizes him into sudden—and decisive—action.

Like all metaphors this reveals only part of the truth. Crocodile tactics have one serious disadvantage: they encourage the free play of centrifugal forces especially in parties without clearly-defined programmes. Therefore, Hitler had to combine crocodile tactics on ideological matters with a beaver-like policy of centralization designed to bind the members more closely to the charismatic leader. This was absolutely essential once the party started to make headway outside Bavaria. New members, while accepting Hitler as leader, were not under his spell like the Munich crowds in the old days. Only if he could rely on blind automatic obedience from all his followers, could Hitler afford to drift along downstream confident that the rank and file would accept without question his supreme right to move in whatever direction he thought expedient. In other words, he did not indulge his natural indolence and indecisiveness too much when his political interests were at stake but did, in fact, display considerable tenacity and perseverance in pursuit of them.

Thus, after Bamberg Hitler pressed ahead as vigorously as possible with the transformation of the party into a highly-centralized bureaucracy structured on quasi-military lines and wholly dependent on himself. What remained of the elective principle was purged out of the party. All other local parties recognized at last the primacy of Munich. The *Gauleiter* were brought more and more under central control. The party programme was declared immutable, not because Hitler greatly cared about it but because he simply wanted to discourage 'revisionism' by pretending that the twenty-five points were the Ark of the Covenant of the movement. The SA was reformed, forbidden to maintain ties with other right-wing bodies and subordinated (in theory at least) to the party leader. New departments proliferated at party headquarters, each handling some aspect of public affairs and busying itself producing draft legislation for the *völkisch* state of the future. And to cater for youth, students, teachers doctors and women, several special associations were formed, all in full communion with the party.

Hitler's position as Führer was enormously strengthened by these changes. In his own hands he carefully retained exclusive right to appoint and dismiss the personnel staffing this huge bureaucracy as well as the right to appoint election candidates at national and local level. That he often acted quite capriciously in exercising these rights, being inclined to prefer intuitive judgement to hard fact, only increased still further the degree of dependence of those fortunate enough to win his favour. The personal feuding and scrambling for office, which was an inevitable concomitant of such a system, did not greatly bother Hitler. At times he seems to have encouraged it, shrewdly appreciating that party rivalries enhanced his own position as supreme arbiter and diverted energies away from divisive policy matters. More fundamentally, internecine warfare was evidence of the smooth functioning of the principle of natural selection which gave the party its leaders. Those who rose to the top were presumably those who ought to do so by virtue of their superior strength and advancement of the Nazi cause, though Hitler was well aware that it would take a long time to produce a perfect leadership cadre.[57]

Another important development in the mid-1920s was the elaboration of the ritualistic side of the movement. The all-embracing nature of the new party structure, the flags and emblems, the uniforms and quasi-military demonstrations such as the Nuremberg party rally of 1927 impressed the rank and file and reinforced their loyalty to the party. And because party was equated with Führer, displays of the party's power and might reinforced personal faith in Hitler and institutionalized his charisma. The pomp and circumstance did something else; it innoculated the members against political reality and gave them the grand illusion of proleptic participation in the Nazi state of the future. It was especially important to give the rank and file a glimpse of future glory at this time for apathy was fairly widespread and a shortage of funds curtailed propaganda activities.[58]

As long as Germany was relatively prosperous, the messianic appeal of the Nazi Party was strictly limited. Sitting on the fence until the times did alter was not weakness on Hitler's part, but the only option open to him. Meanwhile, he allowed the strongest faction to have its own way over electoral tactics. Thus, despite the Bamberg defeat, the Strassers continued with the anti-capitalist 'urban plan', trying vainly to establish power bases in the industrial cities of the Ruhr, Saxony and Thuringia. By the end of 1927 it was clear that this policy was failing to win working-class support but was alienating potential middle-class voters. Accordingly, the party shifted its interest to the broad middle class and to the countryside, where disgruntled farmers in some areas were beginning to express their discontent forcibly as the first shadows of economic malaise fell across Germany.[59] The 1928 elections brought scant comfort with a mere 811,000 votes compared with 907,300 in December 1924 and a total of twelve Reichstag seats. Paradoxically, the Nazis did better in rural areas where the full impact of the new electoral strategy had not yet been felt. It is illustrative of Hitler's style of leadership that only now when it was crystal clear that the 'urban policy' was a fiasco, did he feel confident enough to order its complete abandonment in favour of a policy geared to the farmers and the broad middle class. Only in retrospect does this tactical change assume significance. In the summer of 1929 Hitler was still no more than the leader of a small if growing splinter party, scarcely known outside Bavaria and very likely doomed to remain for ever on the periphery of political life.

Six months later Hitler was a household word in Germany. His opportunity arose out of the political polarization following the elections. The Socialist and Communist vote increased while the German Nationalists, under the disastrous leadership of Alfred Hugenberg, regressed to the intransigent anti-republican posture of the immediate post-war years. In July Hugenberg persuaded Franz Seldte, leader of Stahlhelm, or 'Steel Helmet', a prominent ex-servicemens' association, and Heinrich Class, leader of the Pan German League, to form a national committee to oppose the Young Plan, a settlement of the reparations problem recently negotiated by Stresemann. The committee also demanded the repudiation of the war-guilt clause which saddled Germany and her allies with sole responsibility for the outbreak of war in 1914. Hitler was invited to join them because they needed a 'drummer' to beat up support. Like other right-wing politicians later on, they anticipated little difficulty in containing a small-time Bavarian politician. An opportunity to beat the nationalist drum fitted in excellently with the Nazis' new middle-class strategy and Hitler agreed to help, though only after hard bargaining which gave him control of substantial funds for propaganda.

The situation in 1929 was uncannily reminiscent of 1923 without the violence. For the second time in his career Hitler allied with the 'reactionaries' he despised to undermine the republic they all hated. When only six million

Germans supported the bill 'against the enslavement of the German people', the right wing suffered a sharp reverse. Not Hitler. For the second time in five years he turned defeat into victory. Through the Hugenberg press network his name reached every middle-class breakfast table in Germany. He emerged from the campaign as the most forceful figure in the 'national opposition', completely overshadowing Hugenberg, Seldte and Class. Any lingering fear of Nazi 'socialism' was dispelled for good and all by his association with respectable right-wing politicians and by the singular vehemence of the general offensive he launched on the republic. On the eve of the greatest crisis in the history of the Weimar Republic Hitler had already built a bridge across to the broad middle class on whose support he was ultimately dependent if he wanted power. And Hitler managed to have the best of both worlds. Because of his tight grip over the party machine, Hitler was able to commit it to the campaign despite the uneasy feelings many 'radical' Nazis had about flirtations with the 'reactionaries' of the right. Hitler took care not to strain their loyalty too much. Once Hugenberg, Seldte and Class had served their purpose, Hitler tossed them aside. As usual, he laid the sole blame for the campaign's 'failure' at the door of his allies, much to the satisfaction of the 'radicals'. All in all, it was a highly successful, sophisticated and thoroughly unscrupulous political operation which would have gladdened the heart of Machiavelli's Prince.

There were immediate dividends. Between July and December 1929 party membership rose from 120,000 to 178,000. In the communal and *Land* elections at the end of the year the Nazis made substantial gains largely at the expense of the German Nationalists, although by then the effects of the Depression complicated the electoral arithmetic. In Thuringia the Nazis entered a coalition with the bourgeois parties with Hitler's full approval. Finally, substantial financial contributions flowed at long last into the party coffers from industrialists. Hitler's considerable debts were wiped out. He rented a comfortable flat in the fashionable Prinzregentenplatz, and the party moved from cramped quarters in the Schellingstrasse to the Barlow Palace, the so-called Brown House, in the Briennerstrasse.

Despite these signs of a Nazi revival, it is inconceivable that Hitler could ever have come to power had not the Weimar republic been subjected to the unprecedented strain of a world economic crisis. Though the most likely, perhaps the only, outcome of this crisis, given Germany's past history, was the establishment of a dictatorship to protect the economic interests and social privilege of the middle classes, this does not necessarily mean that Hitler's personal victory was assured. As the crisis deepened in 1932, Hitler might have been outmanoeuvred by his opponents. And if Gregor Strasser had been made of sterner stuff, might he not have carried the bulk of the party into an accommodation with Schleicher? Under a Schleicher-Strasser-Roehm coalition or even under a Papen-Hammerstein military dictatorship events would probably have followed the same broad course given the socio-economic pressures of the 1930s and the political and cultural traditions of twentieth-century Germany. Without Hitler parliamentary democracy would still have been snuffed out; the Jews would almost certainly have been the object of some discriminatory legislation and Germany would have intensified her efforts to revise the Versailles treaty. But as far as Hitler's personal survival was concerned, the manoeuvres of the Papens and the Schleichers and his response to them as well as the absence of formidable rivals in the Nazi Party were probably factors of crucial importance. It is in this narrowly circumscribed area that the element of 'accident' or 'chance' seems to operate in history.

Hitler's powers of leadership were subjected to their most severe test in the early 1930s. Once the Nazis became a major factor in German politics, the dichotomy between their putschist origins and personal inclinations and the ostensible commitment to parliamentary methods (since about 1928) became acute. By the end of 1932 Roehm's SA had grown into a formidable private army of 500,000 men, coexisting uneasily with the party's political organiza- tion headed by Gregor Strasser. In the wave of demonstrations and disorders that accompanied the breakdown of parliamentary democracy in Germany the Brownshirts played a leading role. Bloody street brawls with 'Marxists' and the corrupting violence of Nazi propaganda encouraged these unsophisticated street hooligans to believe that with each electoral triumph a seizure of power was imminent.

Much as Hitler believed in physical violence as a means of intimidating opponents and impressing ordinary citizens with the irresistible might of the Nazis, he was well aware that an SA putsch without army backing would be the highroad to disaster. And as the middle class was now turning to the Nazis, Hitler had every reason to suppose that he could bring about the 'National Revolution' via the ballot box. Accordingly, he had to exert all his political skill to hold the exuberant SA men in check, while avoiding condemnation of their often appallingly brutal attacks on opponents. Sometimes he had to go far beyond what political prudence recommended; for example, having held the SA back after the disappointment of mid-August 1932, he had to stand by the Nazi hooligans who brutally murdered a Communist at Potempa at the cost of alienating middle-class support. On two occasions, in August 1930 and in April 1931, Hitler faced local revolts of SA men disgusted by the Führer's timidly 'bourgeois' policies. The first revolt was only quelled after Hitler rushed round SA haunts in Berlin pleading tearfully with his men to return to the fold. What accentuated Hitler's dilemma in 1932 was the plain fact that, despite impressive electoral successes, power still eluded him. If he could not succeed in obtaining power by peaceful means and dare not risk a putsch, how could he escape the relentless logic of his own destruction?

The answer is that he was saved from political annihilation by a fundamen- tal shift in the balance of political power in Germany between 1930 and 1933. Fascism did not begin with Hitler, as Ernst Thälmann, the Communist leader, shrewdly observed. Under the impact of 'the general crisis of capitalism' parliamentary democracy was paralysed and superseded by an authoritarian- style presidential government. From the spring of 1930 chancellors relied on the president's emergency powers, buttressed by the ultimate sanction of military force, to promulgate essential legislation. And as the balance of electoral advantage moved steadily towards the Nazis, the men in the corridors of power close to the president sought to exploit Hitler's poujadist movement as Kahr and Lossow had tried to ten years before. General Kurt von Schleicher, head of the ministerial bureau and influential liaison man between Reichswehr and presidency, and Freiherr Franz von Papen, crafty intriguer and personal friend of Hindenburg, both needed Hitler's support in order to disguise the naked force on which their own regimes rested. Naively they believed that they could buy support without giving Hitler real power. Hitler, for his part, was working assiduously to ingratiate himself with the king-makers in accordance with his long-standing conviction that the 'National Revolution' would only succeed with the support of the forces of law and order. Already he had done much to reassure the army that it need not fear the Nazis, chiefly by his testimony at the trial in Leipzig in April 1930 of young officers accused of spreading Nazi propaganda in the army. It is illustrative of his more active political style that he spent most of the summer of 1931, not in the mountains with Geli Raubal or idling away his time in Munich cafés, but in visiting influential industrialists trying to persuade them that he would not allow the radical wing of the party to exert influence once he was in power. Only in this highly favourable atmosphere is Hitler's coming to power intelligible. It was not the 'triumph of the will' but the return of fear and disorder that brought Hitler to the chancellery. It is no part of this book to analyse in detail the complicated web of intrigue in 1932–3. What is of interest, in an examination of the interaction of personality and politics, is the way in which Hitler responded to the exigencies of a quickly-changing political scene which called for something more than the crocodile tactics of the 1920s.

The mixture of new and old in Hitler's style is illustrated by the episode of President Hindenburg's re-election in 1932. Anxious to weather the storms that lay ahead, Chancellor Heinrich Bruening sought the agreement of the party leaders to a renewal of Hindenburg's term of office without exposing the old man to the rigours of an election. Hitler was elated at this opportunity to tread the corridors of power and immediately agreed to negotiate. Before deciding what to do, Hitler conferred with a small group of top leaders. This habit of discussing tactics with an inner cabinet of key men—Strasser, head of the political organization, Roehm, leader of the SA, Goebbels, head of the propaganda department, Wilhelm Frick, leader of the Reichstag fraction, and Goering, general factotum of the party in Berlin—was a regular feature of Hitler's leadership style in the early 1930s. On this particular issue they were divided. Roehm and Goebbels sharply opposed an agreement, believing that Hitler must not be seen to shrink from confrontation even with the mighty Hindenburg. Strasser, however, counselled caution, warning that Hitler was likely to be defeated. When Hitler sided with Roehm and Goebbels, one is almost tempted to speak of 'collective leadership' at the top of the party. But without detailed knowledge of the discussions one cannot determine the extent to which Hitler dominated the debates.[61] Nor should it be forgotten that Goebbels and Goering were completely committed to Hitler and probably impervious to opponents' arguments. It is interesting also that, notwithstanding the 'collective' decision, Hitler still tried to avoid confrontation. This may have been clever tactics. Instead of bluntly rejecting the Bruening plan, as the Nationalists had done, Hitler wrote to Hindenburg declaring that although Bruening was at present acting unconstitutionally, he (Hitler) was perfectly prepared to support an extension of the president's term of office, provided that Bruening was dismissed and replaced by a more right-wing administration. The old man rejected the proposal and left Hitler no hiding place. That he was still the procrastinator of old is clear from the way he wrestled with the problem for a month, swayed first one way by Roehm and Goebbels, then the other by Strasser before finally deciding to stand, much to the general relief of the party.

Once he had overcome his doubts he threw himself wholeheartedly into the fray. When the results gave Hindenburg a clear lead (but not the absolute majority required) the party was despondent. Not Hitler. He immediately announced his willingness to fight in the second round and did so with unflagging enthusiasm. Without doubt Hitler's vigorous electioneering did much to increase his personal vote from 11·3 millions in the first to 13·7 millions in the second round as opposed to Hindenburg's 19·3 millions. It is no coincidence that in later life Hitler described 1932 as one of the happiest years in his life. As the crisis deepened, unemployment soared and the middle classes turned towards him, he was able to play before an ever growing audience the role that gave him the greatest emotional satisfaction—the *Trommler zur Deutschheit*. Between March and November 1932 he fought five major election campaigns. Flying from city to city—a novelty thought up by Goebbels—and sometimes addressing two or three mass meetings a day, he reached the peak of his oratorical powers.[62] After months of frustration when the party, though growing locally, had been marking time in national politics, the Führer and the party were once again in the limelight. Again Hitler could mobilize the magic of the spoken word to bridge the credibility gap between political reality and his own mounting ambitions. Possibly, too, this burst of frenzied activity, which carried him from one corner of Germany to another, helped him recover from the great personal tragedy which occurred in September 1931 when Geli Raubal committed suicide.[63] So shaken was he by her death that he had to be restrained from taking his own life.

Yet the Nazis were no nearer power after the presidential elections than before. On 14 April they suffered an unexpected and humiliating reverse when Bruening under pressure from the *Land* governments, banned the SA and the black-shirted SS or *Schutz Staffeln*, an élitist corps commanded by Heinrich Himmler, as a threat to public order. Hitler's authority was strong enough to force the SA to obey but not to prevent rebellious murmuring at the failure of the legality policy. From this embarrassing situation Hitler was rescued by Schleicher, who had ousted first Groener, the minister of defence, and then

Bruening from office. Schleicher offered to raise the ban and to dissolve the Reichstag provided that Hitler supported a cabinet of the general's choosing. Hitler, who cared not at all about the complexion of the new government nor about his promise to support it, readily agreed. For, as Goebbels wrote in his diary: 'The important thing is that the Reichstag is dissolved. Elections! Elections! Direct to the people! We are all very happy!'[64] Another burst of feverish electioneering fitted Hitler's mood exactly as every portent promised another great victory.

Hitler's confidence was amply justified. On 31 July the Nazis polled 13·7 million votes and with 230 seats became the largest party in the Reichstag. True, they did not have an overall majority. And the fact that the total Nazi vote did not exceed that of April suggested to some observers that, having won the middle classes over to them, the Nazis had reached their maximum strength from which they must decline as conditions slowly improved. All the same, it was an impressive demonstration of power and Hitler not unnaturally expected to come to power in the near future.

How was this to be achieved? The obvious road to power for a politician without an overall majority was via a coalition. With the middle-of-the-road parties virtually wiped out, the Catholic Centre Party with seventy-five seats was again a key factor in the Reichstag. If the Nazis could come to terms with the Centre, between them they would command a majority and Hitler could expect a substantial share of power in a parliamentary cabinet. On 2 August Hitler discussed this possibility with his associates and allowed Goering to mastermind negotiations with the Centre. However, on 5 August when Hitler met Schleicher, he adopted a very different line; he insisted on the chancellor-ship, some other posts for colleagues and an enabling bill to rule by decree. These conditions were unacceptable to the men in the corridors of power. On 13 August Papen offered Hitler the vice-chancellorship and one other post in the present government, whereupon an enraged Hitler threatened to let the Brownshirts go on the rampage. Papen and Schleicher were unmoved by Hitler's histrionics. Called to the presidential palace, Hitler reiterated his demands, to be informed coldly by the president that they were totally unacceptable. The most the old man would offer was the inclusion of some Nazis in a coalition government. There was no disguising the fact. Hitler had overplayed his hand and the Nazis had suffered a severe setback. To make matters worse the official communiqué implied that Hitler had asked for 'complete power' (which was not strictly true though that was his ultimate intention) and that he had broken his promise to support the Papen govern-ment (which was absolutely correct).

Why did Hitler adopt this intransigent posture, from which he did not budge for the next four months? Partly, it reflected his natural arrogance and overweening ambition inflamed by a surfeit of rhetoric in recent months which blinded him to the realities of power. There were other reasons. Hitler could not ignore the mood of the party or at any rate of the SA in 1932 any more than in 1923. To maintain his hold over his restless followers he had to negotiate pistol in hand and hold out for the big prize. Anything less than the chancellorship armed with emergency powers to 'smash Marxism' might fatally disillusion a party of protest which expected immediate alleviation of its grievances. Whether it made political sense or not, Hitler had to live up to the image he had created of the fearless leader and tireless crusader who scorned compromise in the battle for the soul of Germany. Haggling in committee was the stock-in-trade of shabby bourgeois politicians and completely unbecoming in a messiah called to recreate the face of the earth.[65] There were personal considerations also. Speaking to a *Gauleiter* colleague in the spring of 1932, Hitler expressed the fear that recurrent stomach pains might be cancerous. He went on: 'I have no time to wait . . . I must get to power in the near future in order to solve the gigantic tasks in the time remaining to me. I must. I must.'[66] This deep sense of urgency may have played a part in turning him against time-consuming coalitions in which he would have to struggle for months—or so he may have feared—before obtaining a monopoly of power. Considerations of this sort help to explain why he was ready to jeopardize the chances of a coalition on two occasions—firstly, on 5 August—because the Centre would have Hitler as chancellor only if Hindenberg did not object—and secondly, on 12 September when he ordered the Nazi deputies to defeat the Papen government and precipitate elections rather than work within the existing Reichstag to replace Papen by a Nazi-Centre coalition. Furious though he was over the rebuff at the presidential palace, Hitler did not lose his head. Immediately after the interview with Hindenburg, Hitler summoned the SA leaders and warned them against precipitate action. For despite everything he remained quite confident that it was only a matter of time before Papen and Schleicher were forced to come to terms. When an American correspondent asked him in late August if, in view of the setback, he would march on Berlin, he retorted:' Why should I march on Berlin? I'm there already. The question is . . . who is going to march out of Berlin?'[67]

The obstinate belief in victory on his own terms remained with him even when the tide turned against the Nazis. In September the new Reichstag was promptly dissolved after Papen was defeated by a Communist no-confidence motion carried with Nazi support. There were ominous signs of fatigue and strain in the party after months of ceaseless agitation always ending in a *cul de sac*. Strasser and Frick feared that the party must lose seats in the coming elections. Difficult though it is to gauge the extent of this feeling, it is likely that Strasser was expressing a view held quite widely by officials.[68] Frick was speaking for at least a substantial minority of Nazi deputies, who for obvious reasons doubted the wisdom of an election but had deferred to Hitler's orders on 12 September. Funds were desperately short because the radical line the party was taking against Papen alarmed those industrialists who earlier in 1932 had contributed quite generously. In these depressing circumstances it is something of a tribute to Hitler's personal magnetism that he was able to rally the exhausted party and infuse it with some of his own enthusiasm. But to little purpose: the party lost two million votes and thirty-four seats, a welcome confirmation of the decline some observers predicted after the July election.

Despite the gathering gloom in the party and the weakening in his bargaining position *vis-a-vis* Papen, Hitler remained obdurate. When Papen invited him to join in a government of 'national concentration'—for the rising Communist vote underlined the urgent need for an understanding with the Nazis—Hitler was unhelpful. Then, for tactical reasons, Papen suddenly resigned. Hitler, as the leader of the largest party, was invited to try to form a government with a Reichstag majority. A majority, whilst not impossible, would be difficult to construct, as Hindenburg and Papen were probably well aware.[69] And it was easy for Hitler to decline the invitation because Hindenburg imposed conditions, including the right to nominate the ministers of foreign affairs and defence, which were incompatible with the formation of a parliamentary government. But in any case, Hitler still wanted to be a presidential chancellor. And that was not on offer in November any more than in August. Hindenburg saw no reason for replacing Papen, whom he liked, by Hitler, whom he mistrusted, especially when the Nazi leader either could not or would not break the constitutional deadlock. Hitler's demand was again rejected and he came away empty-handed from the presidential palace. By any objective standard Hitler's continued refusal to come to terms was beginning to verge on mulish stupidity.

Hitler's obstinacy was no temporary aberration quickly abandoned but marked the beginning of a new phase in his political tactics which lasted for several months. No longer did he lapse into despair and apathy after reverses as he did in May and November 1923. The knowledge that the odds against success on his terms were mounting now served only to heighten his resolve to pursue an intransigent line relentlessly to the bitter end. Absolute victory or absolute defeat were the only alternatives acceptable to the Führer: the tougher the enemy's resistance, the greater the effort required to win the day. A reverse was not the occasion for a reappraisal of objectives but a reason for one more offensive. Or, as he put it in the thoroughly inappropriate mores of the battlefield: 'The more events move to their climax, the more sacrifices are called for in the battle. The battle will be decided by the man who leads the last battalion onto the battlefield.'[70] Resignations and expulsions from the party at the end of 1932 confirm the view that Hitler's rigidly messianic attitude and the corollary that the rank and file were expendable in battle—often literally—in the endless war of attrition for the will o' the wisp of final victory had begun to disillusion members.[71]

The psychological strain of his impossible position began to tell on Hitler by early December. That was probably the real significance of the Strasser crisis, caused more by Hitler's neurotic suspicion of opposition than by the objective situation in the party, serious though discontent with his policy was. The crisis followed quickly on Schleicher's appointment as chancellor on 2 December. Before his appointment Schleicher tried in vain to interest Hitler in becoming vice-chancellor under him. Strasser urged Hitler to take what looked like being his last chance of office. Goebbels and Goering still remained hard liners—

whether out of loyalty to Hitler or genuine conviction it is impossible to tell. On 3 December the dramatic fall in the Nazi poll in the Thuringian local elections underlined the unwisdom of intransigence. The same day Schleicher offered the vice-chancellorship to Strasser in a calculated bid to split the Nazis. As usual, Hitler discussed the offer with his lieutenants; as usual, Goebbels and Goering opposed the offer while Strasser, supported by Frick, urged acceptance. At last there were faint signs that Hitler might be willing to allow one of his henchmen to enter a Schleicher cabinet. For the offer was not rejected out of hand; instead Goering—not Strasser—was authorized to conduct further negotiations with Schleicher. Two days later at another meeting in the Kaiserhof Hotel, Hitler's Berlin headquarters, the Führer suddenly accused Strasser of systematic intrigue to replace him as leader. Strasser replied indignantly that it was Hitler who was leading the party to destruction. Next day Strasser left the party. Hitler was plunged into deepest despair. For a moment it looked as if Strasser might split the party asunder. In fact, such ambitions never entered his head. Instead of organizing resistance to Hitler, he went off to Italy with his family. Hitler recovered quickly. The party was put in the hands of Goebbels and Ley. On 9 December at a meeting of *Gauleiters* and other high officials Hitler exerted all his rhetorical skill to confirm himself as leader. Even so, the effects of the crisis lingered on. Hitler, Goering and Goebbels visited many local parties in December to reassure the rank and file. The crisis flared up again in mid-January when it became known that Strasser had informed President Hindenburg of his readiness to enter the Schleicher cabinet. Nothing came of it but Hitler was extremely worried at the effect this might have on the party. Luckily for Hitler the Strasser crisis ended without disaster. But it must surely cast some doubt on Hitler's capacity as leader. At a time when solidarity was the need of the hour, given his intransigent line, he wantonly jeopardized party unity by an ill-considered outburst. There is no firm evidence that Strasser was deliberately undermining Hitler's position, or that he would have accepted Schleicher's offer against Hitler's express wishes. It could be that Goebbels and Goering poisoned Hitler's mind against Strasser in one of the endless intrigues going on around the person of the Führer. Almost certainly Strasser's persistent opposition to Hitler's 'all or nothing' tactics irritated him and made him susceptible to their insinuations. Although there is no proof, is it not conceivable that Hitler exploded with rage and frustration precisely because he was beginning to wonder whether Strasser might not be right?

Eight weeks later Hitler became German chancellor. Does this mean that Hitler's intransigent tactics had been right all along? Not necessarily. Hitler was rescued from the dead end of permanent opposition through a stroke of good fortune and despite his own obstinacy. Papen's offer of a joint chancellorship—a constitutional impossibility—would not have done the trick on its own. Without a significant shift in the attitude of many industrialists and great landowners towards National Socialism at the end of 1932, Hitler's appointment would scarcely have been possible at that point in time. Only when these circles threw their weight behind Papen's efforts to draw Hitler into the government, did the situation change decisively in his favour.

The precise nature of the functional relationship between fascism and capitalism has been the subject of much, often quite heated, controversy in recent years. Without wishing to enter into a detailed discussion inappropriate in this context, this writer is of the opinion that interpretations which eschew theoretical foundations and treat the issue largely as one of personal relationships between Hitler and a handful of leading industrialists are no more satisfactory than the classic Marxist-Leninist definition of fascism (in 1935) as 'the openly terroristic dictatorship of the most reactionary, most chauvinistic and most imperialist elements in finance capitalism', bent on war to achieve their expansionist objectives. Hopefully, further empirical research into the political attitudes and business strategies of individual firms will reveal more clearly the complexities, subtleties and possibly contradictions in the relationship between industry and National Socialism, hidden from us at present by extraneous ideological considerations which have intruded overmuch into the academic argument. Yet one cannot remain entirely aloof from this continuing debate if merely because meaningful discussion of Hitler is, as indicated earlier, only possible in a conceptual framework. The interpretation advanced below does not, of course, pretend to be more than a working hypothesis but possibly one with more development potential in it than alternative interpretations.[72]

German industry did not react uniformly to the National Socialist phenomenon. Throughout the 1920s when industry hoped to restore Germany to her former greatness by winning new export markets, it showed virtually no interest in the economic nationalism prescribed by the Nazis as a panacea for all economic ills. Even when the Nazis became a considerable political force, most industrialists and landowners supported Bruening and Papen, not Hitler. For Papen was remarkably sensitive to the wishes of industry and agriculture; he imposed quotas on foreign food imports, promised tax reductions and credits to stage an economic revival, and removed wage and taxation policy from Reichstag control. But while the economically viable and export-oriented firms (a category including, at the time, I. G. Farben) showed no interest in Nazism, the 'lame ducks' in the coal and steel industries paralysed by the crisis as a result of the high degree of rationalization carried out in the late 1920s, reacted quite differently. Quite early on in the crisis the coal and steel magnates and the bankers associated with these industries recognized that their economic salvation lay in rearmament (as advocated by the Nazis). Accordingly they were very active in the Harzburg Front, a loose association of right-wing organizations including the German Nationalists and Stahlhelm which came into being in the autumn of 1931 to agitate for the dismissal of Chancellor Bruening and the holding of new elections.

However, according to this interpretation, only in 1932–3 when it began to dawn on German industry as a whole that there was no hope of a quick recovery in world markets, and that their salvation also lay in massive state aid and in internal markets, did the *Grossraumwirtschaft,* or self-sufficient economy, stretching into Southeastern Europe, which the Nazis favoured, suddenly became an attractive proposition.[73] It was symptomatic of the changing attitude of large-scale industry that the powerful chemical combine I. G. Farben and the German car industry, both previously export-oriented industries, now subscribed to this view.

What probably forced the issue out into the open was the appointment of Schleicher as Chancellor. The 'social general' planned to revive the economy through a programme of public works—channelling funds not into industry but into municipal authorities' pockets—and on the basis of close cooperation with the trade union movement. The possibility that Schleicher might halt negotiations to return the Stahlverein, the most influential steel cartel in Germany, to private hands may have been an additional worry for the steel industry. What the Nazis offered was not only assured markets at home but the prospect of high profit margins. As cartelization prevented any significant fall in prices during the economic crisis, the only way to maintain profits was by the depression of wages. Through the destruction of parliamentary democracy and the suppression of the trade union movement the Nazis would make it possible to reduce drastically the social contributions which had added to production costs in the 1920s and to hold wages down to the depressed level of the crisis. With the Nazi vote falling, the 'lame ducks', who happened to be the most powerful sector of industry in terms of political influence, redoubled their efforts to rally the whole of industry round a Hitler chancellorship.

Whether industry on its own would have been influential enough to persuade Hindenburg to appoint Hitler may well be doubted. The alienation of powerful agrarian circles from Schleicher—because of the attempt to revive Bruening's resettlement plan—was a factor of great importance in the final stages. What is fundamental to this interpretation is the belief that by the beginning of 1933 a general consensus of opinion in industry and agriculture was beginning to form in favour of a fascist dictatorship. The fact that Hitler had broken at last with the 'radical' Strasser probably helped to overcome any lingering doubts about Nazi bona fides.

Most certainly this interpretation is not without weaknesses.[74] Its merit is that it does not fall into the error of overpersonalizing the coming to power of Hitler, by attributing this event to the machinations of a small group of conspiratorially-minded politicians with or without (depending on personal preference) the support of a few powerful industrial magnates and Junker landowners. On the contrary, the actions of individuals and groups are seen in the proper context of the underlying socio-economic trends which shaped the general course of events in the early 1930s. At the same time, individuals are not denied their proper place in the historical process. To return to Hitler: it was most fortuitous for him that German industry was moving towards the conclusion that National Socialism was the only viable economic alternative precisely at the time when Hitler's followers were becoming restive. Had industry taken longer to arrive there, some other Nazi leader might just conceivably have been the beneficiary. Nor is one bound by this interpretation to believe in the inevitability of fascism. Had the world economy recovered more quickly, there is no reason to suppose that Germany would still have opted for armaments and autarky.

Hitler played a modest role in the 'conspiracy' because success depended not on his 'determination' but on other people's estimate of his usefulness to them. Of course, he contributed his widow's mite in the shape of the Lippe-Detmold election where, by a supreme effort, the Nazis managed to win 39 per cent of the votes in this miniscule *Land,* still less than the July poll but sufficient to give some credence to the strident Nazi claim that the party was 'on the move' again. Three days later Hitler told Papen that he would not share the chancellorship. This time he was knocking at an open door. Papen helped Hitler persuade Oskar von Hindenburg, the president's son, and Meissner, the president's secretary, that they should persuade the old man to appoint Hitler. On 28 January Schleicher resigned, having failed to obtain a Reichstag majority or persuade the president to dissolve the Reichstag but postpone fresh elections. Papen, asked to mastermind the formation of a new government, made rapid progress. For the 52 Nationalist deputies agreed to support the Nazis largely because Hugenberg was incensed by Schleicher's land colonization policy and offended by his refusal to give him the economics ministry. And Hitler was prepared to join a conservative-dominated cabinet provided fresh elections were promised. That demand aroused Hugenberg's suspicions; with a rare flash of insight he guessed that Hitler would make a bid for absolute power with the state apparatus on his side and then dispense with his 'reactionary' allies as he had done in 1929. Only in the ante-chamber of the presidential palace did he reluctantly agree to this condition. Minutes later Hitler was appointed chancellor of Germany.

It is often said that Hitler was not a presidential chancellor.[75] This is untrue. He had the full support of the president. Legislation passed in the next two months was not submitted to the Reichstag but promulgated as decrees by using the president's emergency powers. Certainly Hitler promised to seek a majority in the Reichstag but that had been expected of other presidential chancellors. Even if Hitler was more likely to find a majority—a factor which must have weighed very heavily with Hindenburg when he appointed Hitler—there could be no certainty of success. And what Schleicher had been denied was promised Hitler—the dissolution of the Reichstag. Good luck more than good tactics put Hitler in the chancellery. That he was able to establish a party dictatorship and completely destroy political freedom in the next few months was again due as much to favourable circumstances as to Hitler's political skill.

He had no need to exert himself greatly to outwit his conservative allies. Outside the democratic left no one was prepared to defend the parliamentary system. Even the official Communist Party tried to console itself with the myopic belief that Hitlerism was a transient phase on the road to socialism. In the cabinet no one disagreed with Papen's observation that a return to parliamentary government was to be avoided.[76] Hitler's deliberate sabotage of the negotiations with the Centre Party—the failure of which was the technical reason for the Reichstag's dissolution—was accepted without demur in cabinet. When he addressed a meeting of industrialists on 20 February appealing for funds for the election campaign, his assurance that this would be 'the last election' resulted in generous donations to party funds. The Reichstag fire on 28 February was an additional bonus. At the correct psychological moment he was given a stick with which to beat the Communists, and with his customary skill as *Trommler* he stampeded the middle classes into a grand reaffirmation of their faith in him. So fortuitous was the fire, that it is difficult not to believe that it was instigated by the Nazis, a view for which there is much historical evidence. The important consequence was the suspension of civil liberties by presidential decree—without cabinet protest—and the commencement of a savage reign of terror against opponents of the regime. In the hectic atmosphere of the March Days Hitler secured the passage of a bill legalizing the dictatorship to follow. Some chicanery was required to obtain the Centre's support but even without it the bill would have been passed. One should not overlook here the considerable benefit Hitler derived from the resurgence of national feeling in the spring of 1933 and the widespread sense of relief that the Weimar system had been superseded—sentiments much in evidence at the impressive Potsdamer Tag, a great display of right-wing solidarity held on 21 March. The speed with which the democratic parties—the Centre, the Nationalists and the Populists, a small right-wing party much favoured at one time by industrialists—dissolved themselves in the summer of 1933 without the slightest resistance is final proof that the broad middle classes had no regrets for the passing of parliamentary democracy. Even Hitler was surprised at the swiftness with which he had been able to establish the one-party state.[77]

2

The dictator 1933–45

Propaganda machines in all totalitarian countries habitually depict the dictator as the saviour of his people from some danger real, or more usually imaginary, and as the man of action who decides what is best for his country with clarity of mind and singleness of purpose, and can always rely on his orders being carried out with devotion and meticulous care by an army of well-disciplined robots. So it was with Hitler. Seen through the eyes of the Goebbels propaganda ministry, Hitler was always the far-seeing and benevolent Führer, the man of genius, concerned about the cares and worries of every German, and steering the ship of state with unerring eye towards the goals of National Socialism.

There is, in fact, abundant evidence that the smack of firm government was conspicuously absent from the chancellery. Before attempting any assessment of Hitler's role in the Third Reich it is, therefore, absolutely essential to examine at some length the structure of goverment under the Nazis and in particular the administrative style Hitler evolved for himself as well as the consequences of this for the broad pattern of policy-making after 1933.

For the first year or so, as long as Hindenburg was alive, Hitler conformed to the irksome restriction of regular office hours. Very soon after the old man's death the pattern of decision-making at the level of Führer and chancellor became disorderly and somewhat haphazard as the business of state started to revolve around the erratic personal habits of the dictator. Hitler, like William II, disliked Berlin, the huge souless metropolis, and before the war contrived to spend as many weekends as possible in Bavaria. On Fridays and Mondays he was, therefore, frequently inaccessible to Berlin officials. In the summer it was much worse for he spent longer periods at the Berghof. And even when he was in Berlin his habit of rising late and spending two to three hours over lunch drastically reduced the working day. When he emerged from his room around midday, having breakfasted and perused the newspapers, the chancellery sprang to life. Officials and visitors, many of whom thronged the ante-chamber for hours, vied with each other for a few minutes with the Führer, either to press pet schemes on him or to expedite essential business. If lucky enough to catch the Führer, callers often had to conduct business either walking alongside him on his way to lunch, or buttonhole him in some corner where he was surrounded by members of his immediate entourage. Pressed for decisions on matters which the suitors thought urgent, Hitler often displayed a marked aversion to clear concise orders; as in the old days he took refuge behind open-ended generalities or even evaded a decision completely.

Further confusion arose because of contradictory orders emanating from the Führer's circle. In the company of party officials—*Gauleiter, Reichsleiter* and SA and SS dignataries, all of whom had a standing invitation to lunch with him—Hitler felt more relaxed, less on his guard and more inclined to act impulsively if a table companion persuaded him to endorse a line of action running counter to established policy. Divergent interpretations of the Führer's 'irrevocable' decision on a particular issue might well be in circulation at a given moment, each representing what individuals who had discussed the matter, however casually, with Hitler, genuinely supposed were the Führer's intentions. Confusion of this kind had a debilitating effect on the smooth running of government departments and turned administrative policy into the plaything of warring factions.

Confusion about the direction of policy was not restricted to the immediate circle round the Führer. The whole structure of government has been aptly dubbed 'authoritarian anarchy'.[1] The popular picture of the Third Reich as a monolithic unity with all parts of the well-oiled machine responsive to the Führer's will has long been discredited by historians.[2] A more exact parallel would be with feudal society, where vassals great and small struggled endlessly with each other and with their overlords to establish themselves as the king's chief adviser. The administrative structure of Nazi Germany formed a complex mosaic of party and state agencies with ill-defined and overlapping jurisdictions, sometimes complementing each other, more often mutually anagonistic, all striving to obtain a monopoly of power in their own domain. For example, in the field of foreign affairs, no less that three party agencies were in direct competion with the foreign office and with each other. There were similar rivalries in the economic field. By 1936 Hermann Goering's central office for the Four Year Plan seemed to have established its complete ascendancy over the ministry of economics under Hjaldemar Schacht. But as Goering's reputation declined during the war, he faced fresh competiton from new rivals—the army economics and armaments office headed by General Georg Thomas, and the ministry of armaments and munitions set up by Hitler in 1940 to deal with severe munitions shortages. Under Fritz Todt and then Albert Speer this ministry became the most powerful economic agency in Germany. Even inside his own central office Goering's position was further weakened when Hitler handed over to Fritz Sauckel plenipotentiary powers over labour forces in 1942. Rivalries inside the party were every bit as fierce as those between state and party agencies; witness, for example, the constant friction between Hitler's personal staff and party officials or the smouldering animosity between the Führer's chancellery, headed by Gauleiter Philipp Bouhler, and the party chancellery under Rudolf Hess. These are only a few of the more obvious examples of the friction and duplication of effort riddling the entire administrative structure of Nazi Germany.

The chaos would have been quite intolerable had the Nazis been committed to a far-reaching programme of social change designed to shift the balance of power away from a privileged minority towards the mass of the people. Such programmes call for constant and purposeful direction at the highest level and predicate the existence of an integrated machinery of government strong enough to break down the tenacious opposition of vested interests to radical social change. Nazi objectives, ostensibly ambitious, in actual fact required minimal changes in the politico-economic structure of Germany. Territorial expansion—by fits and starts—and the persecution of opponents, especially the Jewish community, were attainable with much less than the total mobilization of Germany's resources. To put it another way: Hitler's rambling style of leadership and the quasi-anarchical administrative structure as it emerged after 1933 were perfectly compatible with the creation of Grossdeutschland and the expulsion from public life of the Jews. Whether it would have been adequate for the management of a vast racial empire where true Aryans lorded it over subject peoples is another matter. For the time being the machinery of government continued to function adequately enough. This because, despite the air of confusion, ministers, *Gauleiter* and *Reichsleiter* were in practice free to proceed as they saw fit, interpreting Hitler's cryptic comments or silences to suit the needs of the immediate situation or the exigencies of the particular power struggle they were engaged in. The daily charade at the chancellery and the superficial deference paid to the person of the Führer scarcely disguised the basic reality of life in the Third Reich. Powerful party officials were able to do much as they pleased within the broad and infinitely flexible framework of the Nationalist Socialist ideology, justifying their actions, when challenged by opponents, with reference to one or other interpretations of what the Führer had said (often without giving the matter much thought). If these men were strong enough they could even obtain post-hoc approval for their illegal action. They were encouraged to hold the law in contempt by the sure knowledge that Hitler hated jurists, regarded the law as nothing more than administrative convenience, and often interfered quite arbitrarily with its due processes. It is not surpising that the firm foundations of the old bureaucratic state were progressively undermined by the application to government of the party doctrine that the will of the Führer was the supreme law.

This analysis of government in Nazi Germany leaves unanswered the key question which a study of Hitler's personality cannot ignore: why did he allow the government of Germany to be conducted in this quasi-anarchical fashion? It is tempting to explain it all in terms of Hitler's rather bohemian life style. Reference was made in the last chapter to his unpunctuality, his erratic work routine and his failure to keep appointments—a source of much embarrassment to party officials who usually found him in the late afternoon in one of his Munich café haunts, eating cream cakes and regaling naive admirers with tall stories from the early stuggles of the movement. On his own admission a day spent poring over official documents was a day wasted. Baldur von Schirach, the Nazi youth leader, also recalled that he never saw papers spread out over Hitler's desk.[3]

It is unwise to make too much of personal idiosyncrasies. The fact is that Hitler was not always unpunctual and casual in his attitude: on official occasions—especially military ones—he appeared on time. When receiving foreign statesmen he invariably came well-briefed and argued a case persuasively as Sir John Simon and Anthony Eden recalled after their conversations in Berlin in March 1935.[4] Even his notorious aversion to routine work was probably no great disadvantage in a man who could and did cross-examine officials closely and skilfully. This ability coupled with a mercurial intelligence compensated to a large extent for the neglect of the documentation that came his way. Nor should one forget that Hitler displayed exemplary devotion to duty during the war years, throwing himself wholeheartedly into the struggle, surely a final proof that he could keep his natural indolence within bounds whenever it was necessary for the attainment of his objectives.

It has been said that Hitler deliberately encouraged confusion and uncertainty as a means of consolidating his own power.[5] By increasing the number of agencies or individuals operating in a given area and playing one off against the other—the classic *divide et impera* policy—Hitler prevented the emergence of serious rivals and established himself in government as the supreme arbiter, the role he already played in the party. There is certainly some evidence suggesting that he tolerated power struggles at the lowest level in the party in order to prevent the consolidation of opposition and to increase the dependence of jealous rivals on the Führer's favour. At the highest level Hitler undoubtedly contributed to the duplication of effort characteristic of Nazi Germany, his favourite device being the appointment of special plenipotentiaries to handle specific problems. For example, instead of leaving the construction of *Autobahnen* to the ministry of economics, he appointed Fritz Todt in 1934 with special powers to carry out the assignment and made him directly accountable to the Führer alone. This was the origin of Organisation Todt, an agency which came to play a significant role in economic affairs yet remained outside the jurisdiction of Schacht's ministry and Goering's central office. In foreign affairs Hitler frequently by-passed the foreign office (which he deeply mistrusted) and made use of special envoys such as Joachim von Ribbentrop and Papen. It was also characteristic of the 'Führer style' that Hitler often appointed envoys without the knowledge of others actively engaged in the same field; this was in accordance with his general belief that subordinates needed to know only enough to perform their own task, a practice which naturally enhanced his own position and added to the general confusion surrounding his personal initiatives.

On the other hand, one of the most recent historians of the administrative structure of Nazi Germany argues convincingly that Hitler did not consciously pursue a policy of 'divide and rule'.[6] Such a policy is normally followed by rulers who fear the emergence of rivals. This fear does not, however, appear to have preoccupied Hitler once Roehm and his associates had been murdered. It would be more accurate to say of Hitler not that he divided in order to rule, but rather that he stood aside during inter-party and inter-agency disputes until the outcome was in no doubt. Then he promptly came out on the side of the victor. It could easily be argued that a man who disliked making up his mind would behave in this fashion. Probably it also reflected Hitler's order of priorities; he was much more interested in architecture than in interminable party wrangles. But above all the practice was in accordance with his Social Darwinist beliefs. Nature could be safely relied upon to reveal who was the weaker party in any power political conflict; all one had to do was wait patiently until the struggle had ended.[7] A practice which permitted men such as Himmler and Goering to build up immensely powerful bases by combining party and government office was not, of course, without attendant dangers. Quite illogically, Hitler supposed that the strong, once they had survived the trial by battle, would serve him loyally, in other words that the struggle for power would not be directed against him. Incredibly he was proved right. The powerful vassals surrounding him never conspired against him, perhaps because he always handled them with care and succeeded in exerting his old magic and charisma over them individually and collectively until the very end.

Some degree of administrative anarchy was probably inevitable in the Third Reich whatever kind of man Hitler had been. The restless and ambitious men thrown up by the convulsions of the early 1930s were almost certain to continue to struggle against each other in a closed political system riddled with corruption and offering few constructive outlets for their energies. It must be remembered that the party as such exercised no specific governmental function in the Third Reich. After 1933 Hitler consigned it to a political limbo where it was little more than a propaganda agency ancillary to the Goebbels ministry though of some use to the Führer when he encountered resistance from state agencies. Only party officials who succeeded in securing government posts exerted real influence at the top in Nazi Germany. It was precisely this consciousness of the party's greatly diminished status that spurred on others, especially the *Gauleiter,* to usurp state functions wherever possible. Duplication of effort, demarcation disputes and internecine warfare between party and state agencies were inevitable consequences of the relentless struggle for status. It suited Hitler to tolerate a polycratic system which originated quite independently of him and which he could hardly have changed short of conferring on the party a monopoly of state power—which he was not prepared to do for the sufficient reason that the present system guaranteed him a very considerable degree of freedom of manoeuvre.

Having said all this, it seems anticlimactic to enter the important caveat that one must not exaggerate the effects of this atomized system of government on the processes of policy-making. It would be quite wrong to suppose that the mass of the people was aware of these structural defects or lukewarm in its support of the regime on that account. On the contrary, the Goebbels ministry took good care to propagate the image of a united, efficient and monolithic state and did this so successfully that many foreigners as well as Germans were inclined to think the Nazi state a good deal more efficient and powerful than it really was. Secondly, for all its faults the structure of government was never so anarchical that Hitler could not get his way once he had made up his mind to act. Sometimes it took him a long time to make a decision but when he did, his personal orders, or *Führererlasse,* cut quickly through the administrative jungle and the red tape and ensured compliance with his decisions at least on major matters of policy and within the limits of available resources.

This raises a question of fundamental importance for the study of personality. To what extent was Hitler, in fact, responsible for the policies pursued in the Third Reich? In view of what has been said already about Hitler 'the Führer' in the 1920s, can one assume without further investigation that he was at all times and in every area of policy the dominant figure in Nazi Germany after 1933? Is it not at least conceivable that, in speaking of 'Hitler's Germany', 'Hitler's foreign policy' and 'Hitler's Final Solution', one is in danger of doing violence to a complex historical phenomenon and of attributing to one man's initiative much of what might have happened in Germany without him? In the hope of throwing some light on a crucial issue, so often glossed over in the biographies of Hitler, some attempt will be made in this chapter to try and assess the actual extent of Hitler's influence on policy, taking as examples three vital areas—foreign policy, economic development and the treatment of the Jews.

Before doing so, it may be helpful to identify the dramatis personae, the institutions and groups of individuals which in the ever-changing balance of power in the Third Reich may have exerted some influence on policy. First and foremost, one thinks of the leading agencies of state power—the foreign office under Foreign Minister Konstantin Freiherr von Neurath (up to 1938) and Secretary of State Bernhard von Bülow; the ministry of economics directed by Schacht from 1934 to 1937; the ministry of the interior under Frick (up to 1942); the newly-formed ministry of enlightenment and propaganda under Goebbels; the armed forces under the pro-Nazi minister of war, General Werner von Blomberg, and his chief assistant, Colonel Walther von Reichenau; the navy under Admiral Erich Raeder; and the airforce under Goering. Nor should one overlook the chancellery itself where Dr Hans Lammers, the chief secretary, aided by a small staff, attended to the correspondence between the ministers and the chancellor and was in a unique position to influence the course of events. Secondly, but no less important, there were the great industrial combines which, if not directly then at least indirectly, may have exerted influence on economic policy and on the course of foreign policy as well.

Thirdly, there was Hitler's personal entourage. From the earliest days of the movement Hitler surrounded himself with a motley crew chosen less for their ability than for their personal friendship with the Führer. At its most extensive in the hey day of the Third Reich between 1933 and 1941, it included between sixty and seventy individuals—*Gauleiter, Reichsleiter* and prominent SA and SS officials. This group can be narrowed down to a much smaller group of about a dozen men having easy access to Hitler at all times. These were all long-serving party members, all roughly the same age as the Führer and mostly with administrative experience in the party. The composition of this 'kitchen cabinet' changed over the years but included at least for some of the time the following—Hermann Goering, prime minister of Prussia, commander-in-chief of the Luftwaffe, economic overlord of the Four Year Plan and a powerful figure from mid-1935 to about 1940 after which his influence rapidly waned; Heinrich Himmler, head of the German police and *Reichsleiter* of the SS who remained a powerful and sinister figure from 1936 to the end of the Reich; Josef Goebbels, minister of propaganda and *Gauleiter* of Berlin who was on very friendly terms with the Führer to the end apart from brief interludes in 1937–8 and 1943–4; Rudolf Hess, Hitler's deputy since April 1938 and minister without portfolio, in British captivity after 1941; Adolf Wagner, Bavarian minister of justice and *Gauleiter* of Bavaria up to his death in 1944 and a close personal friend who read the Führer's opening proclamation at the party rally because he had the same Upper Austrian accent; Erich Koch, Reich commissioner for the Ukraine during the war and *Gauleiter* of East Prussia; Fritz Sauckel, plenipotentiary for labour between 1942 and 1945 and *Gauleiter* of Thuringia; Karl Kaufmann, Reich commissioner for shipping and *Gauleiter* of Hamburg; Josef Bürckel, Reich commissioner for the Saarland, Austria and Lorraine; Franz Schwarz, the party treasurer; and last but not least, Martin Bormann, chief of staff to Hess and, after the latter's flight to Scotland, one of the most powerful figures in Germany.

Fourthly, Hitler was served by a small personal staff which handled his private affairs and regulated his appointments.[8] This staff grew up piecemeal over the years and included Julius Schreck, first leader of the SS and up to his death in 1936 Hitler's chauffeur; Julius Schaub, a founder member of the SS appointed Hitler's adjutant in 1923 (in place of Ulrich Graef who was badly wounded in the putsch) and still with him at the end, a man of limited ability who acted as a personal bodyguard and looked after Hitler's houses in Munich and Berchtesgaden; Wilhelm Brückner, who joined the staff in 1930 and was chief adjutant from 1935 to 1941; and Fritz Wiedemann, Hitler's old commanding officer who served from 1935 to his dismissal in 1939 and was probably the most influential of them.[9] Before the war the Führer's adjutants, though completely lacking institutional foundations, became an intermediate body between state agencies and the party and were in a position to exert some influence on events depending on the temperament and ability of individual adjutants. For example, Lammers used to visit Hitler daily in 1933; by the end of 1934 he was waiting weeks for an interview as the Führer now preferred to give orders to heads of departments via his adjutants. High officials and party members seeking redress of grievances quickly got into the habit of approaching the adjutants directly, by-passing Hitler's private chancellery run by Hess, and the Führer's chancellery set up in 1934 under Philipp Bouhler. The rise of Bormann saw a sharp decline in the influence exerted by the adjutants.

After Hindenburg's death Hitler, now supreme commander of the armed forces, felt the need for officers in his immediate entourage who would liaise with the ministry of war. In 1934 Colonel Friedrich Hossbach was appointed as liaison man with the army. In 1935 Captain Karl Jesco von Puttkamer was appointed to liaise with the navy (up to 1938) and Captain Mauritius with the airforce (up to 1937 when Captain Nicolaus von Below replaced him). In 1938 Hossbach was dismissed and replaced by Colonel Rudolf Schmundt. But General Walther von Brauchitsch, the new commander-in-chief of the army, refused to sanction joint representation of the army command and the high command by one man, so Major Gerhard Engel was appointed to liaise with the army (up to 1943) while Schmundt represented the high command. On the whole, the military adjutants do not appear to have exerted any significant influence over Hitler. Nevertheless, he seems to have been extremely frank in discussion with at least one of them.[10] But once war broke out and Hitler devoted his energies to military matters almost exclusively, then their importance grew.

Finally, for off-duty hours Hitler chose quite different companions. The group which sat with him into the early hours around the fireplace at the Berghof consisted for the most part of old Munich friends such as Heinrich Hoffmann, the party photographer. Eva Braun was in this circle, so was Morell, Hitler's doctor, and Albert Speer. Of them all only Speer exerted any real influence over Hitler, and that in his capacity as minister of armaments not as a member of this intimate circle, which existed only to provide Hitler with the adulatory audience he needed.

The subjects which fascinated Hitler more than any other were military strategy and foreign affairs. In the 1920s and early 1930s the iniquity of the Versailles treaty and the coming resurrection of Germany were his favourtie themes on public platforms. After 1933 he continued to regard foreign policy as his own personal province. It is not, of course, in dispute that Hitler exerted a major influence in this field. But was his influence the decisive factor in the 1930s? Can one say that Hitler imposed on Germany a distinctive foreign policy which she would not have followed had he fallen on the Odeonsplatz or been outmanoeuvred by Strasser? Were there 'alternative' foreign policies which might have been adopted? How far was Hitler forced into expansion—if at all—by internal pressures? These are the questions one must ask in attempting to define more precisely Hitler's own role in policy-making.[11]

It is important to bear in mind at the outset that the international situation was exceptionally favourable for Germany in 1933. Bruening and Papen had already contributed significantly to the further dismantling of the Versailles system. At the Lausanne Conference in July 1932 reparations were virtually scrapped while Papen's intransigent stand in November forced the great powers to woo Germany back to the Disarmament Conference with a promise of equality in armaments. And as Germany began to recover some of her old power, the fragility of the post-war settlement was thrown into sharp relief. In Southeastern Europe where Austria-Hungary had been superseded by a medley of small states suspicious of each other and beset with economic difficulties, serious resistance to German expansionism whether under Papen, Schleicher or Hitler was unlikely to develop. The old Triple Entente which kept Wilhelmean Germany at bay in the early twentieth century could not be resurrected. In place of Tsarist Russia stood the Soviet Union, a young and weak state, ostracized by the powers because of its (dwindling) commitment to world revolution, preoccupied with grave internal problems, and in urgent need of a period of uninterrupted peace free of all international entanglements. Britain, France and Italy had little in common beyond a hearty dislike of Communism. When it came to the problem of resurgent Germany, they had convincingly demonstrated their lack of unity over reparations and disarmament. Nor was the United States prepared at this time to play a role in Europe commensurate with its tremendous economic power. The overall effect of American isolationism and Russian disengagement was to fatally weaken the peace settlement by depriving Britain and France of the extra-European dimension they needed to preserve the status quo. Into this promising situation stepped Chancellor Hitler. The balance of advantage was in his favour internationally as it had been in his favour locally when he entered Munich politics fourteen years before.

And if it was his intention to continue the active and increasingly abrasive foreign policy of Papen and Schleicher, then he could rely on solid support from foreign office, diplomatic corps, army command and industry. When he informed the Reichswehr commanders on 3 February 1933 that only when Germany smashed Marxism, developed a martial spirit in her people and built up a large army, would she 'regain political power' and be able to 'fight for new export possibilities' or seek 'the conquest of new living space in the east and its ruthless Germanization',[12] his audience did not demur at an oversimplified analysis which summarily discounted the probability that, as political and economic conditions changed, much more of the Versailles treaty might be amended by international agreement. The men in the corridors of power in Berlin, who had grown up in the sabre-rattling days of William II, never doubted that force would very probably be needed one day to alter the eastern frontiers, the feature of the treaty which most offended official Germany. As for the vast Nazi empire stretching to the Urals, much of what Hitler said on that subject—and in public he rarely talked about it—was discounted as idle chatter. So that for a good part of the way at least, Hitler could rely on the wholehearted support of his permanent officials.[13] Thus Germany's withdrawal from the Disarmament Conference and from the League of Nations, an event of major international importance, cannot be attributed to Hitler's personal influence alone even in respect of the timing. When it became clear in the autumn that Britain and Italy intended to support a tougher French line on arms control to test German good faith before general disarmament, Blomberg and Neurath were just as anxious as Hitler to withdraw, because the scope of the rearmament being planned was incompatible with the acceptance of any international arms agreement even in the short term. No doubt Hitler was hankering after a prestige victory to swing the German people onto his side in the impending struggle with Roehm's Brownshirts and to take their minds off the continuance of high unemployment—but these were relatively minor considerations. It is significant, too, that when President Hindenburg had to be talked round, Papen was as eager to play his part as Neurath. It may be that Blomberg's arguments were the decisive ones in convincing Hitler that Germany dare not tarry at Geneva.[14] But that was purely a matter of tactics and does not alter the salient feature of the operation: this was 'consensus' foreign policy carried out in full agreement with the men in the corridors of power.

On the other hand, in some areas where a different policy might well have been pursued, Hitler was already taking a personal initiative. In the case of Austria, it was Hitler, not Neurath, who decided to try to overthrow Chancellor Engelbert Dollfuss by unorthodox methods. After the March elections the euphoric Führer hit upon the novel idea of mobilizing the Nazi party machine in a great propaganda drive to force Dollfuss to hold fresh elections. Hitler's sanguine and quite unrealistic expectation was that the Austrian Nazis would become a major political force so that their country could be assimilated quietly into Nazi Germany at a time when the very word *Anschluss* (union with Germany) would have set the alarm bells ringing in Paris and Rome. Whether Hitler was encouraged in these wild hopes by Hess and other excited party colleagues in Munich we do not know. The result was a noisy propaganda campaign which lasted on and off for over twelve months, utterly failed to achieve its goal, and seriously damaged Germany's international standing into the bargain. Though largely short-circuited over the Austrian affair, the pliant Neurath quickly approved of the unofficial campaign; after all, it was designed to secure one of the traditional objectives of the revisionists—the union with Austria forbidden in 1919.

The abandonment of Germany's longstanding animosity towards Poland was also of Hitler's doing. Tension between the two states was growing before he came to power. Early in March Poland increased the garrison on the Westerplatte near Danzig hoping in this way to pressurize Germany into recognizing the eastern frontier. The Germans refused to be drawn and the crisis died away. In late April the Poles renewed the war of nerves. This was an inconvenient moment because Neurath's intransigent tactics at the Disarmament Conference were antagonizing the Western powers. Hitler felt a compulsion to act. Meeting the Polish ambassador on 2 May, a conciliatory Führer expressed his wish for an agreement and spoke of Poland's role as a bulwark against Bolshevism in Eastern Europe, a line he adhered to up to March 1939. Contacts were renewed in the late autumn and the Polish-German Non-Aggression Pact was signed in January 1934. Some doubts were expressed about the *volte face* both in the foreign office and army command. But even the most prejudiced anti-Polish nationalist had to concede that Hitler's adroit diplomacy had breached the French *cordon sanitaire* in the east, ended German isolation at a stroke, and neutralized a serious military threat along the eastern frontier. Possibly the pact had a long-term as well as a short-term perspective for Hitler. Though he had by no means written off Danzig and the

Corridor like a second South Tyrol, he may have been looking beyond a settlement of German claims on Poland to the possibility of a new political constellation, with Poland as a junior partner in that great anti-Russian crusade which, however vaguely formulated, was probably never far from his mind. Hitler was not alone in thinking along these lines; this solution of the Polish problem also commended itself to several high-ranking Nazis among them Goering, Hess, Rosenberg, Koch and Rauschning.[15]

Similarly over Russia. Hitler was very largely responsible for the discontinuation of traditional German policy towards that state. Weimar Germany and Soviet Russia were appreciative of the mutual advantages to be derived from remaining on tolerably good terms with each other, ideological differences notwithstanding. Nothing need have changed in 1933. The Russians wished to maintain the German connection despite uneasiness about the anti-Russian bias of the Nazis. And at first Hitler raised no objections. In February he authorized a credit agreement for 105 million *Reichsmark*. In April the treaty of Berlin, signed by Germany and Russia in 1926 to re-establish friendly relations between their two countries, was extended. And as late as May 1933 German generals were still visiting Russia. Then in the middle of 1933 Hitler began to insist on proper recognition being given to the 'natural antagonism' between Nazi Germany and Bolshevik Russia. Possibly the need to justify the dictatorship was uppermost in his mind; it was the politician's instinct to keep before the eyes of the people—especially at a time of continuing economic crisis—the 'Russian bogey' from which he claimed to have saved them. It also fitted in quite well with the new Polish policy. Therefore, nothing was done to halt the deterioration in Russo-German relations caused by the fiercely anti-Soviet line of the ministry of propaganda, and by the Nazi failure to protect Soviet property in Germany. Neurath, as usual, accommodated himself to the new line.

Finally, it was Hitler's initiative that led to the Anglo-German Naval Convention in June 1935. The foreign office was not particularly enthusiastic about an agreement which it believed conceded too much to Britain. The navy, though in favour of an agreement, wanted to hold out for 50 per cent of British strength instead of the 25 per cent Hitler was ready to accept, while the foreign office, once committed to negotiations, wanted to exploit the diplomatic possibilities more thoroughly before coming to an agreement. So Hitler and his special envoy, Ribbentrop, had to work hard for the convention—an agreement to which Hitler attached great importance, seeing in it a first step towards a British alliance.

By the end of 1934 Hitler had established his own free and easy style in the conduct of foreign affairs. After the death of Hindenburg he felt fewer constraints operating on him. The dictatorship was more firmly established and rearmament was getting under way. The day was long past when he worked closely with the foreign office on all matters. Now he preferred to brood over the situation at the Berghof and, when his mind was made up, issue the appropriate orders to foreign office and army command. According to one of his secretaries, he once claimed, dramatically, that all his most important decisions were made in the majestic setting of the Bavarian Alps:

> I get the feeling there of standing in a high tower looking down on earthly misery, on the incomparable trials which beset my people and on the annoyance and difficulty which each day brings anew. In the broad horizons of the land around Berchtesgaden and Salzburg, cut off from the everyday world, my creative genius produces ideas which shake the world. In those moments I feel no longer part of mortality, my ideas go beyond mortal frontiers and are transformed into deeds of great dimensions.[16]

That was typical hyperbole. In fact, Hitler did not neglect to sound out opinion in foreign office, diplomatic corps and army command before making up his mind as, for example, over the re-occupation of the Rhineland.[17]

As Führer and chancellor, Hitler continued and extended his old practice of assigning special missions to individuals of his choosing, often—but not always—party men. There are innumerable examples of this practice which could not fail to undermine the influence of the foreign office. In the Austrian affair Hitler relied on Theo Habicht, a Nazi Party official, as liaison man with the Viennese Nazis. To establish contact with leading statesmen in Britain and Italy, his prospective allies, he sent Alfred Rosenberg to London and Goering to Rome in May 1933. To conduct vital negotiations with the Vatican, and later to mollify the Austrians after the abortive putsch in 1934, he used the wily and resilient Papen. Goebbels was employed, with little success, at the Disarmament Conference and in negotiations with Poland. A rising star among the special envoys was Joachim von Ribbentrop whose useful contacts with British and French statesmen brought him to Hitler's notice during the Disarmament Conference. In March Ribbentrop was appointed special emissary for disarmament. Shortly afterwards he established the Dienststelle Ribbentrop, an agency which soon became a serious rival to the foreign office. In the summer of 1935, as indicated above, it was Ribbentrop who bore chief responsibility for the Anglo-German naval talks. And in 1936 he was appointed ambassador to Britain, a post he combined with the directorship of the Dienststelle, another illustration of the combination of state and party office which was an infallible recipe for success in the Third Reich. These private envoys were clearly in a unique position to influence policy, and sometimes did so. For example, the most recent research on Ribbentrop reveals that he exerted much influence on Hitler, causing him to modify his attitude in the winter of 1937–8 and sanction a new alignment, the Rome-Berlin-Tokyo Axis, directed against Britain.[18]

Another characteristic of Hitler's style was the considerable latitude allowed party agencies for dabbling in foreign affairs. In 1933 he established the Aussenpolitisches Amt, or Foreign Political Office, under Rosenberg, his old mentor and tutor on foreign affairs, for the purpose of conducting the anti-Bolshevik struggle, building up a northern 'community of destiny' with Scandinavian countries, and working out detailed plans for the partition of Russia. In like manner he gave his blessing to the Auslandsorganisation, or

Organization for Germans Abroad, set up under Gauleiter Ernst Wilhelm Bohle to establish links with all Germans living outside the Reich. These were not accidental by-products of the ceaseless power struggle going on inside Nazi Germany. Hitler's instincts probably told him early on that the radical objective of a great racial empire could not be entrusted to foreign office personnel who, for the most part, he mistrusted deeply. Party agencies, each acting independently of the others—for Hitler had no interest in reconciling warring factions—would contribute in ways which could not as yet be foreseen to the establishment of the Nazi New Order of the future. Meanwhile, party agencies would perform an essential function in awakening the German people inside and outside the Reich to a realization that racialism was not an optional extra but was intended to be the rock-solid foundation on which the whole edifice was to stand for a thousand years.

The clearest example of a party agency influencing the making of policy occurred in 1936. When the Spanish Civil War broke out, the foreign office, though alarmed by the situation, decided to preserve an attitude of strict neutrality. There the matter might have rested—at least for the time being—had it not been for the activities of Bohle's organization. Johannes Bernhardt, one of Bohle's agents in Spain, saw economic possibilities in the sale of war material to the rebels. With a colleague he flew to Berlin hoping to persuade the foreign office to aid Franco. They failed to secure even an interview. However, through the good offices of Gauleiter Bohle, they met Hitler at Bayreuth, fresh from a performance of Wagner's *Siegfried*. Whether Hitler offered help to Franco without further consultation or whether, more likely, he decided only after conferring with Blomberg and Goering (both in Bayreuth on the same errand as Hitler) is not absolutely clear. A desire to acquire Spanish raw materials obviously moved Goering to press for intervention, whereas in Hitler's mind ideological considerations seem to have been uppermost. As he saw it, civil war in Spain was not an isolated incident but the latest in a chain of events commencing with the doubling of Russian military expenditure in January 1936. In February a Popular Front government came to power in Madrid; in March the Franco-Soviet Pact was ratified; and in June a Popular Front government came to power in Paris. It is hardly surprising that Hitler should have feared the establishment of yet another 'red regime' and felt moved to join in the 'fight against Bolshevism'.[19]

All the same, it would be most unwise to make too much of what was, after all, an exception to the general rule that Nazi Party agencies were seen but not heard when it came to major policy decisions. After the Austrian crisis of 1934 revealed just how dangerous it was to follow the advice of party zealots, Hitler relied less and less on them and more on a mixture of conventional diplomacy and military action (or the threat of it) to get his own way. Even the Volksdeutsche Mittelstelle, or Office for the Repatriation of German Ethnic Groups, an agency controlled by the SS and set up in 1937 to strengthen Berlin's influence over German minorities in surrounding countries, proved a broken reed in practice. The threat of military intervention, and the readiness of the Western powers to capitulate did much more than the abortive uprising of Konrad Henlein's men in the Sudetenland to disrupt Czechoslovakia.

One must be careful to distinguish between Hitler's role as the executant of German foreign policy in the 1930s and his personal responsibility for the policy itself. As far as the first is concerned, his leading role is not in dispute. When conscription was re-introduced in March 1935 and when the Rhineland was re-occupied in March 1936, it was Hitler who decided the timing of the operations, and it was Hitler who helped to allay the fears of the great powers about future German intentions by applying to international relations those propaganda skills of which he was a past master. In terms of his own personality, success confirmed him in his ability to move 'with the assurance of a sleepwalker' towards his objectives.[20]

It is when one begins to speak of 'objectives' that doubts arise. Because Hitler played a leading role in foreign affairs, it does not necessarily follow that he was proceeding in accordance with some master plan of his own invention though it has often been assumed by historians that this was the case. It is very doubtful if the grand notions for a Nazi new order fermenting within him added up to a coherent policy. Certainly, one could argue that the work of the party agencies, the pro-Polish alignment and the antipathy to Russia were straws in the wind pointing to a determination on Hitler's part to do all that he possibly could to prepare the way for eastward expansion one day. Against that, it might be argued that in practice Hitler acted within the framework of the existing revisionist policy pursued since the days of Stresemann. The withdrawal from the Disarmament Conference, the re-introduction of conscription and the re-occupation of the Rhineland (enabling Germany to strengthen the western frontier) were all dictated by sheer military necessity and had been strongly advocated by a preponderantly non-Nazi army command which was as anxious as Hitler to have a large army in the shortest possible time.[21] It may well be that Hitler never wavered in the belief that the sole purpose of the army was for war against France and Russia in that order, as specified in *Mein Kampf*. But it is at least arguable that the use to which the large army would be put—whether as a weapon of diplomatic coercion to complete the revision of the treaty (not excluding local wars), or more likely, to pursue by force much grander and indefinite objectives—was by no means finally and irrevocably decided in the summer of 1937.

This leads us to the problems posed by the acceleration in the pace of German foreign policy in the winter of 1937/8. At the trial of the major war criminals at Nuremberg the so-called Hossbach Protocol was accepted by the Military Tribunal as proof positive that Hitler was a 'planner', who revealed to his commanders-in-chief and his foreign minister far-reaching plans for expansion no later than 1943–5 and possibly earlier in respect of Austria and Czechoslovakia if circumstances were favourable. Was this a classic example of a restless dictator giving a decisive twist to events, dragging his reluctant followers along paths they would not otherwise have ventured down? Did a 'neurasthenic craving for sheer movement' lead to a totally unnecessary war eighteen months later?[22]

To believe this would be to attribute far too much importance to the personality of one man. The truth surely is that by the late 1930s a combination of factors, economic, military and diplomatic, coalesced to force the Nazi leadership as a whole to modify the pace of German foreign policy. Up to 1936—possibly up to May 1938—German policy functioned very successfully within the limits set by Germany's lack of coercive power. German tactics had been cautious and flexible, the Rhineland episode being the only notable exception to this rule. When Hitler feared international repercussions over Austria in 1934 he did not commit himself still further, as he was to do over Czechoslovakia, but at once abandoned the forward policy.

But by 1937–8 the assumptions on which the early policy had rested were crumbling away. Economic factors will be referred to in the next section. Suffice to say here that what Hitler said on 5 November 1937 was the inescapable consequence of an acceleration in the pace of rearmament in the summer of 1936. Furthermore, there were signs in the autumn of 1937 that Germany was moving towards a serious internal crisis. Secondly, the military measures being undertaken by other powers threatened to impose limits on the relative freedom of manoeuvre enjoyed by Germany in the early 1930s. Thirdly, Britain's attitude since 1936 persuaded a reluctant Hitler that his high hopes for an Anglo-German alliance were misplaced. War with Britain could no longer be excluded as a possibility should Germany start to expand. Ominous signs that the United States was moving towards an actively anti-German posture was another factor in the reassessment process. When Italy joined the anti-British Anti-Comintern Pact in November 1937 a fundamental re-orientation of German policy, starting with the Rome-Berlin Axis of November 1936, had been completed. And it was a re-orientation which did not correspond with the *Mein Kampf* strategy which Hitler is commonly supposed to have adhered to. There is no evidence that Hitler held regular councils of war with close associates to review the deteriorating situation. What we do know, however, is that he frequently discussed the economic aspects with Goering, the diplomatic situation with Ribbentrop, and the domestic scene with Goebbels. It is, therefore, fair to assume that a general consensus of opinion in the top echelons of the party favoured the view that time was running out for Germany. On 5 November 1937 Hitler—who undoubtedly possessed an acute sense of the interdependence of economic policy, military strategy and foreign policy—was simply articulating what was probably in the minds of his associates already. The only purely personal factor was Hitler's undoubted concern about his health. Fear that he might be suffering from cancer preoccupied him at this time. One cannot quantify such a factor; all that one can safely say is that at the very least it must have confirmed Hitler in the view that the changing balance of power forced Germany to run greater risks to attain her 'objectives'—and whether the 'objectives' were the completion of the revision of the Versailles treaty, or expansionism for its own sake, or the first steps on the road to a new order, is a quite separate issue which may not have been decided one way or the other at this stage.

In other words Hitler and his associates were not in possession of a blueprint for aggression as the Nuremberg Tribunal believed. Hitler had no clear idea how to acquire Austria and Czechoslovakia. One might well argue that the Austrian crisis in the spring of 1938 was not the beginning of a new and reckless policy. On the contrary. The Berghof agreement in February 1938, virtually dictated by Hitler to the Austrian chancellor, Kurt Schuschnigg, paved the way for a close coordination of Austria's foreign policy and economic development with that of Nazi Germany, and reinforced Hitler's personal view that a non-violent solution of the Austrian problem was perfectly feasible.

There is at least something to be said for the view that the March crisis was precipitated by Schuschnigg's sudden dash for freedom. It is significant that there was nothing remotely reckless in Hitler's behaviour. To the very end he was full of doubt and hesitation. It was Goering, not Hitler, who pressed throughout for the radical solution of annexation, largely because he wanted to secure control of Austria's raw materials and foreign exchange reserves. Can we be sure that Hitler would have done more than unseat Schuschnigg had it not been for Goering's unremitting pressure? And only when Hitler was absolutely certain that the Austrians would not resist, and that Italy, Britain and France would not intervene did he order invasion. And only after a tumultuous reception in Linz did he finally decide to annex Austria. Hitler's talk in November 1937 of running greater risks was hardly borne out by the Austrian affair. The evidence suggests that he stumbled prematurely into Austria which is not, of course, to deny that he, like all revisionists, hoped to control Austria one day, very probably in the near future. But the risks he ran were minimal, probably fewer than in 1936 over the Rhineland. In a real sense Austria was the end of the old policy of 'limited liability' pursued so successfully since 1933.

The Czechoslovakian crisis, on the other hand, signified the beginning of a new phase because the decision to 'smash Czechoslovakia by military force' and the elaborate preparations to carry this out exposed Germany to graver risks than ever before. On purely strategic grounds the neutralization of Czechoslovakia made good military sense after the conquest of Austria, and would have been the aim of any revisionist government. But the decision to achieve this end by war was Hitler's, and arose out of a mood of post-*Anschluss* euphoria, a deep and abiding hatred of the Czechs and a desire to test out his army in a swift victorious campaign. Initial doubts whether Germany dare attack Czechoslovakia unless Italy was simultaneously engaged in a Mediterranean adventure were swept away during the weekend crisis in May. Anger at the diplomatic victory Britain and France were claiming after their joint démarche in Berlin, and maybe also a conviction that the speed of the Czechs' partial mobilization made it a matter of urgency to strike quickly at the little country, are sufficient to explain the personal decision in the directive of 30 May 'to smash Czechoslovakia by military force in the near future'.[23] And throughout the summer of 1938, as the tension in Europe mounted, Hitler's resolve to go to war never weakened. For the first time in the field of foreign affairs he displayed the same obstinate determination to attain an objective as he had shown in the summer of 1932 when he held out for the chancellorship despite mounting criticism in the party and ominous signs of Nazi decline in the country. His newfound intransigence was directly related to an important change in the internal balance of power. The neutralization of what opposition there had been to his policies and the concentration of power more and more in the Führer's hands placed him in an impregnable position by the late spring of 1938. The timid Neurath had been replaced by the able but sycophantic Ribbentrop. In place of the obstinate General Werner von Fritsch the pliable Brauchitsch was in charge of the army. In short, conservative influence in the corridors of power had been quite sharply reduced, and Hitler was now surrounded by men such as Ribbentrop, Himmler and Goebbels who also wanted to crush the Czechs by force and encouraged Hitler to think it could be done without fear of western intervention. And once again the attitude of Britain and France seemed to confirm the belief that Czechoslovakia was isolated. Warnings from worried army officers about the dangers of a two-front war fell on deaf ears in this euphoric atmosphere. Goering, now on the side of the 'doves', was temperamentally unable to restrain the Führer (until the very end) despite his enormous power as economic overlord.[24]

Towards the end of September it was Hitler who deliberately intensified the crisis. At Bad Godesberg on 22 September he tried to shake off Chamberlain by demanding the cession of the Sudetenland between 26 and 28 September (though he later agreed to delay action until 1 October). Talking to Sir Horace Wilson, one of Neville Chamberlain's advisers, on 26 September, Hitler suddenly demanded an answer from the Czechs by 2 p.m. on 28 September. At the Berlin Sportpalast the same evening he committed himself publicly to this position, warning his audience that if he did not receive a reply on time the Germans would go and liberate the Sudeten Germans. It was almost as if Hitler was screwing up his courage to sticking point, deliberately placing himself in an exposed position and blocking all lines of retreat. Whether he was bent on war, as most historians believe, or bluffing all the way to the brink, there can be no doubt that he played a major role in the Czech crisis.

Equally the decision to avoid war and settle at the conference table was a personal one on Hitler's part although, of course, events conspired together to force his hand on 28 September. In the face of Czech mobilization, troop movements in France, rumours of impending British action, Mussolini's intervention, the tempting (and improved) offer dangled before him by the Western powers, and not least the apathetic reaction of the German people, Hitler grudgingly acceded to the arguments of the 'doves' and pulled Germany away from the brink of war. To pursue the parallel with 1932, Hitler was rescued from the probable consequences of his warlike stance by the intervention of the great powers just as the agrarian-industrial axis had rescued him from the *cul-de-sac* of hopeless opposition in December 1932.

It has been argued that a man who could act as rationally as Hitler did at the height of the crisis must have been bluffing all the time. Not necessarily. The evidence that he would have preferred a local war is overwhelming and scarcely suprising in view of his belief in the therapeutic value of (controlled) blood-letting. Still, whatever view is taken of his intentions, it is a measure of his real power that, had he persisted in his warlike attitude, war would certainly have broken out on 1938 and might conceivably have become a general conflagration. Because the Nazi leadership as a whole was willing to run such risks, one is justified in maintaining that German policy had entered a new and aggressive phase.

Similarly, Hitler's decision to invade rump Czechoslovakia in March 1939, his fury at the Anglo-French guarantees to Poland, and more especially his decision to smash the Poles by military force, were all factors of the highest importance in determining the direction in which German expansionism manifested itself in the twelve months between the Munich agreement and the outbreak of war.

Continuing German pressure on rump Czechoslovakia was inevitable after Munich if only to complete the military neutralization of that little country and secure Germany's rear in the event of war in the west. But a revisionist war against Poland was an interesting departure from the *Mein Kampf* strategy and one for which Hitler was very largely responsible. And it landed him in a war against Britain he did not desire and one in which his Italian ally refused to participate. Nor was war the only alternative open to the Nazis. Even after the entry into Prague and the breach with Poland the British government was still anxious for an understanding with Germany. And the German demands on Poland were not so unreasonable that the dispute might not have been settled round the table had Hitler been willing to negotiate. In the summer of 1939 the 'doves' tried desperately to build a bridge to London when Helmuth Wohltat, an emissary from Goering's Four Year Plan Office, conferred with Sir Horace Wilson. The British government was willing enough for economic cooperation and for some frontier revision in the east. It was Hitler who peremptorily rejected any alternative to war.

Nor was any attempt made to exploit the diplomatic potential in the Non-Aggression Pact signed with Russia on 23 August. Both 'doves' and 'hawks' helped to push a somewhat reluctant Hitler towards agreement with the Bolshevik enemy. Since April Goering had favoured an agreement to obtain essential raw materials and food supplies. Ribbentrop was also interested because of his deeply anti-British policy, which predicated a Russian agreement as a first step towards the creation of a great Euro-Asian block from the Atlantic to the Pacific directed against the British Empire. Only towards mid-August did Hitler finally overcome ideological doubts and accept the need for an agreement which, while it would have no ultimate validity, would scare the Western powers off Poland leaving that country to the mercy of the Germans. Yet the possibility of exploiting the highly favourable situation created by the pact in order to obtain a peaceful settlement never occurred to Hitler and Ribbentrop. Is it not conceivable that Britain and France, already deeply embarrassed by the promises to Poland, might have had second thoughts if they had been given time to reflect on the new situation? Time was what the Nazis refused to give them. The last minute offer to negotiate with Poland on 25 August was playacting, a subterfuge to put the blame for war on the Poles much as Bethmann-Hollweg had tried to put the blame for starting the war in 1914 on Russia. The truth was, as Ribbentrop remarked coldly to Count Galeazzo Ciano when the anxious Italian foreign minister inquired on 11 August whether Germany wanted Danzig and the Corridor: 'Not that any more. We want war.'[25]

Enough has been said to demonstrate the major importance of Hitler's role in the eighteen months before the war. Yet to suppose that the emotive reactions (and the rational calculations) of one man (Hitler) or of a group of men (the Hitler-Ribbentrop-Goebbels-Himmler axis) can on their own explain the outbreak of a great war is to underestimate the extent to which individuals are conditioned by forces and circumstances largely outside their control. More fundamental reasons for the outbreak of war lie embedded in the economic and strategic situation of Nazi Germany in the summer of 1939.

It cannot be doubted any more, in the light of recent research, that the economic situation was rapidly deteriorating in 1939.[26] Shortages of raw materials and skilled labour had become critical while government expenditure (chiefly on armaments) continued to grow, thereby creating dangerous inflationary pressures. Publicly, Hitler obstinately refused to accept the facts of economic life. To keep on insisting on the highest priority for armaments seemed to show no appreciation of the harsh choice that would have to be made sooner or later to avert economic collapse. On the other hand, it may well be that his sensitive antennae detected with uncanny accuracy the unavoidable political consequences of a steadily deteriorating situation. As he told the Reichstag in January 1939: 'In the final instance the economy of the Reich today is bound up with its external security. It is better to see that while there is still time as when it is too late.'[27] In his address to the commanding generals on 22 August, he was brutally frank about the interdependence of economic policy and foreign policy: 'We have nothing to lose, only to gain. As a result of restrictions our economic situation is such that we can only hold out for a few years. Goering can confirm that. There is nothing else for it, we have to act.'[28] In other words, Hitler probably realized that the maintenance of the mobilization capacity of German industry at its present high level for an indefinite period was virtually impossible once the peacetime needs of the armed forces were met. If large-scale arms exports were impossible and if the economic and social disruption consequent upon a switch to the production of other goods was unacceptable, then Germany was left with a clear choice—either to continue to endure mounting inflation to defray the astronomical costs of further rearmament or to create a fresh demand for armaments by waging war.[29]

Having said this, one must also admit quite frankly that there is far too little positive evidence to permit us to determine with any degree of accuracy the importance of such considerations in Hitler's decision for war. Serious though the internal situation was in 1939, one cannot say with absolute certainty that it was impossible for Germany to wait any longer before going to war. One cannot discount the possibility that the steadily deteriorating situation—of which Hitler was kept informed—may have done little more than confirm his own pessimistic long-term diagnosis of Germany's ills and strengthen the case for a war of conquest which he deemed necessary in any case on politico-ideological grounds. It may well be that within a year or two economic pressures would have forced Hitler's hand. What we do not have is sufficient evidence that this was the case in 1939.

It is even more difficult to determine the role of the great industrial combines in setting Germany on the road to war and in nudging Hitler towards expansion. It seems fairly clear that because industry retained, broadly speaking, the essentials of economic independence at a time of rapid industrial concentration, firms such as the Mannesmann-Konzern, the Reichswerke Hermann Goering and I. G. Farben, all closely associated with rearmament, and leading banks, especially the Dresden and Deutsche Banken, were in a postion to develop their own expansionist plans for the domination of central and southeastern European markets. Of course these plans did not necessitate the forcible absorption of surrounding territories in the Reich for their realization. Industrial imperialism and territorial imperialism were distinctive plants. Nevertheless, they were nurtured in the same soil and each was closely affected by the other's growth. Domination of central and southeastern Europe was also a Nazi objective both to attain economic self-sufficiency (the *Grossraumwirtschaft*) and to serve as a base for a future *Drang nach Osten* or Thrust to the East. On this practical foundation a working partnership came into being. There is evidence of this partnership in action both in Austria and Czechoslovakia where certain industrial corporations were able to secure a dominant position in the economies of these countries in 1938–9. To establish more precisely what the relationship was between the forward thrust of the great industrial combines controlling the German economy and the expansion-ist policies of the Nazi hierarchy in 1938–9 we need much more information than we have at present about the policies of individual firms. Provisionally, all that one can say is that economic imperialism on its own would not necessarily have led to war—and did not do so in other capitalist economies. It was only in conjunction with the territorial imperialism of the Nazis that economic imperialism developed 'a particularly explosive power.'[30]

On the scanty evidence available it could be argued quite plausibly that Hitler was at least as concerned about the deteriorating balance of military power as about economics. As Gauleiter Albert Forster remarked to Carl Jacob Burckhardt, the League of Nations high commissioner for Danzig, in the late autumn of 1938: 'Le Führer m'a dit que le temps travaille contre nous et que dans deux ans les autres seront beaucoup plus fortes ques nous.'[31] In other words, on military grounds alone Germany could not wait until 1943–5 to expand but had to act no later than 1940. Military considerations probably exerted much influence over Hitler's post-Munich policy. Certainly over the next few months he maintained more than once that time was running out for Germany.[32] That was not an unreasonable conclusion to arrive at when one examines the state of German armament in 1939. Like the men of 1914, the Nazi leaders must have felt themselves doomed in the long run. At home the internal situation, at the lowest estimate, gave some cause for concern. And once Britain and France, very likely with American support, decided to resist German expansionism, a major war—which Germany could not win—was almost unavoidable. All that remained was a slim chance that a plunge into war would rescue her from the dilemma without plunging her into a life-and-death struggle with the great powers. This was a course of action fraught with appalling risks but, all the same, a decision taken as a matter of rational calculation, not the madman's throw it is sometimes thought to be.

For, despite the much-quoted remark to Goering, *va banque* was not Hitler's 'only call'.[33] Ten years before, discussing the dangers of conducting a dynamic foreign policy, Hitler made a most revealing comment:

> The objection that such an action may have the character of a risky gamble can most easily be refuted by simple reference to previous historical experience. By a risky gamble we understand a game in which from the onset the chances of winning are subject to the fate of chance. This will never be the case in politics. For the more the ultimate decision lies in the darkness of the future, the more is the conviction of the possibility or impossibility of a success erected on humanly perceptible factors. The task of a nation's political leadership is to weigh these factors.[34]

The element of cool calculation, however wrong-headed the conclusions, is as important in understanding Hitler's conduct of foreign affairs as his celebrated outbursts of rage. There is no reason to suppose that he lost his self-control between Munich and the attack on Poland although no doubt the success of German policy in 1938–9 whetted his appetite enormously and strengthened his resolve to have his own way with the Poles, much as the spate of electoral victories in 1932 prompted him to demand what was not then on offer, the chancellorship, and to brush aside all counter-arguments until it was almost too late for his own survival.

What should not be overlooked in trying to assess the extent of Hitler's influence on foreign policy and in particular his responsibility for the outbreak of war, is the plain fact that Nazi Germany was trapped in a situation where internal pressures and external constraints conspired together to force the Nazi leadership as a whole to keep moving forward regardless of mounting risks. This was only 'Hitler's war' in the formal sense that he gave the orders for the attack on Poland. Because he was always acutely aware of the interdependence of foreign policy, military strategy and economic development, Hitler recognized, perhaps more clearly than his close associates, how much future policy depended in fact on factors outside their control. It is within these broader parameters that one must look for a historically-valid explanation, relating

Hitler's personal contribution in a meaningful way to the objective realities which largely determined the course of German foreign policy in the 1930s.

Hitler has often been dismissed as a complete ignoramus in economic matters, a blundering amateur who understood nothing of the intricacies of the subject and cared even less. This is to seriously underestimate him.[35] While it is true that he had no formal training in economics and was certainly not as interested in it as in foreign affairs and military strategy, nevertheless it was an area of public affairs that forced itself on his attention again and again. And because he was alert to the political consequences—or to what he thought were the political consequences of economic decisions—he was able to exert a not inconsiderable influence on broad economic strategy.

Political realism governed Hitler's attitude, and that of other Nazi leaders, to the problem of economic recovery, the most serious challenge facing the new regime. Hitler never doubted for one moment that recovery must be master-minded by the experienced men running German industry and not by party zealots. No sense of gratitude for the intervention of agrarian-industrial axis on his behalf dictated this choice. Ever since 1927 he had been seeking contact with big business and fighting 'socialist' elements in the party likely to scare off middle-class support. The nearer he came to the chancellery, the more he called unruly elements to order and affirmed his belief in the virtues of (non-Jewish) private enterprise. For a man pathologically suspicious of 'bourgeois' professional people, all his life he had a touching regard for the plain bluff entrepreneur whose preeminence in industry he attributed not to inherited wealth and privilege but to the unerring operation of the principle of Social Darwinism.[36]

Hesitation in coming out openly on the side of large-scale industry was due not to lingering doubts about its fitness to effect the recovery or of its rightness to do so, but simply to the exigencies of the confused political situation. Hitler was not master in his own house in the early months of 1933. Many rank-and-file Nazis were agitating for economic change to benefit small retailers and businessmen; party officials bullied employers whenever they could; and middle-class organizations such as NS Hago, the retailer's association, and the Kampfbund für den gewerblichen Mittelstand, or League of Defence for the Commercial Middle Class, were stage-managing noisy campaigns against department stores and consumer cooperatives. Not until the end of May, after the destruction of the trade union movement, did Hitler feel strong enough to come out openly in favour of the traditional masters of German industry. After a meeting with leading industrialists, Hitler readily secured cabinet approval of a most reactionary package deal confirming the blatant class policies of preceding regimes: wages were to be held down to the 1932 levels; industry was promised tax concessions, a reduction in the burden of social payments, and large state contracts; NS Hago and the Kampfbund were called to order; and Wilhelm Keppler, the friend of large-scale industry, replaced Otto Wagener, advocate of the corporate state, as Hitler's party adviser on economic affairs.

In two respects Hitler's personal intervention probably had at least marginal influence on the direction of economic policy in 1933. In the first place, he made it crystal clear from the very beginning that economic recovery must be closely geared to military expansion. This was important for, despite what has been said about the growth of a political 'consensus' in favour of a fascist dictatorship, it would be quite wrong to suggest that there was complete identity of viewpoint about the appropriate measures for overcoming the crisis.[37] When Hitler persuaded the cabinet on 8 February to endorse the proposition that the highest priority in any future recovery programme must be given to rearmament for the next five years, he was in effect preparing the way—possibly more quickly than might otherwise have been the case—for a working partnership between heavy industry, army and party, all three of which had an interest in expanding the armed forces as speedily as possible.

Secondly, Hitler's appointment of Schacht as president of the Reichsbank in place of Luther was probably a step of equal importance. Luther was unwilling to provide the massive credits Hitler demanded for the recovery-cum-rearmament programme. Personal preferences apart, Luther's hands were tied because the Reichsbank was effectively controlled by the Bank of International Settlement, set up in 1930 to supervise the payment of reparations under the Young Plan. It was Schacht, a fervent admirer of Hitler and his chief financial adviser since 1931, who solved the problem. Thanks to his international standing, Schacht was able to persuade the bank to allow the Reichsbank to deal in securities again. Of course, although Schacht employed the Keynesian instrument of deficit financing to revive the economy, one need scarcely point out that the object of economic expansion was not the improvement of the living standards of the German people but the thoroughly illiberal one of creating a powerful army to enslave other peoples.

The economic crisis of 1936 and Hitler's intervention in it have been variously interpreted. The reader is reminded that as the demand for raw materials grew to keep pace with the increasing tempo of rearmament, a shortage of foreign exchange developed. In March the insistence of Russia and Roumania on hard cash for their oil precipitated a serious fuel crisis, revealing the precarious nature of the balance of payments. Those sections of industry still interested in export markets together with Schacht's ministry of economics began to express some concern about the direction of the economy. Voices were even raised in favour of retrenchment and some slowdown in the pace of rearmament. Against this background Hitler wrote the celebrated memorandum of August 1936 in which he firmly relegated economic considerations to second place and insisted that, whatever the cost, the highest priority must continue to be given to armaments to ensure that Germany was ready for war by 1940. To obtain the necessary raw materials for this purpose Germany would have to rely less on international trade and rather more on her own autarkical efforts, until such time as she could expand her territory and solve her economic problems at a stroke.

Was this a decisive moment when the dictator's influence changed the course of events? Hardly that. What he was saying in the memorandum simply reflected a significant realignment of forces which took place in the winter of 1935–6. It has been argued that the tacit understanding between party, army command, ministry of economics and heavy industry on which German recovery rested from 1933 onwards, ended in 1936 when the party established its ascendancy over all its rivals forcing them into a policy of accelerated armament, autarky and expansion.[38] This is a somewhat unsatisfactory analysis. A factor of crucial importance overlooked in these interpretations is the decision of army command, taken in the winter of 1935–6 with Hitler's approval, to move on from the construction of a defensive army (not scheduled for completion before 1938) to the creation of an offensive army, which, as originally planned, would not have been ready before 1942.[39] At the same time the existing balance of industrial power was breaking up with the emergence of I. G. Farben as the leading industrial concern in Germany. And I. G. Farben, which had a long-standing interest in the production of synthetic fuel, was strategically placed through close contacts with the air ministry to play a leading role in Goering's attempts to establish autarky. Indeed, the hysterical outbursts in Hitler's memorandum against the cautious orthodoxy of the ministry of economics—where Schacht, though a believer in autarky up to a point, was opposed to a further reduction of Germany's international ties—betrayed some misunderstanding on the Führer's part of the inescapable commitment of much of German industry to continued rearmament. The fact was that by 1936 industry had become so dependent on internal markets that a return to world markets as an alternative to further rearmament was no longer an attractive proposition even if the world economy had been in a healthier state. And more fundamentally the *raison d'être* of the dictatorship would have been destroyed had the Nazis subordinated armaments to the demands of a consumer-goods oriented economy devoted to the raising of the living standards of working people.

It was the coincidence of army plans for rapid expansion with the objective needs of a large part of industry as well as with the vaguely expansionist mood of the party that determined the new course. The first fruits of the refurbished partnership was the Four Year Plan, an exercise in limited autarky. It was announced by Hitler to party comrades at the party rally; it was deeply influenced by the strategic thinking of the Wehrwirtschaftsstab, or military economics staff, of Colonel Thomas; and it was planned by the staff of I. G. Farben. One must conclude, therefore, that Hitler did not take an unexpected initiative in 1936 that changed the course of events, but simply came out on the side of a new alignment of forces which happened to support the option he personally favoured and had pressed for—the creation of an offensive army in the shortest possible time.

At the close of the 1930s the German economy was in the grip of serious inflationary pressures, caused by massive government expenditure and by the refusal of the Nazi leadership to impose higher taxes or cut back the growth of 'non-essential' consumer-goods industries to make room in the economy for the repayment of the credits which originally stimulated the recovery. Given the socio-political premises on which the dictatorship rested, that was not, perhaps, all that surprising. What does require explanation is the failure of the Nazi leadership to take remedial action to curb the worst effects of inflation at shop-floor level and so ensure the fullest possible implementation of the rearmament plans. A leading authority has recently suggested that the real reason for the Nazi failure was a deep anxiety about working-class reactions to the regime.[40] There is some evidence that this may have been so in Hitler's case.

When, for example, price increases in butter, meat and bread in 1933–4 roused widespread resentment, Hitler's excited protest in cabinet revealed something of these anxieties: 'He had given the workers his word that he would not tolerate price increases. Wage earners would accuse him of breaking his word if he did not take action against price increases. Revolutionary conditions among the people would be the wider result. Therefore he would not permit this wild profiteering in prices.'[41] In 1935, during the so-called 'bread crisis', he supported Darré's pleas for more foreign exchange to buy essential feeding stuff imports and overruled Schacht for he feared the psychological effects of introducing bread rationing. And in 1939 he told Speer that buildings to be erected in Berlin's Adolf Hitler Platz must be equipped with bullet-proof shutters and steel doors for protection against riots which might occur should he 'some day be forced to take unpopular measures'.[42] It may well be that behind these fears lay vivid memories of the 1918–19 revolution which he had witnessed at first hand in Munich. Whatever the Nazis said about 'Jewish wirepullers', they knew perfectly well that the revolution had enjoyed massive support from the organized working class.

Hitler's own attitude to the working class was ambivalent. On the one hand, he hoped that workers untouched by Nazi propaganda would be won over by the welfare measures of the Nazi-controlled German Labour Front. On the other hand, it is clear long before 1933 that he had little faith in the readiness of the German people to endure material privation for any prolonged period in 'the national interest'.[43] It does not seem unreasonable to assume that such fears must have been fairly widespread in the top echelons of the party, and would be intensified in a period of economic crisis. For example, in 1937–8 measures to curb the free movement of labour and fix maximum wage rates in the metal, building and building materials industries were urgently needed, because workers in these key sectors were stoking the fires of inflation by extracting higher wages and improved fringe benefits out of hapless employers forced to bid against each other for skilled labour in short supply. Yet even when the Nazis at last plucked up courage and introduced some essential measures in the summer of 1938, these were half-heartedly implemented, while the wartime package deal introduced in September 1939 was virtually withdrawn by November, so worried were the Nazis by the discontent it had aroused. Whether energetic action could have been taken much earlier to deal with the situation without arousing widespread discontent remains an intriguing question. But in so far as Hitler (and his close associates) did not act for fear of the consequences, then their negative influence on the course of events may have been very great indeed.

At the Hossbach meeting Hitler had already spelt out what he thought the political consequences of a worsening economic situation would be. If rapid rearmament was absolutely essential on ideological grounds, as Hitler insisted it was, what alternatives were open to Germany? An export drive coupled with devaluation was never seriously considered by the regime—and might not have been possible on economic any more than on ideological grounds. But any further reduction in the production of consumer goods or in food imports was categorically rejected by Hitler, leaving Germany with a neatly polarized choice—'on the one hand the great Wehrmacht (or armed forces), and the necessity of maintaining it at its present level, the ageing of the movement and of its leaders, and on the other hand the prospect of a lowering of the standard of living . . . which left us no choice but to act'.[44] Should a food crisis develop suddenly because of Germany's acute shortage of foreign exchange, that, too, would be 'the waning point of the regime'. Rather than depress living standards and face internal disorder, Hitler preferred the alternative of war and the conquest of his neighbours. One cannot, of course, isolate economic factors from the other factors discussed by Hitler at the Hossbach meeting, or exclude the possibility that economic arguments were no more than a rationalization of a desire to expand, arrived at on quite different grounds.

Another puzzling feature of these years was the obvious reluctance of the Nazis to agree to any kind of rational plan embracing the whole economy and mobilizing men and resources to achieve the objectives of National Socialism. The much-vaunted Four Year Plan was a pale reflection of the Russian plan and amounted to little more than a piece of hasty improvization to prepare Germany for war in the near future. A high degree of muddle and confusion remained the characteristic feature of the economic system after 1936 as it had been before. No proper system of raw materials allocation was ever created; the armed forces and industry continued to scramble in an undignified fashion for available raw materials. Industrial investment remained largely unplanned and firms competed with each other for lucrative armaments contracts. And, as indicated above, several rival organizations were allowed a say in the running of the economy, a situation which in itself militated against effective planning.

To what extent were these conditions a reflection of Hitler's personal prejudice against large-scale planning? Hitler was surely too astute a politician not to have realized instinctively that any attempt to mobilize a country's total resources in raw materials and manpower to achieve specific objectives would give considerable power to technical experts and civil servants. To diminish his own stature, in order to enhance that of the bureaucrats he despised so heartily, made no sort of sense to Hitler. And in general, he could not afford to allow the growth of potential centres of opposition to his 'will'. In accordance with that instinct he saw to it that the cabinet never met after 1938, formal contacts between ministers were actively discouraged and top party officials seldom met except at the party rally.

This negative attitude prompts another thought. Did Hitler, because he sensed that the economy could not perform all the tasks demanded of it and that war was therefore the likely outcome, prefer to leave as much as possible undecided in a twilight zone where he could, at will, call for greater efforts without having to fear invidious comparisons between fresh demands and existing blueprints? Was Hitler the ruler still, at heart, Hitler the propagandist, the *Trommler* who trusted in his own power to rouse the people, relying, as always on words and charisma to achieve the impossible, not on cold impersonal bureaucratic machines with their prosaic plans which would demonstrate only too clearly the impossibility of what he might currently be demanding of the people?

It has been argued that Hitler appreciated the economic impossibility of waging a major war, and had very sensibly settled for a series of short wars and quick victories over opponents at whose expense Germany would recoup her losses. A rapid build-up of armaments sufficient for short campaigns with minimal disruption of civilian life, a strategy requiring much less than the total mobilization of resources, was the recipe for success.[45] In fact, nothing as sophisticated or rational occurred. No coordinated military-economic strategy was ever worked out by Hitler with army command and industry. The truth seems to be that the Nazis did all they possibly could, short of total planning, to maximize armaments production in the late 1930s.[46]

One could equally well argue that Hitler's antipathy to large-scale planning was simply a reflection of the limits imposed on the Nazis by the socio-economic assumptions on which the regime rested. To party officials well aware of the grumbles of the working population it seemed absolutely essential not to impose heavy burdens on the people or disrupt the normal pattern of their lives. And through the *Gauleiter* the party could convey its concerns directly to the Führer who was on occasion clearly influenced by them. Nor can industry have felt that its lucrative partnership with the Nazis stood in need of any drastic modification. Having derived substantial and lasting benefit from the destruction of the trade union movement, the industrial combines were hardly eager to become the handmaidens of bureaucratic planners.

Of course, once the period of the short war was over and Germany faced a long struggle, changes in the organization of the economy could no longer be resisted. Even so, the planning measures introduced in 1942 fell far short of what was being done in other belligerent lands. In Albert Speer, Germany found a second Walter Rathenau, a man of drive, energy and ability whose reorganization of industry enabled the Germans to hold out much longer than would otherwise have been the case. In as much as Hitler recognized in Speer the qualities he was looking for in his new armaments minister and supported him against his rivals until almost the end of the Third Reich, he cannot be denied his fair share of credit for what Speer achieved, just as he deserves credit for Schacht's achievements in the mid-1930s.

Essentially, Speer relied on the cooperation of the great industrial concerns to achieve significant increases in production. To man the newly established production committees Speer appointed businessmen regardless of party affiliation and did so with Hitler's express approval. In no sense were industrial concerns subjected to rigid control from the armaments ministry, much less from the party. The old partnership continued throughout the war, with the giant concerns playing an active role in the exploitation of occupied territories while at home swallowing up smaller competitors as the process of industrial concentration went ahead. It was the economic power of the Wehrmacht that suffered a sharp cutback when the soldiers were driven out of the factories where they had exerted direct control over production. Even Speer could not overcome the deeply-rooted conservatism of the Nazi system. It is not surprising that many *Gauleiter* fiercely resisted any attempt to restrict consumer-goods production. What is significant is the way Hitler sided with them. In April 1942 Speer succeeded in cutting back this production by 12 per cent only to discover in June that Hitler had ordered its restoration presumably because of concern about the effects on the civilian population. As late as the spring of 1945 Hitler was still resisting an increase in income tax unless news of a military victory could be announced simultaneously.

Finally, the personal intrigues referred to at the beginning of this chapter continued in an intensified form throughout the war. Speer discovered this to his cost on numerous occasions. When, for example, he wished to establish a central office to handle labour problems, he found the *Gauleiter* solidly opposed to any diminution of their regional powers. And when he finally persuaded Hitler to agree, the Führer did not appoint Speer's nominee, Gauleiter Karl Hanke, as commissioner of labour but Fritz Sauckel, nominee of Martin Bormann, the *éminence grise* who by 1942 had become the most powerful man in the Nazi hierarchy after Himmler. Similarly, when Speer pressed for the conscription of female labour he encountered strong opposition from Sauckel who had behind him both the *Gauleiter* and Hitler. Beneath the lofty ideological verbiage about the place of women in Nazi society lay, as a recent writer points out, fear of the effects upon civilian morale if women were to be conscripted.[47] Only in 1943 did Hitler at last give way in the face of combined pressure from the army and the ministry of armaments. But by December 1943 Speer had to admit that the measure was a total failure because far too many women had succeeded in securing exemptions—yet another example of the way in which ideological prejudice was allowed to frustrate rational efforts to organize the community for a total war. In this matter, as in so much else in the economic field, Hitler merely articulated the fears and anxieties that beset the party hierarchy.

It is sometimes supposed even today that Nazi policy towards the Jews had from beginning to end only one objective in view, and that it moved with relentless logic from the first anti-Jewish demonstrations in April 1933 to the 'Final Solution' in the death camps of Poland. The very enormity of the holocaust encouraged men to search for a 'grand design' or 'master plan' which, as in the case of German foreign policy, could be attributed to Hitler's personal predelictions. Closer examination of the record suggests a rather different pattern, more in keeping with what we know of the highly personalized style of government and the shifting power structure of the Third Reich. On balance it seems much more likely that the pressure of external events, internal power configurations and the influence of powerful individuals were just as important as Hitler's personal inclinations and the inherent radicalism of the Nazi Party in determining the policy adopted by the regime.

Legislation to restrict the freedom of what the Nazis were pleased to call 'alien elements' in German society aroused little disquiet in middle-class circles. The fact is that in no significant particular did the anti-semitic programme of the Nazi Party break new ground. Other right-wing groups were equally anxious to deny citizenship to Jews, expel those Jews who had entered Germany since 1914, and remove all Jews from public office and from the newspaper world. Hitler could, therefore, rely on general support from the broad middle class for the first anti-semitic measures in April and June 1933, which excluded Jews from the civil service and legal profession, restricted their entry into schools and universities, and empowered the government to revoke German citizenship and confiscate the property of Jewish émigrés.

Such difficulties as Hitler faced were caused by party activists dissatisfied with these 'modest' beginnings. Many rank-and-file members were filled with a lively hatred of things semitic and itched to use physical violence against individual Jews and their property. For tactical reasons this intestinal anti-semitism had been held in check between 1930 and 1933. But in the hectic atmosphere of the 'March Days' exuberant activists, with the full backing of the party press, took to the streets, demonstrated noisily for a 'Jew-free' economy, assaulted Jews and invaded court houses demanding the immediate removal of all Jewish lawyers—with whom many of these Brownshirted hooligans had crossed swords in the past. The evidence is too slender to decide whether street pressure was unwelcome to a new chancellor anxious to impress cabinet colleagues and foreign powers with his statesmanlike moderation, or whether he secretly rejoiced and encouraged excesses in the hope that conservatives in the cabinet might be forced to go further. Of his own radical instincts there is little doubt. On the eve of power, while carefully avoiding public attacks on Jewry, he reiterated in private the party's commitment to racial discrimination adding darkly that, if the Jews persisted in propagating democratic ideas, pogroms would 'hit them harder than those described in their Biblical past'.[48]

What must be borne in mind in attempting to explain Hitler's behaviour in March 1933 is that much more was at stake than the fate of individual Jews.

After the Reichstag passed the Enabling Act in March 1933, a measure conferring emergency powers on Hitler, industry came out solidly in support of him. The difficulty was that rank-and-file members of the party were not only anti-semitic and anti-Marxist but anti-capitalist as well. The 'fascism of the lower middle class' was very much in evidence in the early months of 1933. There were vocal demands for the creation of a backward-looking corporate state which would restore the lower middle class to greatness at the expense of department stores and industrial combines, a programme totally unacceptable to Hitler's industrial allies. To divert attention away from anti-capitalism and towards anti-semitism made sound tactical sense in these circumstances. Whether that weighed with Hitler or not we do not know. At all events he summoned Goebbels to the Berghof to discuss countermeasures against 'Jewish atrocity propaganda'. On 28 March the party press was in full cry demanding a boycott of Jewish shops, doctors and lawyers. To organize the boycott Hitler asked Julius Streicher, the notorious Jew-baiter and a close personal friend, to set up a central committee in Munich. The committee never functioned, for the first day of the boycott on 1 April was little short of disastrous. What the organizers had completely overlooked in their ignorance was that many Jewish firms were already controlled by foreign creditors and German banks. A boycott simply inflicted needless damage on a fragile economy and aroused uneasiness in commercial circles. Before the boycott was called off Hitler, characteristically, snatched some political advantage out of defeat. At his personal request and against the background of continuing anti-semitic excesses, the draft law on the civil service being discussed in cabinet was amended to include specific reference to the removal of 'Jewish' not merely 'unreliable Aryan' elements. Even so, Hitler was not master in his own house. Countervailing pressures had to be heeded. At Hindenburg's request, Hitler reluctantly agreed to exclude Jews who had been officials since 1916 or who had fought in the war or whose fathers and sons had fought in the war. These exceptions were not inconsiderable; in practice it meant that only 38 per cent of all Jewish officials in Prussia were removed from office.

Growing concern expressed by conservative ministers, particularly Papen, Neurath and Count Schwerin von Krosyk, the minister of finance, about the adverse international repercussions of anti-semitism may have played some part in restraining Hitler from extending the anti-semitic legislation during the next two years. But undoubtedly a major factor must have been his understanding of the overriding importance of economic recovery. On 6 July Hitler warned the *Gauleiter* that the revolution was over. The next day Hess banned further boycotts of department stores and on 14 July the cabinet decided not to withhold contracts from Jewish firms, so urgent was the need to bring about a rapid fall in the unemployment figures. Economic realism had triumphed over ideological prejudice for the time being at least.

The next important extension of the anti-semitic legislation, the notorious Nuremberg Laws of 1935, was introduced in somewhat dramatic circumstances. In the middle of the party rally Hitler, without consulting cabinet colleagues or permanent officials, suddenly summoned Bernhard Lösener, the civil servant responsible for Jewish affairs in the ministry of the interior, and several of his colleagues to Nuremberg and ordered them to draft on the spot new laws regulating sexual relations between Jews and Gentiles—an aspect of anti-semitism which pornographic publications such as *Der Stürmer* dwelt upon at great length. At a specially convened Reichstag on 15 September three new laws were promulgated: the first forbade Jews to fly the national flag; the second defined German citizenship; and the third—the so-called law for the protection of German blood and honour—prohibited marriage and extra-marital relations between Jews and Gentiles.

One should be careful not to exaggerate the significance of Hitler's initiative.[49] Legislation of this kind had long been anticipated in the ministry of the interior. And from the end of 1934 a wave of popular anti-semitism gave a proleptic hint to the discerning of what was to come. The agitation, actively encouraged by Goebbels, the most influential anti-semite in Hitler's immediate entourage, mounted in intensity in the summer of 1935. Possibly Hitler was not unmindful of the damage anti-semitic excesses could do to Germany's international standing, now greatly improved after the Anglo-German Naval Convention. On 8 August Hitler forbade undisciplined acts by party members, a theme taken up by Frick who a few days later threatened offenders with severe penalties. However, once Hitler had reasserted his authority over the party and the anti-semitic agitation died away in the high summer, he was prepared once again to gratify the wishes of the activists. Not in the economic sphere however: Jewish firms were making too important a contribution in export markets and to rearmament to be sacrificed on the altar of popular anti-semitism. Because Hitler could not yield to party pressure for a 'Jew-free' economy, he was all the more obliging in an area dear to the hearts of all anti-semites. The foreign political situation may also have been a contributory factor. The Franco-Soviet Pact and the Czech-Soviet Pact signed in May 1935 were being represented in Germany as a new form of encirclement. The Nazi propaganda machine was intensifying its attacks on Russia and laying increasing emphasis on Germany's role in Europe as the bulwark against Jewish Bolshevism. As the pacts were attributed to the 'machinations of international Jewry', an intensification of the anti-semitic laws would serve to underline the point. Another factor may have been concern in Hitler's mind about the extent of popular support for the regime.

Whatever the pressures on him may have been, Hitler was a most willing legislator. That he opted for the most moderate of four draft laws and that he specifically restricted the scope of the Blood Law to full-blooded Jews, were little more than gestures. Against that has to be set the fact that he allowed the fanatical anti-semite Gerhard Wagner, head of the NS Studentenbund, the Nazi League of students and a close friend of Hess, to tighten up the draft laws. Presenting them to the Reichstag, Hitler declared—in a passage clearly intended as a warning to permanent officials—that if the Blood Law failed to solve the problem, it would be handed over to the party for 'final solution'.

And his remarks to close colleagues after the party rally leave no doubt about the virulence of his own views: 'Out with them [the Jews] from all the professions and into the ghettos with them! Fence them in somewhere where they can finish as they deserve while the German people look on the way people stare at wild animals.'[50]

The plight of the Jews would have worsened more rapidly than it did between 1935 and 1937 had it not been for two factors, neither of Hitler's making. In the first place ministry officials, sticklers for the law like civil servants the world over, strenuously opposed illegal interpretations placed on these laws by zealous party members. Hitler did nothing to discourage these encroachments, and seems to have welcomed them. What is interesting is that Hitler did not support the party members against the officials. Furthermore, on at least three occasions in 1937, because of technical objections raised in the ministries of finance and the interior, Hitler shelved legislation which he had personally initiated. Secondly, Hitler and his associates still felt the need to respect world opinion. That was no doubt the reason why, when a high Nazi official was assassinated in Switzerland by a Jew in February 1936, Hitler, on the eve of the Rhineland re-occupation, suppressed his natural instinct to deliver a blistering anti-semitic funeral oration. He seems also to have been concerned about the possibility of anti-semitic outbursts endangering the prestigious Olympic Games to be held in Germany in the summer and winter of 1936. It was on his personal orders that anti-Jewish slogans were removed and the display of *Der Stürmer* banned for the duration of the Games.

Nor can one attribute the sudden deterioration in the position of the Jews in 1938–9 simply and solely to Hitler's hatred of them. Only in the context of the changing balance of power in the Third Reich are the events of these years fully intelligible. After the removal of Blomberg, Fritsch, Neurath and Schacht, the door was at last open to a radicalization of policy both at home and abroad. The decline of Schacht and the rise of Goering were particularly significant in connection with the Jews. For Schacht with his extensive international contacts, being acutely aware of the adverse effects 'Aryanization' of the economy would have on foreign opinion, had always resisted it. Goering, economic 'strong man' since 1935–6 and a close friend of the Führer, was less concerned about foreign opinion and quite outspoken in his desire to make a clean sweep of the Jews as quickly as possible. And behind Goering stood the great industrial combines, possibly a factor of some importance in explaining the radicalization of the regime's anti-semitic policy. Prospering in the boom years 1938–9 and glutted with liquid assets, these combines were itching to expand at the expense of smaller units and had begun to cast envious eyes on Jewish firms.

The radical changes that were on the way were revealed starkly during Reichskristallnacht on 9–10 November 1938. Ninety Jews were murdered, synagogues all over Germany went up in flames, and 7,000 Jewish shops were destroyed in an unprecedented outburst of frightful savagery organized by party activists. The origins of this pogrom illustrate vividly the highly personalized style of decision-making and the fierce revalries characteristic of life at the top in the Third Reich. In the confident expectation that Hitler would soon place the Jews under further constraints, Goebbels and Streicher were busily organizing 'spontaneous' demonstrations for a 'Jew-free' economy in the summer of 1938. At the height of the Sudeten crisis the agitation was frankly unwelcome to Hitler. Through Bormann he reminded the party that the existing legislation rendered all independent initiative superfluous. It was the murder of a German embassy official in Paris by a Jewish youth that gave Goebbels his chance to revive the campaign and possibly, too, to restore himself to favour with the Führer, who was at that time sharply critical of his propaganda minister's notorious liaison with the actress Lida Baarova. Although Goebbels instructed the press to play up the incident in the editions of 8 November—whether with Hitler's approval or not we do not know—to his surprise Hitler made no reference to it in the annual speech at the Bürgerbräukeller. Whereupon Goebbels hurried to Munich and buttonholed Hitler at a gathering of party leaders on 9 November. Having listened to Goebbels, Hitler declared that 'the SA should be allowed its last fling'.[51] One can only speculate about the motives. Perhaps it was simply a visceral reaction by a man frustrated since the Munich conference had robbed him of his local war: burning synagogues were a surrogate for burning Czech villages. Yet from the subsequent course of events it is clear that Hitler quickly decided to use the incident as an excuse for expelling the Jews from the economy.[52]

As usual Hitler avoided direct involvement in the savagery leaving Goebbels to organize 'spontaneous' demonstrations in villages and towns throughout the length and breadth of Germany. It is significant that Hitler did not inform Goering, Himmler or Reinhard Heydrich his deputy—all deeply interested in the fate of German Jewry—of the pogrom because he obviously realized that they would oppose it. Goering, a long standing rival of Goebbels and resentful of the latter's ambition, protested to Hitler about the damage done to the economy. Himmler and Heydrich were equally critical of its adverse effect on emigration plans. But all attempts to engineer Goebbels's dismissal misfired. Hitler ostentatiously demonstrated complete solidarity with the propaganda minister, and the protests died away. In any case the whole Nazi hierarchy was very soon absorbed in the congenial task of hedging Jews around with new restrictions. Goering quickly forgot his objections and took the lead in plundering the Jews. A spate of discriminatory and often spiteful legislation deprived them of the means of livelehood: a huge fine of 1,000 million marks was imposed on them;[53] all Jewish firms and real estate holdings were compulsorily sold;[54] Jews were forced to surrender all shares and gold and silver possessions; they were totally excluded from schools and universities and even from cinemas, theatres and concert halls, sports stadia and swimming pools; and by 1939 able-bodied and unemployed Jews were forced into labour battalions engaged on public works. The evidence suggests that Hitler took a lively personal interest in these measures, and frequently adjudicated on points of detail referred to him by Goering.

As the war clouds gathered, there were ugly signs that the Nazi leadership was prepared to make the Jews pay a heavy price should hostilities break out. Nevertheless, it is probably an oversimplification of a complex situation to construe Hitler's bloodthirsty and ferocious comments to foreign statesmen as an unequivocal commitment to the physical annihilation of the Jews at the earliest possible moment.[55] Even the celebrated remark in the Reichstag on 30 January 1939 that, if 'international Jewish finance' plunged the world into war, the result would not be 'the bolshevization of the earth and the victory of Jewry' but 'the annihilation of the Jewish race in Europe', might be interpreted either as a blunt warning to Germany's enemies that the Jews would not be spared the horrors of war or perhaps as a clumsy attempt to put the blame for war on the Jews.[56] One must resist the temptation to read back into Hitler's remarks sinister undertones of a policy not decided on until 1941. Just as one must pay due regard to 'alternative' foreign policies which to some extent modified Hitler's own concepts, so, too, in studying the holocaust one must allow for the possibility that there were other 'final solutions' before the gas chambers.

The weight of the evidence suggests that Hitler had no very clear idea of what should be done with the Jews apart from turning them into pariahs. Therefore, he was perfectly prepared to fall in with whatever 'solution' of the 'Jewish problem' was currently in vogue in the corridors of power. Emigration is a case in point. Hitler looked with favour on this solution because it was supported by Himmler, a rising star in the Nazi firmament. By combining high office in the party with control of the German police, Himmler had turned the SS into an organization of immense power by the late 1930s. One of the units under his command the Sicherheitsdienst, or SS Security Service, happened to have been sponsoring the emigration of Jews to Palestine since 1935. In February 1938 Hitler gave his formal approval to this policy despite foreign office objections to the creation of a Zionist state in the Middle East. That Hitler, who may in the first place have been following the line of least resistance, became convinced of the viability of this 'solution' is suggested by his approval of private negotiations—not entirely pleasing to Ribbentrop—which Schacht was allowed to conduct in 1938–9 with Rublee, the chairman of the International Committee for Political Refugees; this was an (unsuccessful) attempt to finance the emigration of 150,000 German Jews through Jewish payments for German exports. And in January 1939, when Goering called for the acceleration of emigration 'by every possible means', he clearly had Hitler's approval. The fact that a total of 247,000 of Germany's 503,000 Jews had left Grossdeutschland by September 1939—78,000 in that year alone—is proof that the Nazis pursued this policy with energy and conviction. Far from holding on to the Jews as an insurance policy to keep foreign powers off their backs, the Nazis did their best to be rid of the 'plague bacilli'.

The brutalization of life which war brings in its wake could not fail to affect the position of the Jews, now virtually outcasts in German society. Proof beyond all doubt that Hitler was a man of instinctive violence capable of the most frightful deeds came at the beginning of the Polish campaign: he ordered four special commandos into Poland in the wake of the German armies with orders to execute thousands of prominent citizens, in a cold-blooded attempt to destroy the fabric of the Polish ruling class. No specific order to execute Jews was given but the Einsatzgruppen or special commandos, took it upon themselves to shoot any Jews they could find. When the military authorities protested at the disastrous effect these horrors were having on army morale, and Himmler restrained the murder gangs, Hitler at once intervened and relieved the military of all responsibility for the civilian population, making it abundantly clear that he would tolerate no criticism of Himmler's work. By the end of the year the special commandos had recommenced their indiscriminate shootings.

Even so, the systematic extermination of the Jewish race was probably not finalized in Hitler's mind at this stage. As emigration was impracticable while the British fleet ruled the seas, Hitler seems to have toyed with some other 'territorial' solution to the problem. While the Einsatzgruppen were still at work in September 1939, he informed Himmler, Heydrich, Forster and later Rosenberg that he wanted all Polish Jews—some three millions in all—to be concentrated in ghettos in specified towns (to facilitate overall control of them), as a prelude to the creation of a huge Jewish reserve between the rivers Vistula and Bug, that is, on the eastern frontier of the new Reich. On 7 October Himmler was given full powers as Reichs commissioner for the strengthening of Germanism (in other words, for settling Germans in the conquered territories) to carry out this task—a sure sign of Hitler's complete confidence in the Reichsführer SS. Between December 1939 and February 1940 large numbers of Jews were transported to the area south of Lublin which the Reichssicherheitshauptamt, the headquarters of the SS security service, had earmarked as the reserve.

This 'final solution' lasted barely six months. Quite why Hitler lost faith in it is a mystery. It is hardly conceivable that he turned against it because overcrowding in the reserve would make it impossible for the Jews to maintain tolerable living standards.[57] Probably Goering informed him of Governor Hans Frank's representations in February 1940 that the transportation of Jews should be halted because of the intolerable strain being placed on limited food supplies in German–occupied Poland. It is safe to assume that when Goering finally stopped all transportation on 24 March 1940 it was with Hitler's approval.

Three months later, during the closing stages of the French campaign, Hitler toyed momentarily with a second territorial solution—the so-called Madagascar plan.[58] The proposal, worked out in a foreign office memorandum, was to ship all western Jews to Madagascar leaving the eastern Jews in Poland as a pledge of continuing American neutrality. Himmler was immediately enthusiastic, a factor which probably weighed heavily with Hitler, and with the Führer's approval the Reichssicherheitshauptamt drafted a scheme for transporting three-and-a-half million Jews to the island after the war. During the summer Hitler mentioned the plan to several prominent figures including Mussolini, Raeder and Otto Abetz, German ambassador in Paris.[59] As late as June 1941 he told a Croatian collaborator that he intended to send all the Jews to Madagascar or Siberia.[60] The fact that he was still talking of the Madagascar plan to close friends in the summer of 1942, when extermination was already under way, certainly weakens the argument but does not necessarily mean that he was not in earnest in 1940. Had Britain surrendered that summer, the plan could have been implemented.

The exact point at which the decision was taken to murder the whole of European Jewry is shrouded in obscurity and still a matter of dispute amongst historians. Some have argued that Hitler did not decide on the 'final' solution until late October–November 1941 when it dawned on him that the Russian campaign was running into difficulties. In the face of stiffening Russian resistance all hope vanished for the foreseeable future of transporting the Jews from the ghettos of Poland to the area east of the Urals—a 'third' solution Hitler toyed with in the summer of 1941 according to Goebbels and Rosenberg.[61] Yet precisely at this point when doubts were beginning to assail him, Hitler ordered the acceleration of the deportation of the Jews which had greatly slowed in pace since the first half of 1941 when preparations for the attack on Russia had prior claim on available transport. In October the first mass deportations from German cities to Lodz commenced. Had the entire Jewish population of Europe—three million Polish Jews and two million from other lands—been crowded into the ghettos the Nazis would have been unable to contain the situation. To relieve the pressure on overcrowded and typhus-ridden accommodation some local SS commanders had already begun to execute Jews by shooting as soon as they arrived from the west. When Himmler discussed these executions with Hitler it seems likely that the latter ordered the extension of this 'final' solution to encompass the whole of European Jewry, the visceral reaction of a fanatical racist determined to be rid of the Jews *so oder so*. It is interesting to note that he had not allowed an emergency to arise through negligence or preoccupation with more pressing military matters. On the contrary, he had deliberately deepened the crisis by accelerating the deportations. One is reminded of other occasions in 1932 and 1938 when he purposely sought confrontation as if to overcome his own doubts and hesitations about the course of action he was about to embark upon.

However, other historians maintain that Hitler decided on mass extermination not in the autumn but in the summer of 1941. The Russian campaign was the decisive factor. Already in March Hitler declared that this would be a racial war of annihilation different in kind from the campaign in the west; for example, political commissars were to be shot on capture. Five Einsatzgruppen followed the German armies into Russia in June with specific instructions to murder 'the Jewish-Bolshevik ruling class'. The murder squads executed all the Jews they could lay their hands on whether 'Bolshevik' or not. Encouraged by their success, Hitler probably approved orders through Goering to Nazi agencies to begin preparations for the wholesale annihilation of all Jews.

Confusion arose because Hitler was too impatient to await the completion of the arrangements and ordered the acceleration of deportation before the death camps were ready for their victims. All that happened in October–November was that Hitler formally approved the arrangements already being worked out. This second interpretation does seem to fit such evidence as we possess rather better than the former.

Now that Germany was at war with the 'Jewish-Bolshevik' state, the very *fons et origo* of world revolution, it was psychologically much easier to take the decision to murder millions of Jews. Physical extermination of the enemy must have appeared to Hitler as nothing more than a logical extension of the life-and-death struggle against the same enemy without the walls. But what made it objectively possible to turn a nightmare into sober fact—and this was a factor of the utmost importance—was the existence of a highly organized police apparatus controlled by another fanatical racist and a man thoroughly loyal to the Führer. Himmler's Einsatzgruppen had already proved their mettle and were, by sheer coincidence, beginning in the autumn of 1941 to experiment with gas, a silent and swift method of execution making it technically feasible to dispose of millions rather than thousands of victims. In short, the machinery of destruction and the accomplices to operate it already existed, thus enabling Hitler to realize his ambition to 'expel' the Jews from Europe despite a worsening external situation.

Once committed to this barbarous course, Hitler showed no sign of relenting. In private conversation he avoided the subject out of a need to preserve the utmost secrecy. As mentioned above, he pretended on occasions that emigration was the solution he still favoured. Of course, there is little doubt that Hitler was, as Goebbels remarked, 'the undismayed champion of the radical solution both in word and deed'.[62] As late as 1943 he emphasized to Himmler how necessary it was to continue deportations regardless of the unrest it might cause. As the balance of military advantage turned decisively against Germany, he remained as obstinately determined as ever to win at least one battle—the fight against Jewry. And at the very end of his life he claimed with pride that the extirpation of Jewry was his legacy to the world.

The holocaust is the most macabre monument in the whole of modern history to the power of a myth over the minds of men. The extermination of the Jews made neither economic nor strategic sense. It seems an act of sheer madness to have allocated transport desperately needed on the eastern front to this wholly negative operation. Nor did it make any kind of sense to deprive Germany of a labour force which could have benefited the war effort. However, what to a rational mind is proof of the ultimate irrationality of the Third Reich, must be seen—if historians are to make sense of the holocaust and of Hitler's leading role in it—as a logical though not necessarily inevitable outcome of the Nazi belief in the cosmic struggle between the Aryan race and world Jewry. There is an eerie parallel between the attitude of the ruling élite in Nazi Germany to their frightful task and the Aztec priests of old. As is well known, the latter offered up blood sacrifices to appease their gods and prevent darkness and disaster engulfing the Aztec people. It is, to say the least, an arresting thought that members of the special commandos often calmed their troubled consciences with the reassuring thought that the 'execution' of the Jewish 'criminals' would usher in an era of peace for mankind.[63]

Only in 1944, in a broadcast to the German people on 30 January, the anniversary of his coming to power, did Hitler at last raise a corner of the veil of secrecy surrounding the macabre operation and attempt to justify it as a 'historical necessity'. Anti-semitism was most definitely for export in the universal struggle against Jewry. Scornfully he dismissed the opinion that any state could ever come to terms with their Jews any more than the human body could assimilate 'plague bacilli' in the long run. In a chilling phrase he spoke of his hope that other nations might become acquainted with 'the elements of a scientific understanding and objective solution of the [Jewish] question'. And he expressed the hope that the war would 'open the eyes of the peoples in a few years to the Jewish question and the National Socialist answer and the measures for its solution will seem as worthy of emulation as they are a matter of common sense. The greatness of this world historical struggle will train the eyes and minds of the nations for thinking and acting in mighty historical dimensions'.[64]

3

The military commander

Until fairly recently is was fashionable to dismiss Hitler as a bungling amateur in military matters, the opinionated corporal of the First World War, utterly out of his depth as a supreme commander, a carpet-biting maniac even, who pulled Germany down to defeat through his wholly irrational conduct of the war. This view of Hitler rests very largely on the testimony of certain German generals who rushed into print after the war and blamed the Führer, conveniently deceased, for all that had gone wrong after 1942 while carefully claiming credit, on behalf of the army, for Germany's earlier successes.

In the last few years, with the return of much captured material to the German archives, a more accurate and historically credible picture is emerging. Of course, no amount of research can ever exonerate Hitler from a very heavy burden of responsibility for Germany's defeat. But it is at least possible to detect light and shade in the picture where previously Stygian darkness reigned. Possibly, too, we have now reached the point in time when we can begin to appreciate the dimensions of the personal tragedy that ended with all the trappings of a third-rate melodrama in the Berlin bunker. However, before embarking on any evaluation of the impact of Hitler's personality on the momentous events of the Second World War, it may be helpful to examine, briefly, the strengths and weaknesses of Hitler as a war leader.

From the extensive fragments of the daily war conferences which have survived, it is quite clear that Hitler was no ignoramus pontificating about matters beyond his ken. On the contrary, Hitler had in fact an astonishingly broad grasp of military strategy and an eye for operational tactics in offensive warfare that one would not expect in a layman never initiated into the mysteries of warfare by a spell at staff college. All the commanders and staff officers who came into contact with him, even those most critical of the regime and its leader, were impressed by his understanding of military affairs. Though intolerant and opinionated on many occasions, he generally showed himself to be exceptionally well-informed, thoroughly conversant with troop dispositions and possessed an unusual facility for placing local situations in their general strategic setting. In discussion Hitler invariably defended his point of view coherently and, even if the premises were wrong-headed, with at least superficially relevant arguments.

Surprisingly, for a man without any formal military training Hitler was in possession of a considerable body of technical knowledge. At the lowest level, thanks to an extraordinarily retentive memory, he acquired over the years an astonishingly detailed knowledge of conventional weaponry which would have put most quartermasters to shame. He was thoroughly familiar with the calibre and range of every field piece in the German and other armies and could rattle off figures of ammunition stocks, monthly production statistics and detailed weapon specifications—such information was his favourite bedtime reading—at the drop of a hat. Naturally there was a large element of deliberate theatre in the way he paraded information at every opportunity. Psychologically it was important for him to feel superior to staff officers in whose presence he was never wholly at ease. Exhibitionism of this variety—the mark of the pretentious amateur, not the true expert—seems to have served this psycho-political end very effectively. His habit of raining down a torrent of figures and technical data (usually fairly accurate) when he wanted to change the subject—though a well-known ploy to those who regularly attended his conferences—never failed to impress an audience. And his uncanny facility for exposing inaccuracies in reports could throw even the most thick-skinned general into total confusion. However, it should be noted that when Hitler faced a battery of technical, as opposed to military experts, he did not employ this stratagem. Albert Speer reports that when he visited the Führer during the first year of his appointment as minister of armaments, always with several colleagues in attendance, Hitler listened attentively, had no difficulty in understanding the alternatives put to him and often abandoned his prejudices, much to the surprise of high-ranking officers.[1] It is true that he tired of this. By 1943 he had excluded all but two of Speer's advisers from their regular conferences and considerably reduced the amount of free discussion on these occasions.

Hitler's technical expertise was not all bluff by any means. Sometimes he could see further than military experts simply because the fresh untrained mind can occasionally perceive possibilities where a trained mind, burdened by the sheer weight of subject matter or inhibited by professional conventions, fails to do so. A case in point in the 1930s is the role of armour in warfare. Hitler had an instinctive feeling for the revolutionary potential of armour which would, he believed, if used boldly, restore mobility to warfare and enable Germany to win swift victories with a minimum of bloodletting. It is an interesting reflection on the very real independence enjoyed by the army before 1938, that, despite Hitler's constant pressure for more armoured units, progress was fairly slow. Bottlenecks in industry had something to do with this but the main reason was the scepticism of most generals. They were unwilling to gamble on armoured divisions being the decisive factor in the next war, and preferred the safer course of using tanks in an infantry-support role. Only when he became commander-in-chief of the Wehrmacht in 1938 was Hitler able to get more of his own way in this matter. To break up the log jam he appointed the tank enthusiast, General Heinz Guderian, to the new post of commander of mobile troops with the right of direct access to the Führer.

On the other hand, Hitler's much vaunted technical expertise did not extend very much beyond conventional weaponry. It has been said of him, quite correctly, that he remained at heart the infantryman of the First World War, stamped indelibly with the ideas and experiences of that era.[2] Most certainly he was slow to appreciate the significance of new scientific developments which mushroomed during the Second World War, particularly radar, jet propulsion and rocketry.

This raises a more fundamental question about Hitler's style of military leadership. The truth is that by attempting to run a major war out of his own mental resources, reserving the right to make vital decisions on his own, Hitler set himself a quite impossible task even if Germany had possessed the necessary resources. To ensure a proper balance between strategic realities, operational tactics and the appropriate weaponry, many factors have to be balanced against each other—the state of research into new weapons, their operational possibilities, the probable reaction of the enemy, the morale and state of training of one's own troops, the state of civilian morale, logistical problems and the productive capacity of industry. Hitler could not begin to cope adequately with this task. His tendency to oversimplify situations, an (inevitably) imperfect knowledge of many of the aspects involved in strategic planning, and an often quite unpredictable stubbornness combined to lead him into serious errors of judgment. Two of the major blunders deserve special mention—the failure to develop jet fighters until it was too late to affect the outcome of the war, and the decision to manufacture rocket missiles and bombs instead of ground-to-air missiles.

The revolutionary nature of the Me 262, Germany's first jet fighter, clearly escaped the Führer. At first he refused to allow full-scale production of the fighter possibly because, since the failure of the heavy bomber He 177, he had become sceptical of the claims made for all new prototypes. Not until November 1943 did he relent, and only then because with an allied invasion of Europe a near certainty in the next few months, he was looking for a fast aircraft to pin the enemy down on the beachhead until reserves could be brought up to deal with them. With characteristic enthusiasm he now approved of the full-scale production of the Me 262 but apparently on the understanding—given by the designer of the aircraft, Professor Willy Messerschmidt, in the presence of Goering and of General Erhard Milch of the air ministry and without objections being raised by either—that what was essentially a one-seater fighter could easily be converted into a two-seater aircraft capable of carrying two 500-pound bombs.[3] It is illustrative of the casual and confused nature of decision-making in the Third Reich that Hitler's order was disregarded and production went ahead on the fighter. By sheer chance Hitler discovered what had happened in May 1944, and cancelled the entire project in a fit of temper.

For the next few months he stubbornly insisted on his fighter-bomber while the technical experts maintained a discreet silence despite their belief that his plan was impracticable. He was not short of arguments to justify his stubbornness. Some were quite ludicrous as, for example, that the excessive speed (850 kilometres per hour) would affect the pilot's health; others were remarkably prescient, for instance, that the faster-moving Me 262 would have great difficulty in engaging slower-moving but more manoeuvrable enemy fighters. Then, finally, in October 1944 he relented sufficiently to permit limited production of the Me 262 as a fighter. But not until March 1945, when the evidence suggested that the Me 262 had performed well, did he finally order full-scale production as a fighter. Needless to say, it was then far too late: Germany did not even possess the fuel to put the Me 262 in the air. Thus, as Speer argues, Hitler threw away the one chance Germany had—in conjunction with ground-to-air missiles—of holding in check the mounting air offensive against the homeland.[5]

Similarly, in the case of the so-called V weapons. On seeing the first tests in October 1942 Hitler was carried away with enthusiasm. Without waiting for further confirmation of the weapon's viability, he ordered immediate production of 5,000 rockets. By July 1943 he was supremely confident that he had discovered 'the decisive weapon of the war'. Without reference to Germany's overall strategic needs and acting entirely on impulse, he ordered rocket production to be given absolute priority with tank production. Even so, another twelve months elapsed before rockets and flying bombs were ready for use. In the end the weapon proved an abysmal failure. Between June 1944 and March 1945 1,100 rockets and 2,400 flying bombs were launched at Britain, mostly at the London area. Nine thousand civilians were killed and much material damage caused. But on the course of the war the effect of V weapons was negligible. They did nothing at all to check the allied air offensive over Germany; each missile contained one to two tons of high explosive compared with the 300 tons the allied air forces dropped day in and day out on the Reich. What propaganda value the weapons had—and Hitler grossly overestimated this element—was quickly neutralized by allied bombing and the eventual overrunning of the missile sites. Precious resources had been squandered in producing an offensive weapon of dubious value instead of the defensive hardware Germany needed—in particular the ground-to-air missiles on which experimental work was being carried out in 1942 when Hitler opted impulsively for rockets.

In the field of conventional weaponry, without in any way belittling Albert Speer's immense contribution to the rationalization of the German war effort, it is true to say that Hitler's drive and energy did contribute significantly to the very considerable increases in arms production achieved between 1942 and 1944. Together Hitler and Speer squeezed much more out of industry than anyone thought possible. Nor can one deny that Hitler frequently displayed a rare gift for improvization. As the records of Speer's conferences with the Führer reveal, Hitler issued a stream of orders modifying existing weaponry chiefly in respect of the calibre and range of guns. And when inspecting new weapons he was on occasion capable of flashes of truly inventive genius. On the other hand, many of his decisions were wrong-headed. For example, when the army desperately needed a light tank to outmanoeuvre the Russian T-34,

Hitler insisted on increasing the armour and fire power of new prototypes. As a result the new Panther, originally planned as a thirty-ton tank, ended up a few months later at forty-eight tons. Indeed, to pacify the Führer the designer Ferdinand Porsche actually produced an absurdly superheavy tank, the Mouse, which at over one hundred tons could only be built in small numbers and was of no tactical value. Furthermore, as Hitler had always been mesmerized by numbers, he tended to believe that quantity not quality was the key to victory: faults that came to light in a weapon would, he supposed, be more than compensated for by mass production, a doctrine hardly likely to inspire confidence in soldiers in the field, dependent for survival on weapons of proven inefficiency.

At the same time Hitler remained as always the centre of intrigue and rivalry. Those close to the Führer habitually pressed the claims of projects in which for one reason or another they had taken a personal interest. The upshot was that far too many weapons were under construction at any one time. Consequently there was an acute shortage of spare parts. Logistics was never Hitler's strong point. He completely failed to appreciate the direct relationship between the number of weapon types in production and the problem of ensuring a steady flow of spare parts to service them. To provide sufficient parts for all the weapons in production would have necessitated a cut in production, a reality he never faced up to.

One is left with an overall impression of a man floundering in detail, a quartermaster with a touch of genius making heroic efforts to grapple with a whole range of problems beyond the capacity of one man to master. Even when he did grasp the essentials of a problem quicker than his military advisers—as for example in recognizing by 1942 the need for a basic restructuring of weapons in all branches of the armed forces—neither his expertise nor the state of the economy was equal to the task of resolving the problem. It was typical of Hitler that he oscillated between the sublime and the ridiculous. He was quite capable of taking the most specious ideas in deadly earnest, as witness the order in March 1945 to investigate the possibility of using Greek fire against bridges. And a month later, when he received the news of Roosevelt's death, he immediately declared this to be the turning-point of the war. A basic irrationality forced its way to the surface on these occasions which merits closer examination in a study of personality.

It was not that Hitler could not anticipate the likely effects of military reverses. What he could not do was accept the consequences when the inevitable happened. Of this phenomenon there are many examples. In March 1943 he went on record as saying that unless Germany had room for manoeuvre in Russia she could not continue the war there;[6] yet when Germany was finally driven out of Russia, he argued that a country hemmed in as Germany was in 1944 had certain military advantages.[7] In April 1944 he forecast quite correctly that a successful allied landing in France would spell the end of the war because of Germany's chronic lack of resources;[8] yet when the allied forces broke out of the beach-heads, Hitler fought on. On 29 June he admitted that a war of movement was impossible because of the enemy's superior mobility;[9] yet when the American forces led by General George S. Patton broke out at Avranches, Hitler attempted vainly to wage a war of movement. He was a veritable jack-in-the-box who interpeted every situation to suit himself regardless of inconsistency. This habit points to the profound struggle taking place in Hitler between, on the one hand, his acute intelligence which left him in no doubt about the likely outcome of the war and, on the other, his deeply-held conviction that he was a man with a mission to accomplish whom 'providence' would protect. Again and again he rejected the world as he knew it to be in the cold light of dawn and clung tenaciously to the infantile picture of the world as he wanted it to be.

That was why Hitler was so reluctant to admit that Germany had been forced onto the defensive by 1942–3 and insisted so vehemently that will power—or 'fanaticism' as he called it—was the real determinant of victory. In a revealing comment in December 1944 he declared:

> Genius is a will-o-the wisp if it lacks a solid foundation of perseverance and fantical tenacity. That is the most important thing there is in human life. People who have only ideas and thoughts and so forth but possess neither firmness of character nor tenacity and perseverance will amount to nothing in spite of all. They are merely soldiers of fortune . . . . One can only make world history if one can back up an acute faculty of reason, an active conscience and eternal vigilance with the fanatical perseverance that makes a man a fighter to the core.[10]

Just occasionally Hitler's fanaticism was of positive advantage, notably in December 1941 when his stubborn refusal to retreat from Moscow helped to inspire his soldiers to hold on at all costs, and made possible a new campaign the following year, slim though Germany's chances of winning outright in the east probably were by 1942. But in general he grossly exaggerated the role of will power in history. What he stubbornly refused to admit was that, unlike faith, will power cannot move mountains but is only effective within the limits circumscribed by the balance of forces at a given moment in history. Therefore, although he probably guessed as early as November 1941 that Germany could not win in Russia, he was reluctant to draw the correct conclusions.

In particular, Hitler was notoriously stubborn about withdrawals, and frequently refused to allow commanders to abandon untenable positions until it was too late to avert major disasters, notably at Stalingrad in 1941–2 and in the Crimea in 1944. His experiences in the First World War, which he often spoke about at the daily war conferences, did not help him see reason in this matter. Incidents such as the precipitate retreat of German troops from the Arras-Soissons line in the spring of 1917 when the infantry, aware that prepared positions awaited them in the Siegfried Line, avoided costly rear-guard actions, may well have led him to believe that, if morale was to be maintained in a steadily worsening situation, positions once occupied must never be abandoned. But like may a generalization about Hitler, this needs careful qualification. For although he was never wholly converted to a belief in an elastic defence system, he did modify his attitude in the course of 1942 and accepted at last the need for some withdrawals to prepared positions.

Much has been written about Hitler's deep mistrust of his military advisers, which, so it is alleged, became positively obsessional in the closing stages of the war. It cannot be denied that his dislike of the socially exclusive officer corps was of long standing and that he was always somewhat ill at ease in the presence of staff officers whose expertise he did not possess—and therefore grossly undervalued. As the war started to go badly for Germany, he was frequently irritated by the imperturbable and unemotional professionalism of the staff officers—'ice-cold calculators, defeatist-minded and unreliable' as he once called them[11]—an attitude which seemed utterly alien to the fanatical and unyielding spirit he now demanded of his officers. Increasingly Hitler blamed enemy victories not on the hard realities of the situation of which he was well aware, but on 'defeatism' and 'cowardice'. Officers responsible for unauthorized withdrawals were frequently dealt with ruthlessly on Hitler's express orders. After the July Plot revealed widespread disaffection among his officers Hitler's mistrust of them became positively paranoid.

Here again it is unwise to generalize too much about Hitler's relations with his military advisers. Some, such as General Franz Halder, chief of the army general staff, fared badly at Hitler's hands while others, for example General Kurt Zeitzler, Halder's successor, and Field Marshal Gerd von Rundstedt, could with care and clever stratagems handle Hitler to the end. When Hitler refused point blank to permit the evacuation of the German forces trapped in the Caucasus in November 1942 despite the growing dangers they were exposed to, Zeitzler nevertheless ordered preparations for their evacuation to be made secretly. On the night of 28 December, after the failure of the attempt to relieve Stalingrad, Zeitzler insisted on seeing Hitler. Finding the Führer on the point of listening to Beethoven records, Zeitzler succeeded in persuading him that only prompt withdrawal could avert disaster. Zeitzler at once telephoned the necessary orders to Army Group A from Hitler's headquarters. An hour later Hitler rang Zeitzler countermanding the order pending further consideration. Zeitzler, because of the advance preparations, was able to argue that countermanding the order to withdraw would cause too much confusion. Hitler hesitated, then abruptly accepted the argument and allowed the evacuation to continue as planned.

Similarly, when Rundstedt was forced to retreat to the Rhine in February 1945, he obtained Hitler's reluctant consent by constantly reassuring the Führer of his determination to fight on to the end in what he privately knew to be a completely hopeless situation. In other words, the Führer's 'inflexibility' varied in direct relation to the degree of confidence he reposed in individual officers and to their ability to manipulate him—factors which added an element of unpredictability to German strategy in the closing stages of the war.

Hitler's unassailable position as Germany's military and political leader combining supreme power in his own hands to a degree unthinkable in Britain or in the United States, was not just a matter of charismatic personality, a simple transference to another sphere of his political primacy. The explanation lies in part at least in the tradition of narrow specialization which plagued the German armed forces. Military planners were trained to conceptualize in terms of particular operations within their own branch of the service. Being unaccustomed to thinking in terms of the broad strategic picture, they capitulated all the more easily before a gifted and articulate amateur.[12]

Hitler was quick to exploit structural weaknesses in the system whenever he could. For instance, he rarely allowed the commanders-in-chief of army, navy and airforce to attend the same war conference, much preferring to see them separately, usually in the presence of General Wilhelm Keitel, chief of the high command office, and General Alfred Jodl, chief of operations at high command, but occasionally on his own. Whatever the circumstances, the commanders-in-chief had little opportunity to stray from their brief and develop a taste for broad strategy or even to coordinate their activities with those of the other branches of the service. What coordination there was had to be arranged outside the war conferences, and was further hampered by Hitler's habitual secrecy about his ultimate intentions. He deliberately encouraged compartmentalization: foreign office intelligence was not supplied to the general staff, nor was military intelligence supplied to the foreign office. Just before the attack on Russia, Hitler further strengthened his own position by making the army solely responsible for the Russian theatre of operations and handing over to the high command office all other theatres. Smooth running of military operations was complicated still more by the intervention of powerful men with direct access to Hitler, especially Goering (and Raeder to some extent), who on occasions persuaded Hitler to modify plans to suit their convenience, further weakening the professional advisers.

Finally, one must not overlook a simple factor working in Hitler's favour—the sheer physical exhaustion of senior men in the latter years of the war. Keitel and Jodl regularly spent three hours around midday and never less than an hour in the late evening attending war conferences as well as attending to their own work at high command. Tired men are not in the best condition to resist the arguments of a fanatically-determined supreme commander who, in any case, when he felt he was losing an argument, frequently took refuge behind political and economic considerations to justify what he wanted to do, and always refused to allow any discussion of such factors claiming that they were his exclusive concern as supreme political leader.

To understand properly Hitler's attitude to the army some brief comment on the period 1933–9 is necessary. For at first Hitler handled the soldiers with great circumspection. While he maintained a close liaison with Blomberg, the minister of war, took a lively interest in weaponry, and frequently impressed on Fritsch, commander-in-chief of the army, the need for the utmost speed in rearmament, he did not interfere at all in the running of the army. Whenever he attended army manoeuvres he remained for the most part a silent spectator, so much so that Colonel Hossbach formed the erroneous impression that the Führer was completely out of his depth in a strange world.[13] The transition to the all-powerful war leader really started in 1938 with the Blomberg-Fritsch affair. When it was revealed that Blomberg's wife, Erna Gruhn, was a common prostitute with a police record, Hitler was obliged reluctantly, and out of respect for the outraged feelings of the officer corps, to dispense with the services of a war minister who had done much to maintain good relations between the party and the army. The prospect of having as his successor Fritsch, whose orthodox military thinking had irritated Hitler for years, was too much. Hitler used a trumped-up charge of homosexuality to get rid of Fritsch, personally assumed the role of commander-in-chief of the Wehrmacht, appointed Keitel to run the high command office as the Führer's personal planning staff, and chose as commander-in-chief of the army the pliable Brauchitsch. Taken as a whole, these changes concentrated supreme military and political power in the hands of one man for the first time since the days of Frederick the Great.

That he intended to make use of his new power was soon apparent, partly because of the gathering pace of German foreign policy, but also because he quickly discovered to his chagrin that army command had paid little heed to his constant pressure for a rapid build-up of armoured and motorized troops. For the next eighteen months he exerted himself to remedy what he regarded as a major weakness.

After the annexation of Austria in March 1938 Hitler immediately switched his attentions to Czechoslovakia. As commander-in-chief of the Wehrmacht he personally briefed Keitel on the general principles to be observed in drawing up a plan of attack; he checked the draft plan (Case Green) personally, he supervised the secret build-up of forces around Czechoslovakia in the summer of 1938; and in his first major confrontation with Halder and Keitel in early September he insisted on modifying the battle plan to permit a more imaginative use of armoured units. In other words he displayed a degree of panache in military matters which must have surprised those closest to him. Similarly in 1939, he ordered army command to draw up the plan of campaign against Poland; he again vetted the plan personally; he again paid close attention to the build-up of forces; and on the eve of war called his commanding generals to the Berghof where he harangued them on the objectives of the campaign. However, once Germany was at war, Hitler stayed on the sidelines. He visited the front each day—exposing himself to considerable risks on occasion—showed a keen interest in the course of the campaign, but made little attempt to interfere in the running of it.

If the generals supposed that their supreme commander intended to remain modestly in the background and allow them to determine the strategy of what was now a major war, much as Emperor William II allowed first Count Helmuth von Moltke, then Erich von Falkenhayn and latterly Hindenburg and Ludendorff to dominate the military scene, they were rudely awakened. On 27 September, the day Warsaw fell, Hitler summoned Goering, Raeder, Brauchitsch, Halder, Keitel and General Walter Warlimont, Jodl's deputy, to the chancellery where he informed them of his intention to attack in the west before the winter. On 9 October he ordered Halder to draw up a plan of campaign. While Goering and Raeder were in favour of an immediate attack, Brauchitsch and Halder were staggered by a decision which, as they saw it, failed to take into account the need to re-equip the army after the Polish campaign, and ignored the hazardous weather conditions likely to prevail in the west in the winter months.

Why did Hitler insist on extending the war? Elation after the victory in the east or anger at Britain's refusal to make a peace—a remote possibility as he must have realized all along—were not the reasons. What Hitler was saying loudly and clearly was that Germany had gone to war not merely to restore the frontiers of 1914, but to make Germany the dominant power in Europe from the Atlantic to the Urals while there was still time. For whereas the army general staff assumed from the inactivity on the western front that the French lacked the will to fight and would gladly forget the war if Germany did the same, Hitler's instincts told him that time was 'working for our opponents';[14] France must, therefore, be smashed without delay and Britain forced to make peace before she armed fully and the military balance shifted inexorably against Germany.

Economic considerations probably played a not inconsiderable part in this decision though, as always, it is impossible to quantify this factor.[15] Hitler understood from the very outset that modern war was as much a matter of economics as of military strategy.[16] It was not enough to invade Belgium and Holland in order to stop British trade with those countries, substantial though that was. More fundamentally, Germany's mounting economic crisis had not been solved by the victory in Poland. To keep the German war economy afloat, it was essential to have direct control of the raw materials, food supplies and labour reserves in western Europe. Nor must it be forgotten that the Nazis expected France, Belgium, Holland and Scandinavia to play an important role in the German-dominated continental economy of the future. Unless Germany exploited her temporary military advantage to lay the foundations of this new economic order and satisfy the forward thrust of German economic imperialism, final victory would not be possible over opponents with vast economic resources at their disposal. That was the irrefutable logic of the economic situation which Hitler perceived, perhaps only dimly and imperfectly, when he insisted on carrying the war to the west.

Whether Germany could have defeated France, Belgium and Holland in the winter of 1939–40, it is impossible to say. It may be that had adverse weather reports and opposition from the generals not frustrated Hitler's plans, Germany would have been plunged into an extremely difficult, even disastrous, campaign. Not that Hitler felt in the least grateful for warnings from the army. Behind the technical objections of the general staff he detected only an unmartial desire to avoid any extension of the war as well as lack of confidence in his judgement. Suspicion that high-ranking officers were conspiring to overthrow him (for which there was some justification) reinforced his long-standing aversion for the socially exclusive officer corps and found expression in diatribes against 'the spirit of Zossen'.[17] Psychologically, this was probably an important turning-point in Hitler's relations with the army. Significantly, Goering, Goebbels and Robert Ley, leader of the German Labour Front, all took up the theme in public speeches in which they contrasted the loyalty and devotion of the airforce and navy to the Führer with the unreliability of the army. As long as the war went well, this mattered little. But once the tide turned against Germany after 1941, then Hitler's suspicions were reactivated and an intolerable strain was placed on the relationship between army leaders and the supreme commander.

What emerged from Hitler's decision in January 1940 to postpone the attack in the west until the spring was a new plan of campaign which led the German armies to a spectacular victory a few months later. The change of plan illustrates Hitler's nose for strategic possibilities. The original plan, drafted unwillingly by Halder to placate the impatient Führer, proposed a frontal attack through Belgium to roll back the Anglo-French armies and secure bases for an air and sea attack on Britain. It soon dawned on high command, army command and on Hitler, too, that this unimaginative strategy was certain to lead to an indecisive slogging match between equally-balanced armies in northern France. While Hitler was groping around for an alternative, General Erich von Manstein, chief of staff of Army Group A, managed to catch his ear in the haphazard way typical of much of the decision-making in the Third Reich. The gist of Manstein's plan was to lure the Anglo-French armies into Belgium and Holland by a feint attack in the north while making the main thrust through the wooded Ardennes to cut the enemy off. Hitler was attracted by the element of surprise and audacity in the plan which seems to have coincided with his own thoughts on the subject since November. But at that stage in the war he lacked confidence and the necessary expertise to issue definite orders to scrap Halder's plan. In February Hitler finally adopted the Manstein plan and ordered the general staff to put flesh on the bones.

Hitler had his baptism of fire as supreme commander in Scandinavia, not in the west. The attack on Norway and Denmark in the spring of 1940 was in large measure the inspiration of Raeder, a zealous supporter of the Führer and a passionate believer in offensive warfare, who perhaps for these reasons was able to exert a good deal of influence over Hitler. From the beginning of the war Raeder had been trying to interest Hitler in the seizure of Norwegian bases from which to attack the convoys bringing essential supplies to Britain. To some extent Raeder's eagerness to attack Britain might almost be regarded as part of a much wider 'alternative strategy' which had interested the navy since before the First World War, and proved equally attractive to the foreign office under Ribbentrop. In place of Hitler's anti-French, anti-Russian and pro-British strategy, Raeder and Ribbentrop were seeking, in effect, to unite the whole of Europe, including Russia, against Britain.

Hitler was interested in Raeder's proposition, though not, of course, in the 'alternative strategy', but was much too absorbed in the struggle with the generals to respond positively. In December Raeder returned to the fray with an even stronger argument: there was reason to believe that Britain might soon invade Norway in order to give assistance to the Finns, who had been attacked by Russia in November. If Britain occupied northern Norway, Swedish ore supplies, on which Germany was heavily dependent and which were shipped out through the ice-free port of Narvik, would be endangered. The argument impressed Hitler. But what made him decide in January 1940 to set up a small planning staff at high command to work on exercise 'Weser' under his personal supervision was probably the frustration he experienced over the proposed western campaign as well as a desire for action of some sort to break the deadlock. Even so, the attack might well have been delayed had not intercepted reports indicated that Anglo-French forces were ready to embark for Norway in order to seize the railroad to the Swedish ore-fields.

The brief campaign which commenced on 9 April with the attack on Norway and Denmark, twenty-four hours before the British started to lay mines in Norwegian territorial waters as a prelude to invasion, throws an interesting light on Hitler. From the start he had kept a tight hold over exercise 'Weser'. General Nikolaus von Falkenhorst was appointed commander of the amphibious operation on Keitel's advice and after the briefest of interviews with Hitler, who attached great importance to first impressions. Brauchitsch and Halder only found out about the appointment later when Falkenhorst requested troops from them, so anxious was Hitler to preserve absolute secrecy.

As supreme commander Hitler intervened actively during the Norwegian campaign, and for the first time experienced the shock of sharp reverses. Between 10 and 13 April ten destroyers, half Raeder's entire fleet, were sunk at Narvik, and 2,000 mountain troops commanded by General Eduard Dietl together with 2,000 sailors were left stranded in the port without supplies. On top of this came news of British landings north of Narvik and Trondheim. Hitler lost his nerve and in a fit of blind panic ordered immediate withdrawal of the German forces in Narvik—an order which Jodl, it is interesting to note, quietly suppressed. For three days the crisis raged at Hitler's headquarters until Jodl eventually persuaded Hitler to hold on at Narvik. The sun came out again. By the end of April the Germans were in complete control of Norway and in Germany Hitler's reputation soared.

During the campaign in the west in May 1940 Hitler again displayed excessive caution on two critical occasions. A confident Hitler had effectively demoted Brauchitsch, a man for whom he felt nothing but contempt, and was personally directing the campaign from field headquarters at Münstereiffel. At first the attack went according to plan. General Fedor von Bock drew the Anglo-French armies into the Low Countries while Rundstedt's armour thrust through the Ardennes and by 14 May had crossed the Meuse river. The speed of the advance upset Hitler. Fearing a counterattack from the French armies in the south—a fear shared by Keitel and Jodl but not by army command—Hitler overruled Brauchitsch and Halder and ordered Rundstedt's armour to halt on 17 May until the infantry caught up. Fortunately General Guderian, now a corps commander, pressed ahead under cover of 'forward reconnaissance' and in defiance of the spirit of Hitler's order. On 20 May Guderian reached Abbeville, dragging the German army to victory after him. Thanks to Guderian a plan, which a leading expert has described as 'a lucky series of long-odds chances', succeeded brilliantly.[18] Characteristically, Hitler's mood changed; he lavished praise on the army which, forty-eight hours previously, he had accused of endangering the whole campaign, and ordered the advance to continue.

Four days later he hesitated again. This time the mistake was irredeemable though he was no more to blame for this than were some others. By 24 May the British armies had been driven to the coast and German armour was poised for a last victorious thrust when Rundstedt, having encountered some local resistance at Arras, suddenly halted the advance. As it had not dawned on army command that the British were preparing to evacuate their forces, it made good sense not to risk tanks in the unfavourable Flanders terrain with sixty-five French divisions still in the field. Hitler, like Rundstedt, was absolutely convinced that the British would fight to the last round of ammunition. Therefore, visiting Rundstedt's headquarters the Führer sided with him and countermanded orders from Brauchitsch and Halder that the advance continue. Personal intrigue cannot be excluded as a factor in Hitler's action. Goering may well have persuaded Hitler that it would be a politically astute move to let the airforce, and not the army, have the honour of finishing off the British.

The forty-eight hour delay before Rundstedt resumed his advance turned out disastrously for Goering. Bad weather grounded his aircraft. And when his Me 109s finally took off, the Spitfires proved a match for them. Because of this local air superiority, it was possible to evacuate 200,000 British and 130,000 French and Belgian troops from Dunkirk. Meanwhile on 5 June a major German offensive was launched on the Somme. On 17 June Marshal Henri Pétain, the victor of Verdun, sued for an armistice which was signed on 22 June in the forest at Compiègne, where twenty-two years before in the same railway coach Germany had acknowledged defeat.

The incredible had happened. Mighty France had fallen and Germany was indisputable master of Europe as she had never been before even in 1871. For this Hitler took all the credit. His doubts and hesitations were all forgotten. Had he not chosen the winning strategy? And would the campaign have ever been launched but for his granite determination? Henceforth he spoke *ex cathedra* on military affairs as he had for long spoken on politics. Equally significant, his generals swallowed whatever reservations they had about the Führer and applauded him enthusiastically even if they were not willing to go quite so far as Keitel who, in a fit of euphoria, dubbed Hitler 'the greatest commander of all time'.

What did Dunkirk matter now that Hitler was master of Europe? Like everyone else in Berlin that summer Hitler assumed that Britain would accept the logic of events and surrender gracefully. Elated by his dazzling victory, Hitler's thoughts were already turning eastwards. Whether army command anticipated Hitler's wishes and presented him with an outline plan of attack on Russia before he even requested it, or whether—more likely—it was Hitler who informed Brauchitsch, Jodl, Keitel and Jeschonnek on 21 July that a four to six-weeks campaign could finish off Russia in the autumn is uncertain. What is certain is that by the end of July it had been agreed to postpone an attack in the east until the spring of 1941 because of transport deficiencies. And, as it had been clear since the beginning of July that Britain intended to fight on, Hitler was compelled, reluctantly, to consider the possibility of invading the island kingdom.

From the start there were grave doubts about the feasibility of this difficult amphibious operation which Hitler fully shared. The army doubted the navy's capacity to provide essential cover against the British fleet. And Raeder, acutely aware of the crippling effects of the losses off Narvik and of the notorious unpredictability of the waters in the English Channel, was equally dubious. Only Goering remained confident that he could win mastery of the skies over Britain, thus fulfilling an essential prerequisite for invasion. Faced with conflicting advice, Hitler decided, sensibly enough, to make up his mind about invasion when he had seen what the airforce could do.

Hitler's caution was amply justified. On 13 August, 'Eagle Day', Goering commenced a major offensive aimed at destroying the RAF on the ground and in the air as a prelude to invasion in mid-September. Whether the attacks would have succeeded had they been pressed home, it is impossible to say. Whatever chance there was of victory for the Germans—in all probability a slim one—was thrown away when Goering switched the airforce to the bombing of London's dockland on 7 September, this in retaliation for allied air attacks on Berlin which in their turn were a riposte for an (accidental) German raid on London. The climax of the crucial Battle of Britain came on 15 September when sixty German aircraft—half the total over London that day—were shot down at the cost of twenty-six British fighters. By the end of September Hitler drew the correct inferences from Goering's failure and operation 'Sealion' was postponed until 1941.

Looking back, it is difficult to lay the blame exclusively on Hitler. True, had he attacked Britain in June and July when fighter command was desperately weak, the airbattles might have ended differently. But everyone in Berlin expected Britain to capitulate at that time: no one allowed for what has been called the 'sublime stupidity' of the British fighting on against heavy odds. Nor can Hitler be held responsible for Goering's direction of air strategy; that was one area Hitler rarely interfered in. Where he can, perhaps, be faulted was in ordering Goering to attack London yet at the same time strictly forbidding terror bombing of residential districts. On balance one must concede that Hitler showed an unusual willingness to accept advice about the prospects of invasion possibly because he was never more than half-hearted in his support and clung to the illusion that the British would be sufficiently intimidated by the invasion preparations to come to terms with Germany.

Where Hitler does bear major responsibility is in his failure to see that

Britain would have been seriously—possibly even fatally weakened—by a sustained offensive directed at those sensitive points in the Mediterranean: Gibraltar, Malta and Suez, which guarded her lines of communications with the empire in the east. Admittedly, he showed some interest between September 1940 and May 1941 in the so-called 'peripheral stategy' advocated vigorously by Raeder with some limited support from Brauchitsch and Halder. But at no time did Hitler pursue this alternative strategy with the wholehearted commitment essential for success. Sharp reverses in the Mediterranean followed by a reasonable peace offer might possibly have unnerved Britain and encouraged the appeasers inside and outside the cabinet to assert themselves. And if that seems rather unlikely, defeat in the Mediterranean would surely have forced Britain and her allies to wait even longer before landing in Europe.[19] Not that Hitler was an entirely free agent in the Mediterranean. For example, to capture Gibraltar Hitler would have needed Spanish assistance. By October General Francesco Franco, so eager to enter the war on Hitler's side in June, had changed his mind in view of Britain's continued defiance of the Führer. For as long as British seapower remained unbroken at sea a land attack on Gibraltar was unlikely to succeed.

In North Africa, however, Hitler did miss a golden opportunity to strike a crippling blow at Britain. By November Hitler's Italian ally was in deep trouble in Greece—which Mussolini attacked in October much to Hitler's annoyance—and also in Africa where Marshal Rodolfo Graziani's forces were falling back in disorder before General Archibald Wavell's counterattack in December 1940. Only to help the Italians save face did Hitler agree reluctantly in February 1941 to send a light infantry division and an armoured division, commanded by General Erwin Rommel, to Libya. Even that limited commitment transformed the situation. By April Rommel had driven Wavell back to the Egyptian frontier. As the British were already overstretched by their commitment in Greece, Rommel's offensive called into question the future of the British presence in the Middle East. When Greece fell to the Germans at the end of April and Crete a month later, Britain faced a desperately grave situation. Raeder urged Hitler to reinforce Rommel at once and make a concerted effort to drive Britain out of the Middle East.

His pleas fell on deaf ears. Hitler persisted in the arrogant belief that as long as Germany was unchallenged master of Europe (and the impending attack on Russia would achieve just that) Britain could never defeat her. So the propitious moment was allowed to slip by, never to return. All Hitler achieved in the end by committing more and more men and increasing quantities of raw materials to Africa between 1941 and 1943, as he did in an attempt to bolster up the Italians, was the dissipation of German forces without any hope of decisive victory. By any reckoning Hitler's Mediterranean strategy must surely rank as a serious blunder.

One can say in mitigation, of course, that Hitler was surrounded by military advisers whose outlook was basically Eurocentric. That is only a partial explanation. The fact is that Hitler was not prepared to be diverted from eastward expansion. From the summer of 1940 onwards he pounced on every scrap of evidence that seemed to confirm that decision. And Vyacheslav Molotov, the Russian foreign minister, played right into Hitler's hands. His earthy realism during the conversations with Hitler and Ribbentrop in November 1940 made it brutally plain that Russia, already highly suspicious of German military arrangements with Finland and Roumania, would not be deflected from taking defensive action in the Balkans by the Führer's grandiose talk of partitioning the British empire between Germany, Italy, Japan and Russia. Russian demands for the occupation of Finland and the acquisition of a naval base at the Dardanelles would make German expansion eastwards more difficult, as Hitler was well aware. It also occurred to him that it would not be long before Russia, weakened militarily by the Finnish war, started to modernize her armies.

One must also credit Hitler with some understanding of global strategy. Far from neglecting the United States as a factor in world affairs, as is sometimes alleged, he had been worried for some time by the distinct possibility that by 1942 the Americans would have entered the war on Britain's side. In that event, unless Germany made her bid to dominate Europe to the Urals quickly, she would be crushed by an irresistible combination of Russians and Americans. Time, as always, was not on Germany's side. War with Russia was inevitable in any case, as Hitler saw it. 'Because one day the Russians, the countless millions of Slavs, are going to come. Perhaps not even in ten years, perhaps only after a hundred years. But they will come.'[20] And when the clash came, it would be the decisive battle of world history between the Aryan people and 'the Jewish–Bolshevik enemy of mankind'. Furthermore, Hitler persuaded himself that victory in Russia would unlock the door to that peace with Britain which he still hoped for. All that kept Britain going was (he supposed) the prospect of an alliance with the giant in the east. Remove that hope and Britain would have to surrender because the Americans would be unable to come to her aid as they would by then be facing an infinitely greater peril in the Pacific from the Japanese. As a sop to Raeder, whose opinions Hitler respected even when he did not agree with them, Hitler threw in the thought that if the 'world *Blitzkrieg*' did not force Britain to abandon the war, then a drive through the Middle East to the Persian Gulf might after all be necessary. On 18 December 1940 the die was cast. Hitler ordered work to begin on operation Barbarossa with 15 May 1941 as the deadline.

The role of economic factors in explaining Hitler's decision must not be disregarded, subject to the usual qualification.[21] By the winter of 1940–41 the new continental economy was in poor shape. The exploitation of the resources of Western Europe and the Balkans had still not solved Germany's economic problems. Just the reverse in fact. As Germany extended her control over more and more of Europe, her difficulties intensified. For example, before the war Europe consumed 142 million tons of grain of which 132 million tons were produced in Europe. By 1941 the shortfall had risen to 40 million tons and with no prospect of significant imports from overseas. Secondly, Roumanian imports and synthetic production were insufficient to fuel the German airforce for major offensives against Britain and possibly in the future against the United States. Trade with Russia was not the solution. For although Russia had wheat and oil surpluses, her negotiators drove hard bargains, demanding in exchange production goods and armaments which Germany found it difficult to supply. But if Russia was under German rule, 31 million tons of oil and 95 million tons of wheat would be at Germany's disposal, enabling her to place the continental economy on a viable basis at last, beat the British blockade, and tighten her control over Europe.[22]

There is no way whereby Hitler can escape a major share of responsibility for the decision to attack Russia, which trapped Germany in a two-front war and set her on the road to final defeat. That does not mean that he was solely to blame. A recent study of the operational planning for Barbarossa reveals only too clearly that Hitler's generals shared his optimism about the task before them.[23] Like their counterparts in other European countries, the German general staff grossly underestimated Russian military strength, partly because of the difficulty of obtaining accurate information about the state of the Red Army, and partly because Stalin's purges of the Red Army in 1937-8 had seriously weakened it, judging by its sluggish performance in the Finnish war.

Furthermore, the planners, in the narrow specialist tradition of the general staff, concentrated almost exclusively on operations. The logistical problems an invader would encounter in the vast heart of Russia were, incredible to relate, ignored in the initial stages of planning. The fact that a significant proportion of Russia's industry lay on the other side of the Ural mountains beyond the range of the airforce was discounted because it was lightly assumed that *Blitzkrieg* tactics would dispatch the Red Army before this asset could affect the course of the campaign. When gnawing doubts did begin to assail the planners in the spring of 1941—when for example it was realized that Germany had vehicle oil for only two months' fighting—it was difficult to sustain objections for very long in the presence of a leader who most of the time maintained that 'they had only to kick in the door . . . and the whole rotten structure will come crashing down.'[24]

One question posed most frequently over the years is whether the four-week delay caused by Hitler's decision to attack Yugoslavia in May 1941 spelt the difference between victory and defeat in Russia. Were Brauchitsch and Keitel right to blame the difficulties they quickly enountered in Russia on the effects of the delay? The latest research suggests that there is no easy answer.[25] As far as Yugoslavia is concerned, Hitler can be exonerated from blame; all the combat units deployed in that country were back in their assembly areas ready for the onslaught on Russia by the end of May. What delay there was arose out of the Greek campaign where the operations lasted longer and damage was caused to equipment by the appalling state of the roads. However, in general the delay in starting the attack on Russia was due much more to an overall shortage of equipment than to the fighting in the Balkans.

It would be unfair to attach a disproportionate share of the blame to Hitler for what went wrong during the first six months of the Russian campaign. At first, the three invading armies thrust deep into the heart of Russia, taking hundreds of thousands of prisoners. Army Group North commanded by Field Marshal Wilhelm von Leeb advanced towards Leningrad and the Baltic coastline, Army Group Centre under General Fedor von Bock towards Moscow and Army Group South under Rundstedt pushed on towards the Ukraine with the Caucasus as its ultimate objective.

The initial optimism at army command quickly faded when it became apparent how totally misinformed German reports of Russian strength and morale had been. Stiffening Russian resistance and the inability of unmechanized infantry to keep up with German armour frustrated attempts to encircle and annihilate the Russians first at Bialystok-Minsk and at Smolensk; on each occasion large numbers of Russian soldiers were able to escape from the trap. In view of this, army command proposed a modification of Barbarossa to give absolute priority to the capture of Moscow, resurrecting arguments they had earlier abandoned out of deference to Hitler, who had insisted that its capture was of minor importance. It was now argued that the Russians would probably concentrate their forces in defence of the historic capital, thus presenting the Germans with one last chance of annihilating them before the onset of the winter.

To their dismay Hitler disagreed and precipitated the first major crisis at army command. In mid-August Hitler finally agreed to modify Barbarossa but in a different direction from that advocated by army command. In the north Leeb was ordered to complete the encirclement of Leningrad. But Bock was to halt his advance on Moscow and his armour was switched south to help Rundstedt encircle and wipe out the Russian armies in the Kiev salient. Only when this latter objective had been attained would Hitler permit an attack on Moscow. Was this a great strategic blunder as some German generals have suggested?

It is by no means certain that Hitler was wrong. The Kiev offensive was a signal success. Four Russian armies were defeated and hundreds of thousands of prisoners taken; and Rundstedt was able to occupy the Ukraine, most of the Crimea and the Donetz industrial basin, the latter an area of economic potential which Hitler realized, quite correctly, was absolutely indispensable for Germany if the war effort was to continue into 1942. The alternative of a frontal onslaught on Moscow, even if it had been launched before the mud of October and the snow of November slowed Bock down, would not necessarily have succeeded. Had the Germans captured Moscow, it is unlikely that this would have broken the back of the Russian resistance.[26] And with greatly extended lines of communications to defend, the Germans would have been vulnerable to Russian counterattacks on their flank.

Yet even if Hitler's operational strategy was very probably correct in all the circumstances, that is small merit. Nothing can disguise the hard fact that tenacious Russian resistance had brought the '*Blitzkrieg* era' to an abrupt end even before Marshal Griogrii Zhukov's dramatic winter offensive. What is interesting are signs that Hitler appreciated the deeper significance of events. Despite his defiant boast in October that the foe 'had been struck down and will never rise again', he knew that the Russians could not be finished off by December. The best that could be hoped for was that the present campaign would put Germany in a position to end the war in 1942. It seems that his insight extended further still; by November he had serious doubts about the possibility of outright victory in Russia and hinted guardedly at the possibility of a compromise peace.[27]

To clinch matters for the successful termination of the war in 1942, Hitler was now actively encouraging the attack on Moscow to go ahead as planned, despite ominous signs of adverse weather and stiffening Russian resistance. Political considerations probably outweighed any doubts in his mind about the feasibility of the operation. The fall of a historic city would, after all, be worthwhile if it swung the timid neutrals, Spain, Vichy France and Turkey, onto Germany's side in readiness for war against Britain. Carried away by his own exuberance, he remarked to Admiral Kurt Fricke that the fall of Moscow might even force Britain to make peace at once.[28] And a victory was sorely needed to dispel the mood of gloom in Germany following the slowing down of Bock's offensive and the sharp reverse suffered by General Ewald von Kleist's armour at Rostov at the end of November.

When Zhukov threw one hundred divisions against Bock's soldiers on 5–6 December, 1941 the tables were turned at last and the German forces found themselves in a desperately dangerous situation. One of the most controversial decisions of the war was taken by Hitler during this crisis: on 16 December he issued a 'stand fast' order to Bock's men, followed three days later by his acceptance of Brauchitsch's resignation, and his own assumption of the personal command of the army, a step never taken before by a supreme commander. Opinion is still divided over the correctness of the 'stand fast' order.[29] But on balance Hitler can be given credit for prompt action, which averted the distinct possibility that a general retreat would have cost Germany much more valuable equipment, and might have degenerated into a rout of 1812 proportions in the absence of prepared positions to fall back to. Of course, the tenacity and heroism of countless German soldiers fighting in the most appalling conditions was just as important as the inspiring fanaticism of their new commander-in-chief, who brushed aside 'this little matter of operational command' and believed firmly in his duty to train the army in 'a National Socialist way'.[30] What might properly be criticized is the inflexibility with which he upheld the order; the action needlessly cost many lives and was the subject of bitter conflict between Hitler and Field Marshal Günther-Hans von Kluge, Bock's successor, once it became obvious that the reserves the Führer promised his hard-pressed army were simply not available. In the end Hitler agreed to withdraw the order, and the Army Group Centre stabilized itself, by strategic withdrawals, along a new front by the end of January.

The traumatic experiences of the winter of 1941–2 seem to have left Hitler in no doubt that the war could not now be won by Germany.[31] While it is extremely unlikely that he would have drawn the correct conclusions from the failure of the *Blitzkrieg*, the dramatic Japanese attack on the American fleet at Pearl Harbor in December and the subsequent German declaration of war on the United States, paradoxically enough, strengthened his resolve to go on fighting until 'five minutes after midnight'.[32]

The Japanese attack on the United States was not of Hitler's doing. Japan had, in fact, played a fairly subordinate role in Hitler's global strategy. Prior to Barbarossa Hitler showed no interest in Japanese participation. This is sometimes seen as a major blunder. But whether he ought to have tried to involve them or not, the Japanese had, in fact, their eyes fixed on expansion in the Pacific and were not prepared to be trapped in a mainland war. Realistically, Hitler regarded Japan primarily as a means of keeping the United States out of the war in Europe as long as possible, the calculation being that a Japanese attack on British possessions in the Far East would deter the Americans from intervening against Germany. That this may have been a provisional policy until such time as Germany dominated Europe, was hinted at by Hitler in a conversation with General Hiroshi Oshima, Japanese ambassador in Berlin, in July 1941.[33] Elated by the initial success of the German armies in Russia, Hitler talked at last of Japanese participation in Russia and of joint German-Japanese action against the United States. With Europe virtually in his grasp, so he supposed, he may perhaps have been looking forward to the final struggle with America for world hegemony. But at this stage the Japanese felt they could obtain what they wanted in the Pacific by coming to terms with the Americans. By September Hitler had reverted to the old strategy of relying on the Japanese simply to keep America out of the war until Russia had been defeated. However, when Japanese conversations with the Americans finally broke down, the Japanese cabinet resolved the issue by war. Whereupon Hitler declared war on the United States. The European war had now become a global conflict. No doubt if it had seriously inconvenienced Germany, Hitler would not have reacted in this fashion. But, as he was convinced that President Franklin Roosevelt would almost certainly intervene in the war if Russia and Britain collapsed, Hitler was to some extent anticipating the inevitable: 'The Americans are shooting at us already, we are already in a state of war with them', he remarked indignantly to Ribbentrop when the foreign minister raised the technical question whether the Tripartite Pact of 1940—which committed Germany, Italy and Japan to aid each other only in the event of an attack on one of them by a fourth party—could apply if Japan was the aggressor.[34] A man with Hitler's jack-in-the-box mentality could even argue that there might be some marginal advantage in striking at the Americans before they were ready.

Far from being 'psychologically an extremely clumsy step', one wonders whether Hitler did not secretly welcome the deepening of the crisis.[35] Might there not be a parallel here with his behaviour in September 1938 when he deliberately placed himself in a more exposed and perilous position over Czechoslovakia, as if by increasing the odds against success he could summon up latent spiritual reserves within him to ride out the crisis without faltering or weakening? Having made defeat well nigh unavoidable by bringing America into the war, would he not be forced to make superhuman efforts to win the war in Russia against all expectations?[36] The gnawing conflict between reason and emotion was temporarily stilled by the pretence that once the spring thaw came and mobility returned to the Russian front it would be possible to strike crippling blows at Russia.[37]

It is easy to say that a leader who loses touch with reality to such an alarming extent has forfeited all moral right to remain in charge of a great nation. And it is tempting to suppose that a less fanatical leader might have broken off the struggle in the east in 1942 or 1943, and prepared the way for a compromise peace by political action designed to disrupt the forces ranged against Germany. We should not allow righteous indignation at the appalling cost in human lives of militarily hopeless resistance to blind us to the formidable obstacles which would have faced any leader attempting to change course so dramatically in the midst of a great war. It is a melancholy and well documented feature of modern warfare that once the passions of belligerent peoples are aroused, the very idea of compromise becomes anathema to democrats and fascists alike and the bona fides of any peacemaker are automatically questioned. Total victory or total defeat are the only alternatives on offer.

It follows from this that Hitler's fanatical determination to fight on reflected in some measure at least the prevailing mood of the German people certainly up to the Stalingrad débâcle. In clinging stubbornly to the irrational conviction that, however grim the outlook, providence would preserve him, Hitler was not just responding to the drives of his own personality; a dogged determination to soldier on to the bitter end is a not uncommon reaction when a people is trapped in a total war situation. Goebbels's propaganda machine and Himmler's repressive police system were naturally extremely potent factors in persuading the Germans to drink the bitter cup to the very dregs. It is equally relevant to point out that the insistence of the enemy powers on unconditional surrender in 1943 left the Germans with no viable alternative to fighting on. Added to which, the terrible bombardment of German cities stiffened the resistance of the people much as similar attacks on British cities had steeled the British to resist in 1940–41. So if what happened after Stalingrad reminds one irresistibly of a Greek tragedy in which the defiant dictator struggled vainly against his fate, dragging down an entire people to destruction with him, it is important to remember that it was a people conditioned to expect no quarter from its enemies – especially from the Russians – and left with no alternative but to fight on under his leadership. This is in no sense an alibi for Hitler who showed no readiness to sacrifice himself in the interests of peace. Nor is it intended as a criticism of the German people. It is simply a sober comment on the extent to which the ideological fury of modern warfare reinforced by the apparatus of a police state can blind large sections of a people to the objective reality of its situation.[38]

It has been suggested that ill health may have played a significant part in Hitler's inflexible refusal to face up to reality.[39] Without anticipating the discussion of Hitler's illness in the next chapter, it is probably true to say, in respect of the early stages of the Russian campaign, that his serious illness may well have accentuated his irritability during the long-drawn out dispute with the generals about the desirability of a drive on Moscow. Yet, as he probably arrived at the correct decision in August 1941, one can scarcely argue that illness impaired his judgement. And by the time the Moscow crisis occurred and the 'stand fast' order was given, Hitler had recovered more or less completely from that illness. On the other hand, after 1942 one cannot exclude the distinct possibility that the cumulative effect of the many drugs Dr Morell prescribed for Hitler contributed, perhaps significantly, to the process of mental ossification, a point to be discussed in more detail in the final chapter.

A significant factor which should not be overlooked in this connection was the physical isolation of Hitler for much of the war. While other war leaders lived in or near their capital cities, keeping in touch with a broad spectrum of opinion, a practice which could not fail to strengthen their purchase on reality, Hitler lived for three years in a remote forest in East Prussia, apart from occasional visits to the Berghof. In the highly-fortified Wolfsschanze, or wolf's lair, surrounded by his adjutants and admiring secretaries, he inevitably took a worm's eye view of the war and was conditioned to think exclusively in terms of military operations. One cannot discount the possibility that, as the situation began to deteriorate, Hitler preferred to keep contact with the outside world to an absolute minimum in order to preserve his own peace of mind.

Because Hitler was becoming entombed in a world of make-believe, it does not follow that he could not act perfectly rationally at the level of operational tactics. Quite the reverse in fact. In the spring of 1942 he recognized, sensibly enough, that his forces were too limited to pursue the war in Russia on more than one front. The choice of front was arrived at equally rationally. An offensive to reach the river Don followed by a drive to the Caucasian mountains was absolutely essential, for without the oil of the Caucasus Germany could not continue the war. Oil was just as vital for Russia. If Germany could deprive the Russians of their Caucasian supplies, and of the wheat of the Ukraine as well, they would not be able to fight on. Halder, later a fierce critic of the Führer's strategy, agreed at the time that it was eminently reasonable.[40] And if further reassurance was needed, that could still be derived from the war map. Rommel's desert offensive in May 1942 carried all before it, driving the British back into Egypt; and in the early summer German submarines were at last taking a heavy toll of British shipping.

Although the tactics of the new offensive were rationally conceived, a margin for error was lacking. Even before the operation commenced, the balance of probability was against success. For one thing the Germans only brought themselves up to strength by relying on satellite troops, men of unproven quality in battle. Secondly, the Russians had changed their tactics. After the bloody battle of Kharkov in May 1942 in which they lost 239,000 men and over 1,200 tanks, the Russians avoided large-scale engagements. Throughout the summer they retreated into the wide open spaces. Not unnaturally Hitler was encouraged by hasty withdrawals and reports of mass desertions to think that the Russians were at their last gasp.

There seems little doubt that throughout the war Hitler was very badly served by his intelligence service which was consistently wrong in its appreciation of the tactical situation. Indeed, that factor may well have contributed significantly to Hitler's decision on 23 July to modify the plan of campaign. The attempt to take Stalingrad and the Caucasus simultaneously instead of in consecutive steps was undoubtedly an error. By dividing Army Group South between two objectives Hitler exposed it to grave risks. The northern flank of the Sixth Army, stretching along the river Don to the town of Voronesh, was dangerously overextended and held by inadequately-equipped Roumanian, Hungarian and Italian troops whose reliability was suspect at high command. Thus an enemy counterattack could at any time endanger the entire operation in the Caucasus and at Stalingrad.

It has been suggested that Hitler did begin to recognize the danger and ordered Halder on several occasions in August to strengthen this sector, in particular by detaching an armoured division from the fighting round Stalingrad to support the Italians.[41] Halder apparently disregarded the order which can only mean that Hitler did not rate the danger very highly and had failed to press the matter with his customary vigour.[42] For it is surely significant that even when German intelligence began ruefully to admit in mid-August that it had grossly underestimated Russian strength (now put at 593 divisions with large reserves), Hitler resolutely refused to believe the reports. When he was informed that Russian tank production exceeded 1,000 a month, he flew at the officer who gave the report with clenched fists, literally foaming at the mouth and forbade him read anymore of the rubbish. However justifiable his anger on learning that intelligence had let him down once more, his behaviour now verged on the paranoid. Yet even Halder, who recorded this incident after the war as proof of Hitler's unsuitability to lead the army in the field, still believed in September, at the time of his dismissal, that Russia was so weak that she could not possibly be as dangerous a threat to Germany as she had been in December 1941.[43]

With army command still of the opinion that the Russians were finished, it is not altogether surprising that Hitler failed to appreciate the significance of the Russian decision to make a stand at Stalingrad after retreating steadily throughout the summer. Therefore the more the Russians resisted in Stalingrad in the autumn of 1942, the more Hitler became obsessed with the need to take the city. Ultimately, the capture of the pile of ruins, which was all that remained of Stalingrad, became a matter of personal prestige. When General Baron Maximilian von Weichs, commander of the army group investing Stalingrad, reported that he could not take the city with the forces available,

Hitler brushed him aside. What he manifestly failed to realise—but was not alone in his error—was that the Germans had lost the advantages of mobility and flexibility and were allowing themselves to be trapped in a war of attrition reminiscent of the Verdun battles of 1916. On 19 November Zhukov launched the inevitable counteroffensive which, though long anticipated by the Germans, took them by surprise for which faulty intelligence was once more to blame. On the Don front the Russians broke through the line held by the Third Roumanian Army, and south of Stalingrad powerful forces penetrated that front two days later. By the time Hitler hurried back to the Wolfsschanze after a few days' respite at the Berghof, the Soviet armies had joined forces. Twenty German and two Roumanian divisions were surrounded in Stalingrad. When Zeitzler argued, with full support from Weichs, that the Sixth Army was doomed if it remained in the city, Hitler banged the table and shouted furiously: 'We are not budging from the Volga'.[44]

Why did Hitler order General (soon to be Field Marshal) Friedrich von Paulus, commander of the Sixth Army, to stand and fight in Stalingrad? Is this one further example of a crass refusal to accept the realities of the situation, a desperate attempt to prevent a repetition of what had just happened in North Africa where Rommel, despite Hitler's order to stand fast and resist Field Marshal Bernard Montgomery's offensive at El Alamein at the end of October, had been forced to retreat in the end with the Führer's grudging consent?

The answer must be in the affirmative. The arguments advanced by the most recent writer on the Stalingrad débâcle in support of his thesis that the situation, though grave, was not quite so desperate as it is sometimes made out to be, are not wholly convincing.[45] To say that Hitler's optimism about Manstein's relief column fighting its way to Stalingrad was shared by his military advisers is true only in a very narrow sense. The fact that Hitler preferred the sycophantic Keitel's enthusiastic support to Zeitzler's sober assessment tells its own story. Similarly, when Goering reassured Hitler that supplies could be dropped by air to Stalingrad, Hitler grasped eagerly at this straw despite the Reich marshal's tarnished reputation and the growing scepticism of General Hans Jeschonnek and Colonel Eckard Christian of the airforce general staff about the feasibility of such an operation. Hitler brushed aside their opposition, insisting that 'it was only a question of time: a particularly gifted organizer would be able to manage it using his special powers, if need be, against generals who opposed the airlift [Manstein and Field Marshal Wolfram von Richthofen of the airforce].'[46] It seems only too clear that, having committed himself publicly at the annual rally in Munich's Bürgerbräukeller on 8 November to the defence of Stalingrad, which he believed (erroneously) was virtually in German hands, he was determined to solicit opinions to justify his own feverish optimism.[47]

The unrealistic hopes were quickly dashed. Atrocious weather conditions interfered with airforce operations. By superhuman efforts under the supervision of Field Marshal Erhard Milch, 8,350 tons of supplies were flown into Stalingrad – an average of 100 tons a day but far short of the 300 tons high command decided that Paulus needed. Secondly, the Russians attacked in strength along the Don and sent the Italians reeling back. That made Manstein's task virtually impossible. When the Russians seized the Morozowski and Taizinskaya airfields used by Goering's planes, Hitler had to admit that Manstein could not relieve Stalingrad, though he adamantly refused to allow Paulus to attempt a break-out. Whether Hitler realized that Stalingrad was irretrievably doomed despite his confident talk of relieving it in the spring, it is impossible to tell.

Another danger now faced the Germans—the distinct possibility that the whole German army in the Caucasus would be cut off unless Hitler allowed its immediate withdrawal. Only at the last possible moment on 27 December did Zeitzler succeed in persuading Hitler to order withdrawal, enabling the Germans to extricate themselves from a situation which would certainly have led to a defeat as disastrous as Stalingrad.

Stalingrad's capitulation in February 1943 was an appalling setback for a hitherto invincible army. Perhaps one should not dwell too much on Hitler's lack of remorse or pity for the 91,000 men who passed into enemy captivity (the vast majority never to return home); war leaders as a breed are not much given to worrying about the sacrifices their armies have to make. Towards Paulus, however, Hitler was full of anger and contempt. Why had he not had the vision to see that a spectacular immolation of the entire garrison in true Spartan style would have immortalized the Sixth Army and rallied the German people for the grim struggle ahead? With such thoughts in mind, Hitler ordered Goebbels to report the last days of beleaguered Stalingrad in uncensored detail. What the tragic story of this military operation surely reveals, only too poignantly, is the general corruption of morals under a dictatorship where experienced military advisers suppress their doubts out of fear and respect for the dictator while loud-mouthed sycophants encourage him still further in his folly.

By the spring of 1943 it was imperative for Germany to go onto the defensive. While it is true that Hitler could not bring himself to recast German strategy or think in terms of weaponry for defensive warfare, he did accept the need for defensive tactics on the Russian front as the only way of producing the reserves Germany must have to deal with an enemy landing in the west or in the Balkans in the not-too-distant future.

The argument between Hitler and army command in the spring and summer of 1943 was not about strategy but simply about operational tactics. When army command proposed to shorten the line by strategic withdrawals, for example west of Moscow, Hitler agreed only on condition that the divisions thus released be earmarked for a spring offensive. What he had in mind was a limited offensive to straighten the line in the Kursk sector. This would, he argued, have the additional advantage of inflicting such a severe blow on the Russians that further offensives in 1943 would be impossible. Secondary considerations were the need to strengthen the morale of German's small allies and, by taking prisoners, to provide slave labourers and allow more Germans to be released for military service.

Though Army Group South favoured an offensive, as did the operations section of the general staff (provided it took place in June), Army Group Centre and the Fourth (armoured) Army were doubtful of success in view of Germany's lack of resources. Furthermore, the Russians, anticipating offensive action, were building up their front. Up to a point Hitler heeded the warnings, and postponed the offensive to allow Field Marshal Walter Model, commander of the Ninth Army, to strengthen his forces. But in the end the Führer fell between two stools. He waited so long that the Russians were well prepared for operation Citadel but not long enough for Model's armour to recover completely. The result was a failure for which Hitler, as author of Citadel, must bear much of the responsibility. For although it is true that the Germans repelled a Russian counterattack on 12 July and probably slowed down Stalin's summer offensive, the lesson was clear to all: Germany had lost her freedom of manoeuvre in the east.

It would be a tedious and unrewarding exercise to examine in detail the various military operations during the last eighteen months of the war. No fresh light would be cast on Hitler as a military leader, simply because there were no major strategic decisions left for Germany to make. No long-range strategic planning was undertaken at the Führer's headquarters after the end of 1942 for it was known that the conclusions would only displease him.

Now at last the strain of a hopeless military situation began to take its toll of Hitler. Perceptible signs of physical deterioration after Stalingrad were accompanied by mounting evidence of mental fatigue. His suspicion of the general staff reached paranoid proportions; from September 1942 stenographers took down the proceedings verbatim at the daily war conferences so convinced was the Führer that his generals were deliberately disobeying his orders. His outbursts of fury were more frequent, less restrained and no longer a cunning ploy to disconcert his audience. And because he suspected most generals of 'defeatism', he interfered more than before in the minutiae of military operations; he regularly deployed troops at battalion level, even single tanks on occasions, a practice which robbed local commanders of all initiative at crucial stages of the battle. Overwhelmed by the sheer volume of work he had taken upon himself, Hitler was physically and mentally exhausted, and fluctuated uneasily between snap decisions and the old inability to make up his mind.[48]

His indecision was illustrated over the matter of defensive fortifications on the eastern front. When Hitler did finally acknowledge that Germany possessed too few divisions to hold an extended front and that strategic withdrawals to prepared positions were unavoidable, if only as a means of finding reserves to repel the long-awaited enemy landing in the west, his consent was grudgingly given and conditional in nature. At first he insisted that the new East Wall fortifications be well-constructed, not hastily improvised as Zeitzler suggested, and should not be so far to the rear—for example along the line of the river Dnieper—that large areas of captured territory would have to be abandoned without a struggle. On occasions he was quite capable of reverting to his old intransigence, taking refuge, with childish naiveté, behind the testimony of front-line officers who, when called to headquarters and asked by the Führer whether they wanted to retreat, replied in the negative—a natural enough reaction from soldiers with a worm's eye view of the battle but not an opinion which a supreme commander should allow to influence his tactics over much. And by the time Hitler finally accepted Zeitzler's arguments for the Dnieper line in August 1943, so many objections had been raised by high command, navy and airforce to the abandonment of areas to which they attached importance for one reason or another, that in the end Hitler avoided confrontation by postponing his decision until it was, in effect, too late to affect the outcome of the war in the east.

All the same, it would be quite wrong to suppose that Hitler had completely lost his ability to react promptly to a changing strategic situation. Italy is a case in point. When Anglo-American forces landed in Sicily on 10 July 1943 and the Italian grand council deposed Mussolini a few days later, Hitler's reaction was to order the seizure of Rome and the evacuation of the 60,000 German troops in Sicily, with the intention of making a stand south of Rome. It was the painfully slow reaction of the British and Americans to events in Italy that caused him to stay his hand and remain in Sicily for the time being. However, contrary to the opinion of his military advisers in Italy, Hitler felt in his bones that Marshal Pietro Badoglio, head of the new government, would shortly desert to the enemy. Throughout August plans were drawn up on Hitler's orders to meet this eventuality. Hitler can, therefore, claim some of the credit for the speed with which the Germans seized Rome and disarmed the Italians when it became known on 8 September that Italy had surrendered. Good fortune stayed with Hitler when the Anglo-American armies landed in Italy. Much to the Germans' surprise they landed initially in the toe of the peninsula and fought their way slowly and painfully northwards throwing away the advantages sea- and air-power would have given them for a landing north of Rome. Nor was it all good luck. The dramatic rescue of Mussolini from an hotel on the Gran Sasso d'Italia, where he was held captive, suggests that Hitler, who personally ordered the search for and rescue of his friend, had not entirely lost his old gift for improvisation.

The very success of German resistance in Italy probably misled Hitler into supposing that the enemy landing in Normandy in June 1944 could be decisively repulsed. Like Rommel, whom the Führer had appointed to supervise the strengthening of the Atlantic coastal defences, Hitler believed that an invasion must be smashed on the beaches. But so overwhelming was the superiority of the enemy in the air and the fire power of supporting naval vessels that the Germans were quite unable to prevent the landing, much less the reinforcement of the beachheads. Whatever tactics had been adopted on the German side, and even if the morale of their troops had been higher and the Atlantic Wall stronger, it is difficult not to conclude that the outcome would have been much the same. All one can say about Hitler's remote control of operations for the first few days from the Berghof is that it did not particularly assist matters. In the first hours of the landings two armoured divisions were held in reserve far too long, to some extent because Hitler was not woken up the moment the news arrived, but mostly because he believed on the basis of faulty intelligence reports, that the real invasion had yet to take place in the Pas de Calais area.

Despite desperate counterattacks there was little hope of holding the Americans, who finally broke out of the Avranches bridgehead and trapped the remaining German forces in Normandy in the Falaise pocket. Replacing Rundstedt by Kluge and then by Model made not the slightest difference. The only consequence of trying to hold the line in the first place at Hitler's insistence was to render it impossible later to hold a line on the rivers Somme and Marne, a possibility he had toyed with in July. In the end as a result of the summer campaign in the west, Germany was driven out of France, Belgium and most of Holland, and lost 500,000 men and virtually all her tanks.

Prolonging the fighting as Hitler had done in Russia, in Italy and latterly in France had a rationale only in military terms if it bought time in which to effect a dramatic transformation of the war. At first Hitler had hoped that new weapons would perform this miracle: the revolutionary all-electric submarines that Grand Admiral Karl Dönitz promised him would soon swing the battle of the Atlantic in Germany's favour; or masses of jet fighters, for which Hitler at last ordered the highest priority in the summer of 1944, would sweep enemy bombers out of the skies; or rockets would bombard the British into submission. When the secret weapons failed one after the other, Hitler fell back on political machinations. Speaking to two of his generals on 31 August 1944 he remarked:

The time is not yet ripe, for a political decision . . . I shall not let an opportunity pass . . . but at a time of heavy military defeats it is quite childish and naive to hope for a politically favourable moment to make a move . . .. The time will come when the tensions between the allies become so strong that in spite of everything the rupture occurs. History teaches us that all coalitions break up, but you must await the moment however difficult the waiting may be . . . [I intend to] continue fighting until there is a possibility of a decent peace which is bearable for Germany and secures the life of future generations. Then I shall make it . . .. Whatever happens we shall carry on in this struggle until, as Frederick the Great said, 'one of our damned enemies gives up in despair.'[49]

The idea of a negotiated peace had been maturing in his mind for some time. Back in 1942 Mussolini's pleas for an end to the fighting in Russia had not moved Hitler. Nor had Ribbentrop's attempts to persuade Hitler to contact Russia in the summer of 1943 met with any success. But in September when Goebbels raised the issue with him he was prepared at last to discuss it calmly and dispassionately. His own inclination was, he said, for an Anglo-German understanding but that would only be possible when the British 'come to their senses'. This was his last line of defence, the expectation that the marriage of convenience between the capitalist states and Marxist Russia would not last very long. Of course, his sharp intellect told him at times that there was little hope of the enemy alliance breaking up.[50] Emotionally, however, he refused to believe that his last avenue of escape was bolted and barred any more than Goebbels, Goering and Himmler could. History was to prove them right in their scepticism about the durability of the wartime alliance, but not soon enough to save Germany from a catastrophic defeat.

It was in pursuit of the will-o'-the-wisp of a compromise peace with the west followed by an anti-Bolshevik crusade that Hitler launched the Ardennes offensive in December 1944. In 1917 the collapse of Tsarist Russia had given Imperial Germany a last chance to launch a major offensive. Twenty-seven years later, when the enemy offensive ground to a halt in waterlogged Holland, Hitler had a breathing space which he utilized in an attempt to prove that Germany was still strong enough to be a useful ally against Russia.

Tactically, an offensive made sense for on the ground at least the German and Anglo-American forces were fairly evenly balanced. The disagreement between Hitler and his generals on this occasion was not about tactics but objectives. For Hitler, under no illusions that the offensive was 'a desperate attempt in a desperate situation',[51] dreamt of seizing Antwerp, a key supply port, and driving a wedge between the British and Americans. This was wildly optimistic as Rundstedt and General Hasso von Manteuffel were well aware. The most they hoped for was the capture of Liège. Hitler got his way in the end but with inadequate forces the Germans had little hope of achieving very much even though bad weather impeded the enemy's air operations.

In the event, the Ardennes offensive ended in complete failure. With the return of better weather the Anglo-American airforces started to pound Hitler's lines of communications. Thanks only to the fierce resistance they offered, together with a favourable terrain and good local leadership, were the German forces able to escape encirclement. One thing was crystal clear: the gamble had failed and the end could not now be long delayed.

Without anticipating the discussion of Hitler's health in the last chapter, this would seem the most convenient point at which to comment on Hitler's mental state in the last few days of his life as the Anglo-American and Russian armies closed in on the Third Reich.

What strikes one forcibly from the contemporary accounts are the kaleido-scopic changes in mood: pessimism, euphoria, anger and lethargy followed each other in bewildering succession as the cumulative effect of the strain of war, dependence on drugs, an irregular life style and the unresolved conflict between the dictates of reason and the consuming sense of mission caused Hitler's personality to 'disintegrate' before the eyes of close associates. In Speer's eloquent words, 'he had reached the last station in his flight from reality, a reality which he had refused to acknowledge since his youth.'[52] In this highly volatile mood Hitler clung desperately to the most slender portents. Early in April Goebbels had read aloud to him passages from Carlyle's *History of Frederick the Great* describing how that monarch, having reached a nadir in his fortunes in the winter of 1761–2, was about to take poison when the situation was changed dramatically with the news of the Tsarina's death. The passage profoundly moved both Hitler and Goebbels. The propaganda minister even looked up Hitler's horoscope—a superstitious practice the Führer had always frowned on—and gleefully predicted a great success in April and peace by August. When Hitler heard on 12 April from an exultant Goebbels that Roosevelt was dead, he was at once infected with the feverish optimism of the little minister. Turning to Speer, he shouted excitedly: 'You never wanted to believe it . . .. Here we have the miracle I always predicted. Who was right? The war isn't lost . . . Roosevelt is dead.'[53] However, the burst of euphoria vanished almost as quickly as it appeared when it became obvious that the enemy had no intention of patching up the quarrel with Hitler.

With the Russians closing in on Berlin in early April, Hitler initially decided to make a last stand in Bavaria. Then the old indecision took over; by 20 April, his birthday, he was filled with growing uncertainty, and resisted advice that he leave the capital at once before it was encircled by the Russians. When the first Russian shell landed in the centre of Berlin on 21 April Hitler suddenly forgot his doubts and in a sudden burst of energy ordered a last attack to repel the Russians: SS General Felix Steiner would lead the attack; General Karl Koller, chief of the airforce general staff, was threatened with death if all available forces were not thrown into the battle; and a sanguine Hitler predicted that the Russians would suffer 'the greatest defeat in their history before the gates of Berlin'.[54] Steiner, however, not being particularly keen to sacrifice himself in a hopeless cause, delayed the attack until it was too late to matter.

Only on 22 April was Hitler ready at last to admit openly that the end was near. With the roar of Russian artillery fire rocking the bunker, Hitler flew into a great rage when it was reported at the war conference that Steiner's attack was not yet commenced. Treason, lies, corruption and cowardice surrounded him on all sides; everyone had deserted him; it was all over; let those who wished to do so clear out; he was resolved to stay in Berlin and defend it to the last. Brushing aside protests and ignoring Himmler's telephonic entreaties, he dictated an announcement to be broadcast at once to the people of Berlin, a last pathetic example of the old trick of putting himself in an advanced position from which he could not retreat without loss of face. To strengthen his resolve still further, he invited the Goebbels family to join him in the bunker and immolate themselves on the funeral pyre with him.

Talking to Keitel and Jodl the same day, he vehemently reaffirmed his decision to shoot himself when Berlin fell. In a mood of black despair he flatly refused to give further orders to these loyal sycophants. Bewildered by this negation of leadership, they persisted in their request until Hitler referred them to Goering. When they indignantly protested that no one would fight under him, Hitler retorted: 'What do you mean, fight? There's precious little more fighting to be done, and if it comes to negotiating, the Reichs Marshal can do better than I can.'[55] So violently was he oscillating between despair and hope, that even before Keitel and Jodl had left him, Hitler had resumed 'supreme command', and enthusiastically approved their suggestion that General

Walther Wenck's Twelfth Army on the river Elbe link up with General Theodor Busse's Ninth Army and strike northwards towards Berlin to cut off the investing Russian army.

On 27 April the chancellery building came under artillery fire as the Russian infantry closed in on the city centre. Still Hitler persisted in going through the motions of defending the doomed city in the vain hope that, if he won the battle of Berlin, the Anglo-Americans might yet turn to him as the 'saviour of Europe' against the 'Bolshevik hordes' now hammering at the door. A visitor to the bunker has drawn a vivid if somewhat exaggerated picture of a pathetic old man pacing up and down, the street map of Berlin literally disintegrating in his hands, as he talked military tactics to anyone he could buttonhole.[56] One minute he admitted the hopelessness of the position and handed out poison capsules to his intimates; the next moment he was sending off a stream of imperious telegrams to Keitel demanding an explanation of Wenck's failure to relieve Berlin. Incredibly, he could still inspire an irrational hope in uncritical admirers. On 27 April General Robert Ritter von Greim, newly-appointed commander-in-chief of the airforce and an ardent Nazi, telephoning Koller as shells were pounding the chancellery to rubble, urged the incredulous general not to lose faith; everything would work out: 'I have been strengthened enormously by the power of the Führer and by being with him; it is like a fountain of youth for me.'[57]

For Hitler the last straw was probably the news on 28 April that Himmler had defected. Goering had already fallen under Hitler's severe displeasure a few days previously when he attempted to assume the leadership on the assumption that the Führer would remain a virtual prisoner in Berlin. Goaded on by Bormann, an intriguer to the very end who presented Goering as a 'traitor' (which was certainly untrue), Hitler stripped the Reichsmarshal of his offices and ordered him to resign. When he heard that 'the loyal Heinrich' had put out peace feelers to the Swedish Count Folke Bernadotte, Hitler burst into a terrible rage, his features becoming almost unrecognizable as he denounced Himmler. In one last spiteful act he had General Hermann Fegelein, Himmler's liaison man with the Führer and Eva Braun's brother-in-law, who had slipped off home having no desire to end his life in the bunker, arrested and summarily shot in the chancellery gardens. Hard on the heels of this came news that Russian tanks and infantry were in the Potsdamer Platz. The battle for Berlin was over and Hitler's mind finally made up. A mood of great calm now descended on him. In the early hours of 29 April he married Eva Braun and dictated a last will and testament. At the last war conference that day he listened in silence to the prediction that all fighting would be over within twenty-four hours and then walked out, pausing only to order all troops to break out of Berlin rather than surrender to the Russians. On the afternoon of 30 April he took leave of his associates, retired with his wife to their room where she poisoned herself and he shot himself in the right temple while crunching a poison capsule at about 3.30 p.m.[58] Both bodies were burnt in the chancellery grounds in accordance with the Führer's orders.

It has been suggested that the death of Hitler was a typical case of suicide.[59] He was in his fifties, the age bracket most prone to suicide; born in Austria, a country with the highest suicide rate for years and still ranking second in 1959; a dweller in a city, where the incidence of suicide is higher than in the countryside; and an artist by temperament, a calling with a high suicide rate. He also died in April, a peak suicide month, and on a Monday, the most popular day for self-slaughter. Whatever value one attaches to statistics of this kind, there is certainly evidence in Hitler's case of previous suicide threats at moments of crisis, a not uncommon feature of the successful suicide.

For example, during the abortive 1923 putsch Hitler had exclaimed to Kahr, Lossow and Seisser: 'You must be victorious with me or die with me. If things go badly, I have four shots in my pistol. Three for my collaborators if they desert me. The last is for myself.'[60] Pressing the gun dramatically to his temple, he went on: 'If I am not victorious by tomorrow afternoon I shall be a dead man.' Returning to the main hall of the Bürgerbräukeller, he concluded his speech with the words: 'Either the German revolution begins tonight or we will all be dead by dawn.'[61] During the night of 8–9 November he was several times heard to say: 'If it comes off, all's well, if not, we'll hang ourselves.'[62] After the Feldherrnhalle débâcle Hitler went into hiding at a friend's home. When the police came to arrest him he stood at the top of the stairs waving his revolver and shouting: 'This is the end. Shall I let these swines arrest me? Never. I'd rather be dead.'[63] The friend's wife, in fact, disarmed Hitler and the police led him away. In Landsberg prison he at once declared his firm intention of going on a hunger strike to the death to atone for the fiasco. However, fellow putschists talked him out of this mood of despair, reassuring him that he was indispensable to the movement. And once the trial turned into a great nationalist demonstration, no more was heard from Hitler of suicide.

Eight years later a personal tragedy brought him to the brink of despair again. In September 1931 his niece Geli Raubal shot herself in Hitler's Munich flat for reasons which are likely to remain obscure. Hitler, who had been infatuated by the girl, fell into a depression so severe that his followers feared he might abandon politics completely. While in this mood he appears to have made his one and only recorded attempt to commit suicide. But before he could pull the trigger, Hess tore the pistol from his hand. A year later at the height of the Strasser crisis, when Hitler had brought the party to the brink of dissolution through his own intransigence, Goebbels recorded how Hitler paced up and down the room exclaiming: 'If the party falls to pieces then I will end it all in three minutes with my pistol.'[64] And in January 1935, at a time of unrest in the party, Hitler stunned a conference of *Gauleiter* and *Reichsleiter* by threatening suicide if the party did not remain loyal and enable him to carry out his ambitious plans at home and abroad.

With the possible exception of the 1931 episode, Hitler's threats of suicide should not be taken seriously. Attention has been drawn already to his trick of committing himself to a radical solution of some problem, deliberately cutting off his own line of retreat as if to suppress his neurotic fear of wavering or of revealing the inner uncertainty that so often beset him at moments of crisis. His suicide threats fall into this category. Sometimes he deliberately polarized situations for dramatic effects, as on 1 September, 1939 when he declared to the Reichstag: 'I have again put on that coat which was for me the holiest and dearest. I shall not take it off until victory—or I shall not see the finish.'[65] Or on 23 November, 1939, addressing the generals, he remarked: 'I will stand or fall in this struggle. I shall not survive the defeat of my people.'[66] In neither case did the military situation justify these dramatic undertones, from which one may safely conclude that he was speaking for effect.

Only when Hitler started to doubt final victory did suicide become a genuine alternative, not a rhetorical device. Thus, on 1 February, 1943 he expressed pitying contempt for the life Paulus would lead in Russian captivity. The only life that mattered, he went on, was the life of the people. Individuals had to die. 'But how can one fear a moment that frees him from misery, were it not for a sense of duty holding one back in this vale of tears.'[67] Eighteen months later, with the Anglo-Americans firmly established in the west and the German armies retreating through Poland, Hitler spoke openly of his own end: 'If my life had come to an end', he remarked on 31 August, 1944, 'for me it would be simply a relief from anxiety, sleepless nights and a serious nervous complaint. Only a fraction of a second and one is released from everything and has peace and eternal rest.'[68]

Another reason why Hitler's suicide threats over the years must be treated with considerable caution was his principled opposition to self-slaughter. By nature he was an optimist who firmly believed that by holding on to life, one would discover a path out of the worst situation; it was absolutely deplorable, in his view, that people did away with themselves out of sheer despair. But by the winter of 1944–5 he was quoting with approval Schopenhauer's pessimistic comment that a life full of disappointment was not worth living; if a man was no more than a living ruin, why prolong life? In September 1944, ill in bed with jaundice, he told his secretary that if the pain kept recurring, there was no point in living and he would end it all.[69] The secretary recalls, too, that by 1945 Hitler had lost all interest in conversation of a high intellectual content. He talked endlessly about training dogs or about his diet, and complained monotonously that mankind was not worth living for: 'Animals are much more loyal than men.'[70]

In November 1923 the instinct of self-preservation had told the young putschist that, no matter what he said for effect, if he held on to life, something would turn up. But in April 1945 a prematurely-aged Führer knew in his bones that there was no escape. His political testament, dictated on 29 April, was a genuine suicide note, full of self-justification. According to it, love and loyalty to the German people had motivated all his political actions. For the outbreak of war he resolutely refused to accept the slightest shadow of responsibility. For that the Jews were solely to blame. With the end in sight, he dare not risk being turned into a showpiece by the Russians, and preferred to kill himself when it was clear Berlin must fall. The sacrifices of his followers had not been in vain. One day there would be a resurrection of National Socialism, and it was the duty of his followers to work towards that goal. His very last words were a stern admonition to them to adhere closely to Nazi racial laws, and offer 'merciless resistance to the world poisoner of all peoples—international Jewry'.[71] So in the last hours of his life, writing with posterity in mind, he chose to emphasize the supreme importance of that crude and vulgar anti-semitism which first gained him a hearing on Munich platforms twenty-five years before. Whether this pernicious doctrine on its own or in combination with other intellectual concepts had been the driving force behind this strange man is the subject of the next chapter.

4

Hitler's intellectual world

The belief that Adolf Hitler was a cynical opportunist who lacked firm convictions and lived from hand to mouth in the realm of ideas, shamelessly exploiting intellectual concepts the way he exploited people in his restless search for absolute power, dies hard. It has a long history behind it. The ex-Nazi Hermann Rauschning and the writer Konrad Heiden, both of whom observed Hitler at close quarters, subscribed to this view, and a whole generation of historians has repeated it.[1] Just occasionally scholars have had their doubts, notably Hugh Trevor-Roper who argued, many years ago, that however repugnant a figure Hitler was in the eyes of decent people, the consistency with which he pursued his objectives merited more serious examination of his philosophy of life than it had hitherto received.[2] Not until 1969 did a German historian undertake a serious analysis of this subject.[3] Since then one can no longer subscribe to the Rauschning-Heiden interpretation without considerable reservations. After all, belief in certain principles and skill at tactical manoeuvring are by no means mutually exclusive as the career of many a well-known politician in recent years reveals. 'Principled opportunism' might perhaps be the most helpful description of this marriage of ideas and tactics without which effective political action is doomed to irredeemable failure.

In this chapter some attempt will be made to examine those ideas which, on the surface at any rate, appear to have exerted major influence on Hitler and on Nazi policy in general. Much will be said about Social Darwinism, anti-semitism, and the drive for living space, both from the point of view of the origins of Hitler's interest in these concepts and in terms of the actual influence they exerted on policy in so far as this can be quantified. Cultural influences cannot be ignored either. Comment will be made in the second half of the chapter on his Catholicism, his interest in architecture and his passion for the music of Richard Wagner, though these relate more to his personal pathology than to the direction in which the Third Reich moved.

Two caveats must be entered at the outset. In the first place, the task of tracing with any degree of accuracy the antecedents of intellectual concepts is fraught with immense difficulties. In Hitler's case doubly so, because of his reluctance to acknowledge his indebtedness to others in the world of ideas as much as in practical politics.

Secondly, one should not attach overmuch significance to these antecedents if and when they are established. It would perhaps be going too far to suggest, as the historian Ernst Deuerlein does in his excellent short biography of Hitler, that 'the situation created him, not he the situation.'[4] But the comment is a salutary reminder that defeat in war, the shame of Versailles and rampant inflation were the fundamental causes of Nazism. To give an air of respectability to personal resentments and frustrations young Nazis and other rightwing activists made use of whatever ideas were currently fashionable in the circles in which they moved.[5] To trace the Nazi philosophy back into Germany's past is a fascinating exercise but a seductive one carrying with it a considerable risk of distorting the historical roots of the phenomenon.

We commence our examination of Hitler's ideas with his belief in Social Darwinism. The notion that life is in essence a ruthless struggle for existence, *bellum omnium contra omnes*, was commonplace in *fin de siècle* Europe. The application to social science of the teachings of Charles Darwin, as interpreted by his popularizers—an important qualification—led, in some quarters at least, to the emergence of a highly pessimistic view of man, no longer a moral being infused with a divine spark, but a simple biological organism and an expendable unit in a collective entity. The restraints civilization had placed on human rapacity were dismissed by extreme Social Darwinists as a perversion of the evolutionary processes which decreed that the fittest and the strongest should survive at the expense of the unfit. Humanitarian efforts to protect the weak, the sick and the old distorted the balance of nature. An 'enlightened' state would make it its business to reverse the retrograde trend and positively promote the growth of strong and healthy elements. If traditional moral values counted for nothing, then in the long run the door was open, logically, to the sterilization of the unfit, euthanasia of the old and the physical extermination of any element deemed by the rulers to be 'socially undesirable'. Social Darwinism had important consequences for foreign policy as well. If foreign policy was based on the dubious premise that the biological urges to eat and to procreate were the foundation of all life, it followed that when population threatened to outstrip resources, expansion at the expense of weaker neighbours was a 'right' bestowed on the strong by the laws of evolution and a categorical imperative for the leaders of these peoples.

It would have been surprising if Hitler had not been deeply influenced by Social Darwinism. For in the brash, aggressive and militaristic atmosphere of Wilhelmean Germany, a young, insecure and ambitious state, Social Darwinistic ideas were widely accepted in respectable bourgeois circles. What is interesting in Hitler's case was the tenacity with which he clung to this gloomy view of the human condition. The broader vistas and experiences of public office did nothing whatsoever to expose to him the fallacies underlying this crude philosophy. On the contrary, his entire political programme might be construed as a logical extension of the central belief that

> Victory is to the strong and the weak must go to the wall. She [nature] teaches us that what may seem cruel to us, because it affects us personally or because we have been brought up in ignorance of her laws, is nevertheless

often essential if a higher way of life is to be attained. Nature . . . knows nothing of the notion of humanitarianism which signifies that the weak must at all costs be surrounded and preserved even at the expense of the strong.[6]

Pity was out of place in a world governed by the inexorable operation of biological laws beyond human control. To feel concern for concentration camp inmates, the old and sick being put to sleep in euthanasia centres, subject peoples suffering under the heel of the oppressor, or enemy soldiers dying on the battlefield was sheer sentimentalism, the corrupting legacy of a Christian-humanitarian past. The Nazi was expected to be hard and ruthless in obeying the dictates of the higher law of nature for the sake of his own people.

In the crude and bloody world of the Social Darwinists organized violence was an essential concomitant of political action. 'War', Hitler remarked in 1944, 'is therefore the unalterable law of the whole of life—the prerequisite for the natural selection of the strong and the precedent for the elimination of the weak. What seems cruel to us, is from nature's point of view entirely obvious. A people that cannot assert itself must disappear and another must take its place. All creation is subject to this law: no one can avoid it.'[7] That was the explanation of the deep gulf separating western statesmen and Nazi leaders on the subject of war. To the former, war was an admission of failure, and the supreme tragedy to be avoided at all costs even at the price of what to many seemed a shameful surrender at Munich. For Hitler and his followers war was 'the father of all things', an ennobling experience to be treasured by those privileged to take part in it. Not of course that Hitler wanted a repetition of the long-drawn-out holocaust of the trenches which had drained away the life-blood of the German nation. But while admitting that eternal war was an evil, he insisted that eternal peace was equally undesirable because that would lead to the emigration of the best elements in the people and a decline in the birth rate. The ideal war from Hitler's point of view would be a short victorious campaign which conferred prestige on the army at minimum risk, recaptured the 'spirit of 1914' when class·divisions were temporarily submerged in a great tidal wave of emotion, and secured vital living space for the German people without bleeding it white.

It is well-known that Hitler was a fanatical nationalist. His boyhood and early adolescence was spent in the Branau-am-Inn and Linz districts, a border area where, as is so often the case, national sentiment had a xenophobic edge to it. One of the formative influences in his youth was Ritter Georg von Schönerer, 'the holy knight Georg', leader of the anti-Habsburg and pro-German movement which attracted a strong following in German-speaking Upper Austria at the close of the nineteenth century. Although it is unlikely that Hitler's father, a retired customs official, was a Schönerer enthusiast, the boy's teachers including his history master, Leopold Pötsch, certainly were. From them young Hitler learnt to fear the rising tide of Slav nationalism, despise the Habsburgs for 'betraying' the Germans, and yearn ardently for political union with

Imperial Germany. Pan-German feeling took him from Vienna to Munich in 1913, and then into a Bavarian infantry regiment on the outbreak of war. After the war he entered political life as a nationalist agitator, exploiting contemporary discontent with a peace treaty which separated hundreds of thousands of fellow Germans from the beloved Reich.

However, to describe Hitler as an uncomplicated nationalist whose sole aim was to gather together under one roof all his separated racial brethren as the popular slogan *Ein Volk, ein Reich, ein Führer* suggested, is misleading. German nationalism was already changing in character in the closing years of the nineteenth century as racialism and anti-semitism began to spread in Germany and Austria. Schönerer's nationalist movement, for example, was deeply coloured from the very beginning with a virulent anti-semitism and a savage racialism directed against the Slav peoples.

In the 1890s, as Hitler grew up, the racialist theories of Gobineau and Chamberlain were taking root in central Europe. Count Joseph Arthur de Gobineau's major treatise *Essai sur la inégalité des races humaines*, in which he argued that the rise and fall of races was the key to human history, was published between 1853 and 1856. Not until the 1890s did it exert any significant influence when it was acclaimed by the Richard Wagner circle and by the Pan-German League, possibly because belief in the inequality of men attracted the support of the *haute bourgeoisie* only when their privileged economic and social position was being challenged by the emergence of a powerful working-class movement. Gobineau remained a doom watcher convinced that even the purest race, the white race—of which the German race was the purest part—would in time be contaminated by inferior blood and the spread of democracy; its melancholy fate would be absorption into a universal racial medley incapable of true culture.

On the other hand, Houston Stewart Chamberlain, a Germanophile and an ardent Wagner enthusiast, believed passionately in the redemptive power of the Aryan race. In *The Foundations of the Nineteenth Century*, a work which appeared in 1900 and became the bible of German racialism, Chamberlain identified the Aryan race with the German nation, mixing Social Darwinism, chauvinism and anti-semitism into a poisonous brew. The history of mankind, as portrayed by Chamberlain, was in essence a dramatic struggle of Wagnerian proportions between two pure races—the German and the Jewish. The former embodied all that was superior in the Greco-Roman heritage, the latter was the deadly enemy of mankind bent on world domination. The comforting thought for nationalists who accepted Chamberlain's teaching was his confident prediction that the Germans, being the superior race, would be victorious over all their enemies. One of those who idolized Chamberlain was Hitler. He studied the *Foundations* and was deeply moved on meeting the master, who was Wagner's son-in-law, at the Villa Wahnfried in Bayreuth in September 1923. One of the factors which possibly helped transform the nationalist *Trommler* into the future Führer was the old man's declaration a week later that in Hitler he recognized Germany's saviour.

The fact that reactionary political forces helped Hitler to power and derived great material benefit from the dictatorship should not deceive one into supposing that Nazism was in all respects a counter-revolutionary movement whose *raison d'etre* was the maintenance of a rigid class dictatorship. Theories of fascism that interpret the escalating violence against Jews and Slavs as an inevitable consequence of the class dictatorship, a device for mobilizing the people to wage aggressive warfare in the interests of German imperialism, fail to do justice to the Nazi phenomenon.[8] Although economic and social realities determined the salient features of the dictatorship, ideological prejudices acquired a sinister momentum of their own and helped to plunge Germany into a war which ultimately brought disaster to the very classes hoping to profit most from the regime.

It is here in the fanatical intensity with which the Nazis pursued their racial-imperialist ambitions that the revolutionary character of Nazism lies, and not in any alleged connection with the modernization process. The argument advanced by some scholars that Nazism represented the modern social revolution so long delayed in Germany is difficult to sustain.[9] The plain fact is that the coming to power of the Nazis did not reverse any of the broad trends discernible in German society before 1933. Despite the archaic blood-and-soil nonsense emanating from *völkisch* circles and propagated by the Goebbels ministry, the drift from countryside to town continued and even accelerated under the Nazis. And the process of industrial concentration continued without let or hindrance to the detriment of those small firms which had expected protection from Hitler. While socially the ascendancy of the old professional and business élites continued well into the war years. If some movement towards power-sharing with the Nazi parvenus was unavoidable, this was only an extension of the 'fraternization process', the partial erosion of class barriers normal in a modern democracy, and had little effect on the economic power base of the old order. If the Nazi suppression of local autonomy and the creation of a centralized state are considered evidence of the modernization process, then it must be pointed out that the modern trend is in the opposite direction.

One of the most revealing sources of information about Hitler's racialist fantasies in the early 1930s are the controversial conversations recorded by Hermann Rauschning.[10] At a conference in the Munich Brown House in August 1932 at a moment when he was holding out for what to many seemed the unattainable goal of the chancellorship, Hitler outlined to party officials plans for the future of Europe which were utterly disruptive of the existing order of capitalist society. The ultimate aim of Nazi foreign policy would not be achieved even when Germany regained control of lost territories or acquired the oil, wheat and mineral wealth she needed for self-sufficiency. As Hitler saw it, Europe was 'in the midst of . . . a revolutionary cataclysm produced by the abdication of the old social powers and the rise of the new ones'. Unlike the Marxists, Hitler did not believe the effete bourgeoisie would be replaced by the working class because the worker was 'as much a temporary symptom of a dying social order as the nobility and the bourgeoisie'.[11] The new social order he had in mind for Europe reminds one of the socially-ossified and authoritarian republic of Plato. Hitler went on:

> There will be a *Herren*-class, a historical class tempered by battle, and welded from the most varied elements. There will be a great hierarchy of party members. They will be the new middle class. And there will be the great mass of the anonymous, the serving collective, the eternally disfranchised, no matter whether they were once members of the old bourgeoisie, the big landowning class, the working class or the artisans. Nor will their financial or previous social position be of the slightest importance. These preposterous differences will have been liquidated in a single revolutionary process. But beneath them there will still be the class of subject alien races; we need not hesitate to call them the modern slave class. And over all these will stand the new high aristocracy, the most deserving and the most responsible Führer personalities. In this way, in the struggle for power and mastery both within a nation and outside it, new classes emerge; never, as the professors and bookworms would have us believe, through a makeshift constitution, a government decree.[12]

Two years later, firmly established in office, he reaffirmed, in the presence of high-ranking party officers, that the coming new order could not be conceived of

> in terms of the national boundaries of the peoples with an historical past but in terms of race that transcends those boundaries. . . . Just as the conception of the nation was a revolutionary change from the purely dynastic feudal states and just as it introduced a biological conception, that of the people, so our own revolution is a further step, or, rather, the final step in the rejection of the historic order and the recognition of purely biological values. . . . The process of dissolution and reordering will run its course in every nation, no matter how old and firmly knit the social system may be. The active section in the nation, the militant Nordic section, will rise again and become the ruling element over these shopkeepers and pacifists, these puritans and speculators and busybodies.[13]

Bourgeois morality would have no place in the 'new order'. Slavs would be forcibly removed from their farms and turned into agricultural labourers deprived of education and condemned to toil for their German masters, the new élite of warrior-farmers produced by systematic breeding of the best elements in the aristocracy and the peasantry. Wholesale transportation of populations might be employed to remove undesirable elements such as the Czechs. Sterilization was plainly hinted at to reduce the fertility of the Slavs, a constant source of anxiety to the racialist-minded since the end of the last century. For, as he remarked ominously, 'at crucial periods in history all the tinsel falls away and the great rhythm of life alone rules the hour. I am restoring to force this original dignity, that of the source of all greatness and the creation of order.'[14]

Was this idle chatter quickly forgotten by Hitler and by those who listened to him? By no means. The history of the Third Reich shows only too plainly that the Nazis were determined to transform these racialist fantasies into reality given the opportunity, and—a point to be taken up later—at the cost of economic disruption unwelcome to the forces which had helped Hitler to power.

After the conquest of Poland Himmler, on Hitler's direct orders, murdered tens of thousands of prominent Polish citizens in a calculated bid to rob the Poles of their natural leaders. There followed the forcible colonization of Gau Wartheland and Gau Danzig-Westpreussen. By June 1941 over one million Poles had been transported from their homes to make way for 200,000 German settlers, who took over their farms and small businesses. As part of Himmler's resettlement programme thousands of Polish children, allegedly with Nordic characteristics, were forcibly taken from their parents and handed over to childless SS couples through the agency of the Lebensborn organization.

The attack on Russia opened up new vistas for the SS. In the notorious document 'General Plan East' Himmler revealed what the Nazis had in store for Eastern Europe. The general government of Poland and the Baltic States were to be completely Germanized: a total of thirty-one million Slavs would be moved out of the eastern territories up to a line from Leningrad to the river Dnieper bend to make room for German settlers; and by 1967 there would be three-and-a-half millions of them in the so-called frontier marches living in fortified settlements from which they would lord it over those Slavs left behind to become the hewers of wood and drawers of water for the master race. The primitive brutality with which this programme would have been carried out was revealed on 16 July 1941 when Hitler discussed the eastern problem with Goering, Keitel, Rosenberg, Lammers and Bormann. The entire area up to the Urals was to become an old-style colonial territory administered and exploited in German interests. Order had to be restored there quickly: 'This can best be done by shooting dead anyone who as much as looks askance at us', remarked the Führer.[15]

If the racial imperialists achieved little of their grandiose plans, this was because the resistance of the Red Army and of the Russian people set limits to Nazi ambitions. Even so, the fanatical obsession of some Nazis was truly amazing. As late as August 1944, when the Red Army had already driven the Germans out of Russia, Himmler was still haranguing party leaders in weirdly unrealistic language:

> It is irrevocable that we move our national boundaries forward by 500 kilometers, that we settle here. . . . It is irrevocable that 30 million other Germanic peoples be added to our 90 million, so that we shall increase our blood base to 120 million Germans. . . . It is irrevocable that we shall populate this territory, that we shall found the seedbed of Germanic blood in the east, and it is irrevocable that we shall move our border defences far into the east. For our grandchildren and their great-grandchildren will have lost the next war . . . unless our airforce in the east . . . stands at the Urals.[16]

The sheer irrationality lying at the heart of the Nazi philosophy is also exemplified by anti-semitism. For rank-and-file Nazis the negative campaign against Jewry probably aroused much more enthusiasm than the positive task of creating a race of supermen, an attitude which seems to have been shared by Hitler.[17] Future generations could create supermen if they pleased, whereas the immediate presence of Jews in German cities and towns was an affront to all the party stood for; and on Jews could be vented the resentments and frustrations which had attracted so many to the party in the first place.

Historically, anti-semitism had flourished in the dark undergrowth of German society from the early nineteenth century to the last days of the Weimar Republic. As a political phenomenon (of limited duration) it first erupted onto the political scene in Austria and Germany in the last quarter of the nineteenth century as a result of economic and social pressures generated by the modernization of society. Skilled artisans, shopkeepers and other lower middle-class elements, frightened by the decline in their economic power and social status, were easily persuaded that Jewish financiers and moneylenders were to blame. By the close of the nineteenth century, as indicated above, this form of anti-semitism was being replaced by a more virulent racial form, which was propagated in Germany with especial zeal by the literary circle led by Richard Wagner.

Hitler's story in *Mein Kampf*, that he became an anti-semite in Vienna, has been discounted by some writers as a piece of poetic licence. True, his own father was probably mildly anti-semitic, and as a schoolboy Hitler very likely read the anti-semitic *Linzer Fliegende Blätter*. All the same, at that time Hitler's dislike of Jews was a fairly superficial emotion. Not until he went to Vienna did he encounter anti-semitism as a full-blown ideology, so to this extent the story of an encounter with an orthodox Jew in the inner city which prompted, him, so he alleged, to undertake a serious study of the racial origins of the Jew, has allegorical significance.

What were the causes of Hitler's conversion to rabid anti-semitism? One cannot exclude an element of political opportunism: in Vienna he was able to study at first hand the use made of anti-semitism by Karl Lueger, the mayor of Vienna, in creating the Christian Social Party. But literary influences were probably a good deal more important for a man who read voraciously and indiscriminately all his life. There is insufficient evidence to substantiate Wilhelm Daim's contention that the self-styled Lanz von Liebenfels, a colourful and unbalanced ex-monk, was 'the man who gave Hitler his ideas'.[18] What cannot be denied is that Liebenfels's publications, in particular the rabidly racialist and anti-semitic journal *Ostara. Zeitschrift für die Blonden*, was typical of the literature Hitler read in Vienna. Turning over the pages of this journal, which had a circulation of some 10,000, Hitler entered a weird twilight world where the heroic Aryans were locked in a titanic struggle to the death with sinister dark forces seeking their destruction. Liebenfels flew the swastika flag from the ramparts of his castle (bought with money from an admiring industrialist), and demanded the prohibition of intermarriage with inferior breeds in the new racial order of the future. Castration and even mass extermination of sub-humans were remedies Liebenfels did not hesitate to advocate at one time or another in his writings. The significance of Liebenfels for Hitler was, as an authority on these years remarks, that he 'pointed out directions in which Hitler could find more compelling answers' for the personal difficulties he was currently facing in Vienna.[19]

The deterioration in Hitler's personal circumstances undoubtedly helped to confirm him in his new-found prejudices. The traumatic experiences in 1908–9 will be examined more fully in the next chapter. Sufficient to say here that as Hitler slipped off the secure perch of a fairly tolerable bourgeois existence, based on his orphan's pension and his mother's estate, he entered a world he did not care for. Rootless and alone in a great cosmopolitan city, abandoned by the bourgeoisie he felt he belonged to because of his father's profession yet filled with bourgeois prejudice against organized labour, is it not likely that he rationalized his own plight in terms of the 'Jewish domination' of Vienna?[20]

Looking ahead somewhat, it is worth noting that Hitler's decision to commit himself to full-time political agitation in 1919 coincided with a sharp recrudescence of anti-semitic feeling in Germany. Between 1895 and 1914 as the German economy recovered from the great depression of 1873–95, anti-semitism sharply declined. Only in the aftermath of war was it reawakened by a large influx of Jews fleeing from the disorder and chaos reigning in parts of eastern Europe. Attacks on Jews became a normal feature of right-wing gatherings, and the slogan 'the Jew is responsible' was heard whenever the discontented railed at their economic plight. Fuel was added to the flames by the prominence of Jews such as the Russian Leon Trotsky, the Hungarian Bela Kun and the German Kurt Eisner in the revolutionary socialist camp. Already in April 1919 the Deutschvölkischer Schutz und Trutzbund (German Folkish Defence League) had established a branch in Munich which played a prominent part in the anti-semitic excesses in that city in November and December 1919. The newly founded German Workers' Party, growing up under the patronage of the Defence League and the influential and equally anti-semitic Thulegesellschaft (Thule Society), naturally repeated the parrot cry that Jews and freemasons were responsible for Germany's defeat. So it is not surprising that a newcomer to the party should have exploited the current dislike of the Jews whenever he stood on a public platform.

At the risk of disturbing the flow of the argument, it may be helpful at this point to examine briefly the content of Hitler's anti-semitism which he worked into a coherent doctrine in the course of the early 1920s. This for the very good reason that unless the crudity and naïveté of Hitler's beliefs in respect of the Jews are fully appreciated by the reader it is perhaps more difficult to move on to consider certain other explanations of his anti-semitism advanced in recent years.[21]

The starting point of Hitler's anti-semitic beliefs was the bland assumption that the state was the distinguishing mark of any people, an indispensable organization existing to provide work for all and representing the coercive power without which a people could not assert its right to live. Jews, according to Hitler, were unable to establish states because they did not look upon work as a social obligation and a duty performed for the good of the group as

Aryans did. For a Jew work simply represented an egoistical desire to preserve the individual—hence pillage and brigandage was the Jewish way of life. One wonders, incidentally, what Hitler would have made of the modern state of Israel.[22]

Still, the existence of the Jewish race, held together by the power of Mosaic law, was a fact of history. The Jew, like any other mortal, had to live. But how, if Jews could not establish states? The simple answer was that they lived as parasites on other peoples. Hitler, who was inordinately fond of analogies from nature, once compared the Jew with ivy clinging to a tree, sucking it dry of nutriment and eventually killing it. What was needed, he added ominously, was 'the hand of a gardener to tend the garden as quickly as possible'.[23] Throughout history Jews had lived parasitically, starting off as nomadic tribesmen who eschewed a settled way of life, much preferring to use up pasture land wastefully and move on. In modern times they had become the commercial class, the manipulators of money who bought and sold goods but never produced them.

The Jews were not just simple parasites to be rooted out of Germany 'one way or another', to use a favourite phrase of Hitler's, but beings scheming and plotting behind the scenes to conquer the whole world. No need to look for deep underlying social and economic causes to explain the upheavals of 1789 and 1917—these were simply the work of 'subterranean Jewish wirepullers'. From its new headquarters in Moscow World Jewry was now making a calculated bid to conquer Germany as the next step towards world domination. So once again the fatherland was in the front line, where Hitler loved to be, facing an implacable foe bent on enslaving the people. If Germany was to be saved, time was of the essence—hence the shrill hysterical note that often crept into Hitler's denunciation of Jewry. Whether he picked up this conspiracy theory of history from the writings of Houston Chamberlain or from conversations with Rosenberg, his confidant in the early 1920s, or more likely from the notorious *Protocols of Zion*, a forgery purporting to reveal the world domination plans concocted by the council of World Jewry and circulating in the German Workers' Party as early as 1919, it is quite impossible to say.

By what means did Jews set about undermining the countries they settled in? Their most insidious weapon was 'interest capital' which was currently squeezing Germany to death in the interests of the moneylenders. Hitler, the would-be friend of big business, was treading on very thin ice here but tried to have the best of both worlds by drawing a cunning and nonsensical distinction between 'interest capital' and 'industrial capital', a phrase borrowed from Gottfried Feder, the party's economic expert.

Industrial capital was perfectly respectable, Hitler was at pains to assure his audiences, for without it production was impossible. Any value this capital possessed came from the honest Aryan sweat put into work. The tragedy was that honest German workers were being tricked by their Jewish leaders into attacking industrial capital when the real enemies of the people were the Jewish financiers with their high interest rates, who made fortunes out of human misery, tightened the strangle hold of international Jewish finance on Germany, and by encouraging inflationary tendencies robbed ordinary Germans of all incentive to work.

Secondly, Jews were corrupting the German people by spreading pernicious doctrines of 'internationalism', 'pacifism' and 'democracy'. The odd notion that war was an unmitigated evil was a Jewish device to weaken the will of honest Germans to solve their problems—as virile peoples ought to—by force. As for the nonsensical democratic belief that all men were equal, this conflicted with the basic Nazi principle that 'the best elements' should govern while the majority obeyed them. Party politics were nothing but a sham. 'They all hang on a Jewish string; if a red whip drives them forward on one side, a golden bridle holds them back on the other side. Whether they call themselves middle class, democratic or proletarian or dictatorial they are all without exception Jewish and not one of them is German, even fewer are national.'[24]

Thirdly, Jews were trying to weaken the physical stamina of the Germans. Their financiers exploited hunger by keeping prices up and supplies down. On one occasion Hitler even argued that the 'Reds' were deliberately destroying Russian factories so that as they were being rebuilt, the workers could be driven even harder. Another method beloved of Jews was the age-old traffic in girls. White slave traffic and promiscuity were actively promoted in order to sully Aryan blood. Allegations of Jewish sexual depravity never failed to titilate audiences—an interesting phenomenon to which we will return presently.

Finally, the Jews, having no culture themselves—for, incredibly, Hitler denied that Jews possessed any true spiritual qualities—were bent on destroying the cultural heritages of other peoples. In the early days Hitler was always sure of hearty applause for onslaughts on the modern theatre as a 'breeding place of lasciviousness and shamelessness', and on modern art as a caricature of all that decent Germans had been taught to admire. Unimaginative philistines were reassured by Hitler's confident assertion that the Jew was behind this as so much else in the modern world which they could not understand.

Hitler's conclusion had a certain crazy logic about it. The German people faced a stark choice. Either the Jews were allowed to conquer the world, which would be the end of mankind, for once peoples die out the parasites living on them must die out as well, as every biologist knows; the world would become a dead planet spinning on through space for all eternity. Or, the peoples of the world must awaken to the deadly peril before it engulfed then, and remove the 'cancerous growth' from the body politic.

The crudity and fantastic implausibility of Hitler's anti-semitism leaves one with the feeling that the explanations offered so far in this chapter are not wholly satisfactory. At least one must consider the possibility that equally valid explanations may lie in the hidden recesses of personality, in that irrational subconscious jungle where, according to some schools of psychiatry, much of the motivation of human conduct is to be found. The contribution of psychiatry and social psychology in helping to understand both the pathology of Hitler and, what is more important for the historian, the collective pathology of a society, where sizable groups of people were seduced by such irrational fantasies, will be discussed in the next chapter. Nevertheless, at the risk of some repetition this seems an appropriate point to discuss some of the explanations advanced by psychohistorians to account for the virulence of Hitler's anti-semitism.[25]

To date psychohistory has been largely dominated by the teachings of Freud as a young man. Personality is conceptualized in terms of drives and instincts, partly sexual and partly destructive in nature, and of the need man feels to come to terms with an outside world which is fundamentally hostile to his free development. From this standpoint the psychohistorian Robert Waite and the psychiatrist Walter Langer have both concluded that the intensity of Hitler's anti-semitism was due to some form of perverted sexuality.[26]

On the basis of clinical observation it is also argued that the 'typical' anti-semite usually suffers from an identity crisis: his friendships tend to be precarious; an unresolved Oedipus complex often lies hidden way back in early childhood; he is politically immature and culturally infantile in his tastes; he displays great skill and agility in projecting his own sense of inadequacy onto other people; and, finally, he is sadomasochistic.

Does the historical evidence we possess about Hitler's private life confirm this life pattern? Of sadomasochism there is some evidence, also of an identity crisis which will be evaluated in the next chapter. Hitler's friendships were few in number, shallow in content and might well be termed precarious. As far as we can see, his relations with this mother and father do suggest an unresolved Oedipus complex. That his political opinions were immature by the standards of liberal democracy is fairly obvious. Culturally, one can scarcely deny that Hitler was a philistine who resolutely closed his mind to modern trends in art, architecture and music. But the nub of the Waite-Langer argument lies in the contention that Hitler projected onto the Jews a deep sense of guilt and self-hatred arising out of his own sexual perversion.

Direct evidence in such an intimate area is naturally hard to come by. Putzi Hanfstaengl, a friend of Hitler's in the early 1920s, and Otto Strasser, the brother of Gregor who fled from Germany in 1934, on whose testimony Langer relies rather heavily, were admittedly close to Hitler in the early days. But as both were dedicated opponents of Hitler by the time they gave their testimony, their evidence must be treated with great caution. Nor is there reliable evidence that any of the women Hitler was involved with over the years—Henny Hoffmann, Renate Mueller, Unity Mitford or Eva Braun—killed themselves or attempted suicide because of bizarre sexual demands made on them by Hitler.

On the positive side, however, one cannot ignore emotive passages in *Mein Kampf* full of sexual imagery in which Hitler accuses the Jews of promoting the white slave traffic and prostitution, and of encouraging incest and spreading syphilis in order to pollute the blood of pure Aryans; for the psychoanalyst the language of fantasy is highly revealing. And for what it is worth, August Kubizek, his companion in Vienna, testified to Hitler's incessant chatter about the origins and development of prostitution.[28] It is interesting, too, that in 1938 when shown compromising photographs of Erna Gruhn, Blomberg's wife, Hitler exclaimed that her male partner 'must have been of Jewish extraction'.[29]

Much has been made of Hitler's alleged monorchism. It is perfectly true that such a malformation does not impair sexual activity. However, one cannot discount the possibility that the absence of a testicle (or an undescended one) might have set up anxieties and fears of inadequacy in a young boy. Scanty though the evidence is, one cannot on balance exclude the possibility that Hitler may have suffered from some sense of sexual inadequacy which might conceivably explain the virulence of his anti-semitic outbursts.

A novel explanation of Hitler's anti-semitism has been advanced by the American historian Rudolf Binion.[30] By no means the first to try to establish a connection between Hitler and the Jewish doctor Eduard Bloch who treated Hitler's mother during her fatal illness, Binion had worked his thesis out in considerably more detail.

He maintains that Bloch's treatment of Hitler's mother with iodoform in 1907, the gas attack which temporarily blinded Hitler in 1918 and the Final Solution in 1941 form were, in effect, a 'psychological continuum'. Although Hitler was apparently on good terms with Bloch after the mother's death, it is well-known that relations can harbour subconscious resentment against the doctor when a loved one dies. This repressed resentment of Jews was nutured by experiences in Vienna but only turned into active hatred in 1918 when the mustard gas attack triggered off memories of Bloch's iodoform. Then, following news of Germany's capitulation and the outbreak of revolution, Hitler suffered a hysterical relapse in which—so he claimed later—in a vision from on high he was ordered to avenge the wrongs Germany (and his mother) had suffered. For the rest of his life, so Binion argues, Hitler's primary aim was to relieve the traumatic experience of his mother's death by 'poisoning the Jewish poisoner'. That is precisely what he did twenty years later when he ordered first the euthanasia programme and then the murder of European Jewry.

The historical evidence on which Binion's impressively-researched thesis rests is rather slender. There is no convincing evidence that Hitler supposed that iodoform had poisonous side-effects on his mother or believed that she died of iodoform poisoning and not cancer, or that he associated the mustard gas attack with the iodoform treatment. The evidence for the 'vision' is also weak; the fact that Hitler encouraged his supporters to spread this dramatic story is not proof that it ever happened. Nor indeed, as Binion admits, did Hitler mention in his own account of the 'vision' any divine instruction to kill the Jews.[31] As we have seen already, the origins of the Final Solution are much more complex and even Binion does not dispute that expulsion of the Jews was 'an alternative to exterminating them'.[32] And is it not more likely that gas was adopted for the Final Solution (after shooting had been used earlier on) not because of Hitler's subconscious memories of the events of 1907 and 1918 but simply because gas was a speedier and—for the executioners—less harrowing method of murdering their victims?

Finally, one other theory is worthy of consideration—namely, that Hitler had a Jewish grandparent on the maternal side. Extensive investigation has produced not a shred of evidence that this is so. That is not necessarily the end of the matter. If Hans Frank's testimony can be relied on, Hitler seems to have been sufficiently interested when his disreputable nephew, Patrick Hitler, tried in 1930 to blackmail him, to have ordered the Gestapo to conduct an exhaustive investigation.[33] The fact that the Gestapo could find no proof of the story would not entirely exclude the possibility that Hitler never quite shook off the fear that he might be a quarter Jewish. Incidents such as the order in 1938 to turn the village of Döllersheim, where his grandmother was buried, into an artillery range as well as his constantly reiterated belief in private conversation that German blood was being tainted by the Jews, might be construed as evidence that Hitler had real anxieties in this direction.

From what has been said so far, it might appear that there is dispute only about the possible causes of Hitler's anti-semitism. That is not so. For although one cannot question the crucial importance of anti-semitism in making Hitler the man he was, it must not be assumed that the relative value of anti-semitism, Social Darwinism and eastward expansion in his political philosophy was determined irreversibly long before Hitler entered active politics and never subsequently modified. This does not appear to be true in the case of his anti-semitic prejudices.

In the early 1920s Hitler obviously relied very heavily on popular anti-semitism in establishing his reputation as an orator. When material conditions improved after 1924, anti-semitism declined sharply. The new situation was faithfully reflected in Hitler's speeches in the late 1920s; disquisitions on living space and on the Nazi philosophy of the state became his favourite themes with only occasional references to Jews.[34] This also corresponded with Hitler's changing role in the Nazi Party. For as he assumed the mantle of 'philosopher-king', he was seeking to elevate the tone and content of his message, and quietly abandoned the technique of the *Trommler* whose sole object had been the mobilization of the masses for immediate action by exploiting whatever contemporary discontent lay to hand. Even when the party broke into national politics in the early 1930s, Hitler made no attempt to resurrect the Jewish bogey. Marxism was now the major enemy and appeals to national pride, not anti-semitic tirades, were the keynote of his major addresses.

Was this mere expediencey? Did he choose instinctively the arguments best suited to his immediate purpose? Or had he begun at last to outgrow the vulgar anti-semitism of the early years? And even if expediency was the main reason, did the change of emphasis in itself have lasting effects on his anti-semitic prejudices? Just because he was the chief instigator of the holocaust and laid great emphasis on anti-semitism in his political testament in April 1945—a natural enough attempt at rationalization by a man contemplating suicide—can one automatically assume that hatred of the Jews was at all times the dominant strand in his political strategy between 1933 and 1945? It would be a rewarding exercise for a historian to examine thoroughly all Hitler's speeches and newspaper articles in order to register more precisely the shifts of emphasis in his anti-semitism and provide us with at least partial answers to these questions.

Eastward expansion to secure living space for the German people is generally assumed to have been an essential ingredient of Hitler's philosophy, and the driving force behind the foreign policy of the Third Reich, leading inevitably to war against Russia in 1941.

This was not always the case. When Hitler entered politics in 1919 there was little to distinguish him from any run-of-the-mill Pan-German agitator. His enemies were Britain and France, and his theme-song the revision of the Versailles treaty and the restoration of Germany's lost colonies overseas. Towards Russia he was not unsympathetic and hinted at the possibility of an alliance with her after she had thrown off 'Bolshevism.' Five years later, dictating *Mein Kampf* in the congenial surroundings of Landsberg prison, he spoke of the necessity for alliances with Italy and Britain, firmly rejected demands for the recovery of the overseas colonies, and proclaimed Germany's holy mission to be the conquest of land in the east to satisfy the economic needs and fulfil the racial aspirations of the German people.

It used to be thought that Hitler turned against Russia under the influence of the Geopoliticians, a group of writers and quasi-intellectuals who put to work in the revisionist cause the political geography of the Scandinavian scholars Friedrich Ratzel and Rodolf Kjellen. By popularizing the idea that states were living organisms engaged in ceaseless conflict for living space and that frontiers should change in response to population pressures, Geopoliticians were making a conscious contribution to the battle against the Versailles treaty. Through Rudolf Hess, Hitler was introduced, either in 1922 or 1924, to Karl Haushofer, a prominent Geopolitician and head of the scientific department of the Deutsche Akademie.

A comparison of the passages on foreign policy in *Mein Kampf* with the writings of Ratzel and Haushofer confirms that Hitler did make use of some of their arguments. For example, Hitler's assertion that the security of a state was directly related to the size of its territory came from Ratzel. And from Haushofer came the rejection of internal colonization on the grounds that there were natural limits to the productivity of the soil. But it is significant that Hitler paid no attention whatsoever to Haushofer's general conclusions. For Haushofer, a conservative nationalist of the old school, did not preach aggression against Russia, nor did he despise the Slavs as sub-humans. On the contrary, in a world divided into space-owning imperialist powers and oppressed powers, he believed Russia to be Germany's obvious ally. In control of the heartland of central Asia, an area of vast economic potential, Germany in alliance with Russia could one day challenge the maritime powers and become a world power. Furthermore, Hitler's resolve to expand eastwards preceded his encounters with the Geopoliticians. In the writings of Ratzel and Haushofer he found little more than supplementary arguments to justify a policy to which he was already committed for other reasons. Work in progress on this period suggests that several factors combined to turn Hitler against Russia.[35]

The influence of Rosenberg was, it would appear, a factor of major importance. Under the wing of this pseudo-intellectual and refugee from the Baltic States, Hitler swallowed the conspiracy theory of history contained in the *Protocols of Zion*. Important also was the Brest Litovsk treaty. The domination of wide areas of eastern Europe, including the Ukraine, by German soldiers, if only for a few brief months in the summer of 1918, made a deep impression on Hitler. Was this not the obvious way of acquiring the 'soil and land (colonies) for the nourishment of our people and the settlement of our surplus population' which the 1920 party programme referred to? That the programme contained such a demand as early as 1920 is in itself significant and points to another major factor in the situation—the pervasive influence of Pan-German propaganda which long before the First World War had advocated eastward expansion to obtain 'elbow room' for Germany. Thus by 1922 before he encountered the Geopoliticians, Hitler already believed that 'the destruction of Russia with the help of England will have to be attempted.' Russia would give Germany sufficient land for German settlers and a wide field of activity for German industry.[36]

A very different explanation of Hitler's commitment to eastward expansion has been advanced by Binion. He believes that some kind of psychic connection existed between, on the one hand, the collective trauma of the German people, stunned by defeat for which they were unprepared, and, on the other, the personal trauma experienced by Hitler's mother who, thirty years previously, lost three of her children within the space of a few months. The death of Gustav in August 1887, Otto in (probably) November 1887 and Ida in February 1888 would have disturbed any mother. Therefore, is it surprising that she over-indulged the next child, Adolf, born in April 1889, and that very probably the anxiety she felt lest she lose him 'was fed into his nursing'?

This pre-oedipal experience assumed significance for Hitler only in 1918, so Binion alleges, when the German people was utterly demoralized by defeat. In the aftermath of war the personal trauma of one man was grafted onto the collective trauma of a whole people. Binion concludes that when in 1924 Hitler declared eastward expansion to be the goal of a future Nazi foreign policy, he was responding to the wishes of the German people to relive the trauma of defeat by making a bid once more for world power. Simultaneously he was reliving his mother's trauma that she might lose him as she had lost other children. In short, the pursuit of *Lebensraum* served a dual purpose: it satisfied a people's desire for revenge and provided an individual with a secure 'feeding ground'. By 1922 Hitler's acceptance of the Rosenberg thesis, that 'Jewish Bolshevism' controlled Soviet Russia, signified psychologically the merging of his lust for conquest (feeding ground) with what Binion regards as the decisive factor—Hitler's desire for revenge on the 'Jewish poisoners' of his mother.

This explanation does not carry conviction. Many psychiatrists would maintain that there is no evidence whatsoever that a mother's traumatic experience can be transmitted to her offspring through compensatory feeding. A larger question is whether one can assume that whole peoples react to trauma and display the same propensity to relive them as isolated individuals. One must conclude that there is no convincing evidence to justify the equation of living space with feeding space, exciting though the concept is. Nevertheless, while one cannot accept Binion's conclusions, his attempt to establish relationships between individual and collective phenomena is the most fruitful line of enquiry psychohistory has come up with to date, and one which will be examined in the next chapter.

It was suggested in the second chapter that, although no one would question the determination of the Nazis to turn the Jews into the untouchables of German society as quickly as practicable, it cannot be assumed that Hitler and his henchmen were consciously plotting the physical extermination of European Jewry from 1933 onwards. Much the same questions are posed by the search for *Lebensraum*. Because eastward expansion was the declared objective of the Nazis, it does not follow that Hitler or anyone else in the Nazi hierarchy was at all clear how this would come about. Nor does it follow that the acquisition of living space was uppermost in Hitler's thoughts at all times between 1924 and 1945, or that the reasons he advanced for eastward expansion in public speeches were, in the end, the decisive ones.

Hitler spoke most frequently and frankly about *Lebensraum* in the second half of the 1920s when it superseded anti-semitism as his favourite theme on public platforms. The arguments were pseudo-economic in nature. His starting point was the bland assumption that Germany could not possibly feed, within her present frontiers, a population of 74 millions increasing annually by 900,000. Birth control, as a means of alleviating this 'pressure', he flatly rejected on the ground that it would deprive Germany of her most creative intelligences—which he alleged were the fourth, sixth, seventh and ninth members of large families—while permitting the weak and worthless elements to stay alive. Emigration was equally unacceptable to him because it robbed Germany of her best racial stock. Internal colonization had more to commend it in his eyes but only up to a point as increased yields would quickly be swallowed up by rising demand. The obvious solution of increasing exports to pay for increased food imports could be dismissed as impracticable at a time of acute economic depression. Apart from that, it was militarily undesirable to make Germany too dependent on the outside world, disadvantaging her in wartime. On these highly dubious premises he arrived at the only conclusion that really interested him: 'If you want to feed the German people', he remarked, 'you must always give pride of place to the use of force. Without force you will never be able to give the German people the soil which is its due by virtue of its power, its numbers and the laziness of neighbouring peoples.'[37] That was the only honourable way of providing the Germans with food, land for resettlement of the growing population, and markets for German industry. In fact, once Germany was in the grip of economic crisis, *Lebensraum* as a major theme largely disappeared from Hitler's speeches. To all intents and purposes it was superseded in Nazi publications by the broader concept of the so-called *Grossraumwirtschaft*, that is the creation of a huge German-dominated market based on central and south-eastern Europe, for which there was much support in industrial and commercial circles in the early 1930s.

Indeed once in power the Nazis expended much time and effort not only in dismantling the Versailles Treaty—which could be interpreted as a first step towards a distant goal—but also in extending German commercial and political control over central and southeastern Europe, to create a closed economic system supplying Germany with raw materials and food and reducing her dependence on overseas imports. Even when the pace of German foreign policy quickened in 1937–8 and Hitler, returning to the theme of *Lebensraum*, spoke of the need to solve the German problem by 1943–5, he made no reference to Russia—the only country with vast empty spaces—but only to the desirability of seizing Austria and Czechoslovakia as soon as possible.[38] It almost seems as if living space had a purely symbolical quality for the Nazi Party and its leader, performing the function of 'an ideological metaphor';[39] a mystical *volkisch* goal, ostensibly the objective of all their efforts, was being used to justify in terms of first principles the feverish pace of a foreign policy directed at the attainment of rather different objectives. Of course, one must not push the argument too far. Living space and the continental economy were not mutually exclusive concepts. On the contrary, once war broke out, control of the raw materials and food of Russia became essential in the end as the continental economy ran increasingly into difficulties.

But it is surely significant that the Nazis failed to undertake any serious forward planning for the resettlement of Russia, which one would have expected if overpopulation had been as acute a problem as Nazi propagandists pretended. And when after the attack on Russia, the Nazis started to look for volunteers to take over farmland in the east, no more than a few hundred Germans were ready to return to the soil from which for decades so many of them had been only too glad to escape. Hitler's talk of resettlement in the east was archaic nonsense when he first took up the idea. By the late 1930s economic recovery had accentuated still further the drift to the towns. Nothing is more revealing than the Nazi appeals to Scandinavians and Dutchmen to undertake that *Drang nach Osten* which the Germans had reneged on.

Nor was the movement of populations, planned by Nazi agencies between 1941 and 1943, really compatible with Hitler's assurances in the past that

German industry would find the markets it needed in the east. For if the greater part of the indigenous Slav population was forcibly moved to settlements east of the Urals, how could the fourteen millions left behind, augmented by some seven million German settlers, have provided mass markets for highly-priced German industrial goods in return for cheaply-produced food and raw materials?[40]

These intriguing questions remained in the realms of pure theory. For from the start the eastern territories were in fact ruthlessly exploited in the interests of the German war effort. Russian plant scheduled for dismantlement as part of the plan to de-industrialize the east, was repaired and worked to capacity on behalf of the Germans. Representatives of the great industrial combines were soon deeply involved in the organized and ruthless exploitation of the conquered territories. And far from Slavs being transported eastwards, several millions of them were forcibly moved westwards to work in German industrial plant.

While one is driven to the conclusion that living space for an overpopulated nation turned out in practice to be no more than old colonial exploitation writ large, on the other hand the fanatical zeal with which Himmler and his SS set about their work in the east—with Hitler's full approval—suggests that had Germany won the war the repopulation programme, abandoned so abruptly after Stalingrad, might have been resuscitated. It is clear that what the more fanatical Nazis dreamt of in the east was so out of tune with the aspirations of an industrialized western society that it could only have been achieved by the forcible movement eastwards of Aryan settlers. All one can say for certain is that economic realities would have condemned their fantastic schemes to failure. Had they conquered all Europe including Britain, had they attained world mastery even, it is possible that the repercussions of forcible settlement to move the frontier eastwards would in the end have shaken that empire to pieces as effectively as enemy guns.

For many years historians assumed that Hitler was a continental animal whose sole aim was the domination of the European land mass from the Atlantic to the Urals. More recently this view has been challenged, notably by the German scholar Andreas Hillgruber.[41] A considerable number of German historians, following Hillgruber, now believe that Hitler had much wider ambitions.

Making Germany the dominant power in Europe with the help of Britain and Italy as allies was only the first stage in her rise to greatness. After that stage was completed, the Germans would build a powerful fleet and acquire colonial territory in Africa in preparation for the second stage—a bid for world domination, which might take the form of economic warfare or military confrontation with the United States either on her own or possibly in alliance with Britain. Originally, Hitler supposed that the struggle for world mastery would occur a hundred years after his death. Only when Britain displayed growing hostility to Hitler's policy in the late 1930s did he begin to think that war with Britain, still the world's greatest maritime power, might bring

Germany much closer to the final struggle for world mastery than he had thought likely.

How convincing is the evidence advanced in support of this re-interpretation? Before Hillgruber propounded his thesis, another historian had already argued that a bid for world domination was the logical inference to draw from Hitler's commitment to anti-semitism. If World Jewry threatened the entire universe, it must be defeated everywhere in the world not just in Germany; and to ensure this Germany would have to become the dominant world power.[42]

References to Germany's right to become a world power which are scattered throughout *Mein Kampf* and the so-called *Secret Book* (written in 1928 but never published) should, therefore, be taken seriously as an indication of Adolf Hitler's true ambition. Incidentally, though Hitler's interest in world power was very largely derived from memories of Wilhelmean policies and from Pan-German propaganda before and during the First World War, recent research suggests that Hitler's exposure to Geopolitics after the war greatly strengthened him in his ambitions.[43]

Supportive evidence for the world power thesis has come from an unexpected quarter—Hitler's architectural plans dating back to the mid-1920s.[44] These plans, it is alleged, supply positive proof of an ambition to make Germany not just the leading nation in Europe but the dominant world power. The same writer draws attention to innumerable speeches, hitherto neglected, which Hitler made to army and navy officers after 1933 and in which he constantly reiterated his belief in Germany's right to the status of a world power.

It has been proved beyond doubt that Hitler talked about Germany as a future world power to a much greater extent than historians previously supposed. However, on its own this is not conclusive proof of Hitler's intentions. One cannot exclude the possibility that much of his bombastic talk and exaggerated imagery was simply a device to reassure himself and his followers that he would make Germany count for something in international affairs again.

What suggests that there may have been more to it than idle talk were Hitler's views on naval expansion. Already in the course of 1937 he displayed a decided preference for super battleships, and committed the navy to building six of them. After the May crisis over Czechoslovakia in 1938, when Hitler finally admitted privately that he believed war with Britain and France to be a real possibility by 1941–2, the navy redoubled its efforts to be ready for this conflict. It is interesting, to say the least, that Hitler rejected proposals for an increase in cruiser strength and for the building of substantial numbers of U boats—both of which would have been obvious weapons for interrupting Britain's commerce and bringing her to her knees.[45] Instead, Hitler insisted, against naval advice, on the construction of a battle fleet to be ready for action by 1944 and not in 1948 as originally proposed by the navy. Furthermore, in January 1939 he gave the so-called Z Plan for the building of this huge fleet the highest priority in steel allocation despite the detrimental effects this was certain to have on the army and the airforce. It is difficult to explain this puzzling behaviour unless we are prepared to believe that he had world ambitions. No doubt the fleet he expected to have by 1944 would only have been capable of defending Europe against the Anglo-Saxons and might perhaps have persuaded Britain to change sides. But by laying firm foundations for the second stage before the first stage was over, Hitler would have placed himself in a strong position to concentrate on the building of a massive fleet for the decisive battles for world mastery against the United States.

Though the Z Plan was suspended at the outbreak of war, it was reactivated in the summer of 1940 after the fall of France. It is significant, too, that a proposal to make Trondheim in Norway the greatest naval base in the world with facilities for a huge battle fleet had Hitler's active support in 1940–41. At the same time naval command's forward planning was based on the premise that Germany would soon control a mid-African empire stretching from Senegal to the Congo, and would have at her disposal strong points in the Atlantic from Norway to Iceland. And during the interview with Oshima in 1941, referred to in the previous chapter, Hitler held out the prospect of a joint attack on the United States which, though it may have been no more than a manouevre to encourage the Japanese to commence military operations in the Pacific, might equally be construed as evidence that he was seriously thinking of moving on to stage two in the near future. Once the tide of war turned against Germany these dreams faded rapidly although not until February 1943 was all work on battleships, cruisers and aircraft carriers suspended. To sum up on Hitler's 'world ambitions': while it would be unwise to jump to conclusions at this stage of a continuing debate, at the very least it has been quite clearly established that Hitler took a much greater interest in global strategy than was generally supposed a few years ago.

A man who bears a heavy responsibility for mass murder might not strike one at first sight as being at all a religious person. Unfortunately, recorded history testifies only too eloquently to the melancholy fact that even those who have professed a belief in one of the great world religions have sometimes been guilty of the most appalling crimes: the murder of heretics by the Inquisition and the slaughter of Catholics by Protestant zealots are obvious examples that spring to mind in the case of the Christian faith. Hitler's crimes do not *per se* exclude the possibility that he had a religious streak in his make-up. Indeed, the records reveal that he was fascinated by the phenomenon of Christianity long after it ceased to have much meaning for him. The possibility that religious sentiments may have exerted some marginal influence on his behaviour cannot, therefore, be entirely discounted.

Hitler's early religious background was typical of Austrian Catholicism at the *fin de siècle*. His mother was a pious Catholic, his father a sceptic who appeared in church, resplendent in official uniform, only on the emperor's birthday and on the great feast of Corpus Christi. In the village inn Alois Hitler, though never a violent anti-clerical, spoke out against clerical obscurantism, praised the campaign Emperor Joseph II had waged against superstition in the eighteenth-century church and generally enjoyed the reputation of being progressively-minded and a supporter of 'free', that is secular, schools. In the long run paternal scepticism did more than his mother's conventional Catholicism to mould Hitler's attitude to religion. In the early years it was different. The power and ritual of the Catholic church in all its baroque splendour made a deep and probably lasting impression on the sensitive schoolboy. The ritual of the Nazi movement must have owed something at least to these early experiences of a mighty institution which was a past master in the art of using mysticism and pageantry to maintain its hold over millions of illiterate people. The two years he spent at the Lambach Stift, a Benedictine school in Upper Austria, were extremely happy ones. Hitler sang in choir, served on the altar and was so filled with admiration for the urbane and worldly-wise abbot that he thought of following in his footsteps.

The first turning-point in his religious life occurred at the *Realschule* in Linz where a narrow-minded and unimaginative secular priest, incapable of relating the Christian faith in any meaningful sense to the modern world, took the boys for religious education. Always a ringleader in schoolboy pranks, Hitler was well to the fore in the frequent clashes between exasperated priest and mischievious pupils. Hitler, tongue in cheek, usually questioned Father Francis Sales Schwarz most persistently about his outmoded interpretation of Biblical passages, verbal battles which the Führer recalled with relish forty years later. Schwarz epitomized for Hitler all that he loathed and detested in the clergy. By 1904, the year of his confirmation, Hitler's ill-nutured faith was fast waning. Contemporaries recalled years later how sullen and morose the fifteen-year old had been throughout a ceremony which he participated in merely to please the mother he doted on. After her death the last of the outward ties of conformity with the church were severed. In Vienna and in post-war Munich he had no contact with the church and consorted with people of little or no faith. But, like his father, he displayed no violent antipathy towards the church. In *Mein Kampf* he expressed grudging admiration for this mighty organization even when he took the Catholic clergy to task for their failure to protect the Germans in the Habsburg monarchy against the rising Slav tide. Clerical celibacy, which he later ridiculed, met with his approval in 1924; this he thought was the secret of the church's vitality and close personal relationship with the masses of the people. He expressly dissociated himself from eccentric *völkisch* groups such as that led by Ludendorff, a bigoted anti-Catholic who wished to revive Bismarck's campaign against the church with the avowed intention of placing it completely under state control. It was no accident that Ludendorff denounced Hitler later on as 'the servile tool of the romish priests'.

Of course, Hitler's restrained language was not an expression of flickering affection for the church of his youth, but simply reflected sound political instincts steering him away from divisive doctrinal disputation. In Vienna he had observed how Schönerer's 'Away from Rome' movement repelled many who longed for the union of Austria and Bohemia with Germany—the Greater

German dream of 1848–9. Hitler insisted at all times that what mattered was not a person's religious creed but his or her allegiance to the German race. Accordingly, the party programme promised religious freedom to all denominations provided that they did not threaten the state or militate against the moral sense of the Germanic race—ominious conditions for those who might be tempted on occasion to put God before Caesar—and committed the party to 'positive Christianity'.

It has even been argued that Hitler's anti-semitism was a natural product of Austrian Catholicism.[46] There is an element of truth in this, however small. Popular preachers, whom Hitler very probably heard as a boy, were often aggressively anti-semitic and did not hesitate to denounce Jews from the pulpit as 'atheists, materialists and capitalists'. Uneducated Catholics held Jews in abhorrence as 'Christ killers'. Not until Pope John XXIII swung the church onto a new axis more in tune with the aspirations of the modern world were offensive prayers for 'perfidious Jews' removed from the Good Friday liturgy. 'Confessional anti-semitism', as it has been called, was exploited ruthlessly and skilfully by Karl Lueger during Hitler's sojourn in Vienna. Though Hitler was repelled by the clericalism of the Christian Social Party and never joined it or any other party for that matter, he was impressed by the electoral appeal of anti-semitism. Hitler's own anti-semitism did not have its intellectual roots in Austrian Catholicism, as has been indicated already in this chapter. That does not mean that confessional anti-semitism may not have strengthened his own convictions. For what it is worth, Rosenberg and Frank both expressed the view during the Nuremberg Trial that some connection existed between their anti-semitism and the confessional variety.[47]

For many years Hitler tried to pretend that anti-semitism was in conformity with the mind of the church. In Dietrich Eckart's pamphlet, published in 1924, which purported to describe a conversation between the author and Hitler, the latter, described in the pamphlet as a believing Catholic, produced Biblical texts in support of the conspiracy theory put forward in the *Protocols of Zion*.[48] In *Mein Kampf*, written about the same time, Hitler bluntly declared that 'by defending myself against the Jew I am fighting for the work of the Lord.' And later, 'the folkish-minded man . . . has the sacred duty, each in his own denomination, of making people stop just talking superficially of God's will, and actually fulfilling God's will.'[49]

Speaking to two Catholic prelates in April 1933, Hitler still insisted that National Socialist policy towards the Jews was in conformity with Catholic teaching. Had not the church herself driven Jews into ghettos? The Jews were enemies of the church as well as of the state and by driving them out of public office and out of the professions he claimed to be doing no more than the church had done for fifteen hundred years. In the same interview Hitler vehemently denied the charge that he and his party were anti-Christian. Christianity would, he went on, be the cornerstone of the new regime as it was basic to the life of the individual. For confessional schools he had a special word of praise; character formation, in his opinion, depended on the inculcation of religious beliefs. In a revealing aside he added that he needed devout soldiers because they would give their all in battle.

On public occasions, too, he drew freely on Christian imagery to defend his policies, as for example in 1936, when he declared to a Nazi gathering: 'My Christian feeling directs me to our Lord and Saviour as a fighter. It directs me to the man who, at first alone, then surrounded by only a few followers, recognized these Jews and called on the people to fight against them. . . . I would be no Christian but a real devil if I did not feel sympathy and did not, as our Lord did two thousand years ago, take a stand against them.'[50]

Sheer expediency is a sufficient explanation of these utterances for it is hard to believe that Hitler had any respect left for the church's teachings. Yet only in October 1937 did he state privately that he was at least completely liberated from any remnant of his childhood concepts: 'I now feel as free as a foal in a pasture,' he declared on that occasion.[51] What that probably meant was that the vague feeling of guilt about his religion, common enough in the lapsed Catholic, lingered on in him well into the 1930s.

There is certainly no doubt that Hitler became increasingly hostile to the church in the last few years of his life. Whatever the reasons may have been, by 1941 he had become bitterly anti-clerical and in private conversation regularly trotted out the threadbare arguments of the nineteenth-century rationalist: Christianity retarded human progress; doctrines such as transubstantiation were totally at variance with modern science; the Bible was 'Jewish mumbo-jumbo'; belief in an afterlife sheer nonsense; and the clergy were at best fools, at worst crafty manipulators. Because he believed the church to be based on a lie, he was certain it must wither away in the next century or so. Like Stalin and Napoleon before him, Hitler appreciated the need to leave the church severely alone in wartime, and restrained the crudities of Bormann on this account. But after the end of hostilities he planned to abandon the church formally, as a gesture of defiance to usher in a new age when the concordat between Germany and the Holy See would be ended, Rome would be forbidden to interfere in German affairs, and the church would lose part of its revenues.

Hitler was no atheist. Religion fascinated him as the *Table Talk* reveals. He was probably a good deal more interested in the subject, crude though his understanding of theology was, than the atheist Stalin (an ex-seminary student) or the nominal Christians Churchill and Roosevelt. Undoubtedly Hitler believed in a God. 'The fact of the matter is we are weak creatures and there is a creative force. . . . To deny this is stupidity. Those who believe something are in a better position than those who believe in nothing.'[52] What kind of God, however? Probably a cross between a vague cosmic force and the rationalist God of his father. At all events, a remote figure who set the world in motion, did not interfere in human affairs, could not be influenced by prayer and was revealed to man through the works of nature.[53]

There was a great deal of the eighteenth-century rationalist in his belief that man's duty was to obey the law of nature. 'Piety for us', he once remarked, 'is to prostrate ourselves unconditionally before the divine laws of evidence as they unfold themselves to men and to respect them.'[54] Oddly enough, he strongly opposed any tendency on the part of the Nazi Party to turn itself into a sectarian movement; National Socialism must remain a sober realistic doctrine, based, so he believed, on a deep scientific understanding of the universe. But it can scarcely be doubted that the great rallies of pre-war days were pseudo-religious occasions both for those who listened to Hitler and for the Führer who drew great inspiration from them.

And regardless of what he said about the remoteness of God and His inaccessibility to prayer, there is no doubt that Hitler's series of successes in the early years of the regime strengthened his conviction that providence took a special interest in him and had marked him out for great things. Throughout the darkest days of the war he retained this unshakeable faith in himself. Speaking to one of his doctors after the bomb plot in July 1944, he remarked that 'if I ever doubted in my mission, which providence has given me, then I certainly have doubts no longer. Every day it seems to me a miracle that I came out of that pile of ruins alive.'[55] Only at the very end of his life did he lose this sense of absolute certainty about his own destiny.

Hitler's interest in architecture was no idle amusement to while away monotony. For forty years it was an abiding passion with him from early adolescence to the last days in the Berlin bunker where, within ten days of his suicide, he was still working into the small hours on plans for the rebuilding of Linz.

As an architect Hitler is not rated very highly by the experts. Self-taught and reasonably competent as a draughtsman, he lacked technical knowledge of the subject and good taste as well. His likes and dislikes were predictably unadventurous and conservative as Speer, his architect extraordinary, had ample opportunity to observe.[56] Judging by Hitler's earliest sketches, his personal preference seems to have been for the ornate and pompous neo-baroque style exemplified in the public buildings of late nineteenth-century Vienna which he studied minutely as an adolescent. On the other hand, his knowledge of and interest in the trends in post-First World War architecture was markedly deficient.

It would be a mistake to suppose that Hitler tried to impose his preference for neo-baroque on the architecture of the Third Reich. There was no 'Führer style'; pragmatism and flexibility was the rule here as in so much else. True, for public buildings Hitler invariably opted for the neo-classical style which, incidentally, was not specifically 'Nazi' but part of a much broader European movement. Only in the 1940s did traces of neo-baroque creep into the plans for the rebuilding of Berlin. Probably the influence of Paul Troost on Hitler was of crucial importance in this respect. For Hitler held this exponent of neo-classicism in the highest regard, made a beeline for Troost's studio whenever in Munich, and mourned his death in 1934 as a major tragedy. An element of the old evasiveness was also present in Hitler's attitude to other styles. Thus, although the stark geometry and concete and glass functionalism of the Bauhaus style was anathema to rank-and-file Nazis who equated it with 'cultural Bolshevism', Hitler never came out very clearly against this style. Indeed, when this style was extensively used in the building of factories, he raised no objection whatsoever and was even impressed with the results. Therefore, in practice a variety of styles flourished in Nazi Germany. Public buildings were neo-classical in style; factories were often pure Bauhaus; in small towns a folkish style, which emphasised regional differences and historical diversity, was freely adopted; and in new military establishments it was not uncommon to see a romanesque style.

What function did architecture play in the intellectual world of Adolf Hitler? That is the important question to ask ourselves in the context of this chapter. The psychological dimension catches the eye immediately. While still a small-time Bavarian politician in the 1920s with no hope of power, he spent endless hours designing public buildings. Designs for the triumphal arch and the massive domed meeting hall standing at either end of a broad avenue in central Berlin, a project on which Speer started work in the late 1930s, were worked out by Hitler in 1925–6. A French psychiatrist has referred, rightly, to Hitler's 'pseudo-vocation . . . the external manifestation, the socialized expression of a more profound aspiration which constituted a vital need, that of remodelling the world'.[57] One is strengthened in this belief by the fact that his interest was quite obviously in design rather than execution even if he did sometimes wander around building sites inspecting progress. For him the visual impression a building made was the decisive factor, not the technique of construction. Nor, apart from a fleeting interest in workers' tenements in Vienna before the First World War, did he make any attempt to use architecture to improve living conditions for the mass of the German people. Primarily, architecture remained a means of satisfying adolescent fantasies and of reassuring himself that he had a great future ahead of him when all the signs and portents pointed in the opposite direction.

However, architecture was most definitely not a substitute for power. Indeed, one is almost tempted to say that he sought power in order to realize his architectural ambitions; to become the 'master builder of the Third Reich' was the alternative to being an architect as he once remarked, admittedly in jocular mood, to a close crony.[58] To this end he devoted much time, energy and very considerable resources after 1933. On the very evening of his appointment as chancellor he announced his decision to have the chancellery rebuilt. In the next few months he was busy conferring with the Berlin local authorities about municipal reconstruction, studying models for the rebuilding of Munich and ordering plans to be drawn up for a huge stadium at Nuremberg.

Foreign political success did not divert Hitler in the least. Speaking to Speer about his plans for Berlin in the summer of 1936, just after the Rhineland coup, he insisted that 'these buildings are more important than anything else.'[59] The most striking testimony to the very high priority building occupied in his thinking is the correlation between the gathering pace of German policy in the winter of 1937–8 and the commencement of a gigantic building programme which never really came to a halt until the spring of 1945. Despite the problem of finding men and materials when rearmament was in full swing, Hitler insisted that work commence at once. After the victory in the west in 1940 a euphoric Führer added to these difficulties by ordering reconstruction work to begin on another twenty-seven cities in addition to the four 'Führer cities'—Berlin, Munich, Nuremberg and Linz.

To rationalize this building mania, Hitler employed various arguments. 'Superdimensionality' was a striking characteristic of his public buildings style. The bridge over the Elbe river, the Nuremberg stadium and the east-west avenue in Berlin, to take a few of the more obvious examples, had to be the largest in the world because size, so Hitler argued, was indispensable for restoring a proper sense of self-respect to the German people. 'Why always the biggest? I do this to restore to each individual German his self-respect', he declared in a speech to building workers in January 1939. 'In a hundred areas I want to say to the individual: we are not inferior, on the contrary we are the complete equal of every other nation.'[60]

Secondly, it must be remembered that of all the arts Hitler rated architecture the highest because through monuments in stone a civilization expressed its national values. Triumphal arches and imposing facades represented the will of the people and the power of the state *vis-à-vis* other peoples. The greatness of the huge Reich of one hundred million Germans, which he intended to create, could only find fitting expression in gigantic monuments built of granite to last for thousands of years. For, as he once remarked to Frank *à propos* of the huge stadium he was planning for Nuremberg, the dimensions must be so gigantic that 'even the pyramids will be dwarfed by the masses of concrete and the colossal stone edifices. . . . I am building for eternity for . . . we are the last Germany.'[61]

Finally, public buildings of hugh proportions had a role to play in the consolidation of the regime. Citizens surrounded by impressive symbols of state power would be intimidated by them and would be less likely to criticize the regime. Furthermore, if in the future the German people should pass through periods of doubt and uncertainty about their historic role the sight of public monuments, possibly even in ruins by this time, would hopefully inspire them once more to greatness.

The element of political calculation is evident enough in some of these arguments. Yet one is still left wondering in the end whether the reasons he advanced in public and in private add up to a completely rational explanation of the phenomenon. Was his building mania, like his tenacious belief in Social Darwinism, part of an elaborate defence mechanism which helped him overcome fears and doubts about his own mission and about his ability to hold on to the conquests he had made and intended to make in the future?

It is difficult to exaggerate the influence Richard Wagner exerted on Hitler, as one of the most recent biographers of the Führer has observed.[62] Many

Germans who grew to manhood before the First World War revered Wagner as the one man who towered over his generation, the romantic artist who symbolized for youth the spirit of revolt against the smug respectability of the bourgeois world and personified the 'man of genius' alienated from that world and achieving great deeds in isolation from it. Hitler's admiration for the man and his works was as longstanding as his passion for building and is equally revealing in terms of his own personality.

As a boy he first encountered Wagner's music and drama in Linz at the age of twelve when he was captivated by a performance of *Lohengrin*. A few years later in 1906, accompanied by his friend August Kubizek, he attended a performance of *Rienzi*, an opera based on the story of Cola di Rienzi who saved medieval Rome from aristocratic tyranny and nobly declined the royal crown, accepting only the title of tribune of the people. For his pains Rienzi was assassinated by the aristocrats, a proleptic hint of the fate the Führer narrowly avoided thirty-eight years later. After the performance Hitler took his friend up to the top of a hill overlooking Linz and held him spellbound with wild talk of leading the German people towards a great future. One might well doubt the authenticity of this tale were it not for Hitler's comment to Ley in 1938 that the music of Rienzi inspired him to believe that he would succeed 'in uniting the Reich and making it great'.[63] At any rate, the Rienzi overture was always played at the beginning of the party congress, suggesting that Hitler at least wanted to establish some kind of connection between the opera and his own soaring ambitions.

What was it that Hitler discovered in the music and drama of Richard Wagner? Again, it is the psychological dimension that catches the eye. It is probably no coincidence that his first encounter with Wagnerian opera was around the time he was clashing with his father about his own future. In Wagner's music Hitler heard 'the rhythms of a bygone world',[64] a pagan world where man lived heroically according to the law of blood, a clean world free from the spirit of Jewish 'commercialism' and lust for gold, a world where man grappled with the forces of savage nature and lived in a state of mental intoxication.

In this world Hitler could recapture the feeling of omnipotence of the small child and play at being the triumphant hero governed by his own code of conduct and taking his revenge, first on his father and later on the smug bourgeois world which had refused him proper recognition. Hanfstaengl, who often played Wagner selections for Hitler, testified to the mesmeric effect the music had on Hitler, and concluded, rightly, that it became an integral part of his personality.

The magic spell of Wagner was never broken in Hitler's case. From the early 1920s Bayreuth became a Nazi shrine and Winifred Wagner, who directed the festival after her husband's sudden death in 1930, became a personal friend of the Führer. After 1933 Bayreuth came into its own as the Führer's 'court theatre' and enjoyed lavish support from public funds, removing for the first time the shadow of insolvency which had hung over the festival. On Hitler's own admission the ten days of the festival were 'the most blessed time of my existence. . . . On the day following the end of the Bayreuth Festival . . . I'm gripped by a great sadness, as when one strips the Christmas tree of its ornaments.'[65] He was not just an estatic spectator either, but took a close personal interest in the minutest details of the productions and discussed them far into the night with the Wagner family.

Nor should one overlook the influence of Wagner and his circle on the formation of Hitler's political philosophy. In his political writings and through the medium of the *Bayreuther Blätter*, the 'master of Bayreuth' poured forth a vitriolic anti-semitism, expounded his belief in Social Darwinism, expressed anti-democratic views and popularized the works of Houston Chamberlain. Given Hitler's early admiration for the great composer, it is legitimate to assume that Wagner's opinions on other matters must have carried great weight with the young Hitler.

Above all, Hitler owed to Wagner the arrogant assumption that the artist by virtue of his genius had an absolute right to pontificate on every subject under the sun including politics. Not for Hitler the mundane definition of politics as collective action to achieve limited objectives. He believed in the 'dictatorship of genius', in the artist intervening like a philosopher-king to impose his will on the people and lead them to some distant and heroic goal.

In the political sphere Hitler was manifestly a man of the theatre. This is strongly suggested not only by the external management of party rallies and other pseudo-religious occasions in the Nazi calendar when light, sound and colour were blended together to make the maximum impact on the eye and ear of the beholder. At a deeper and more personal level it seems not improbable that Hitler identified the dramatic political coups of the 1930s in his own mind with the timeless deeds of his Wagnerian heroes. It is interesting that, returning by train from his triumphant tour of the reoccupied Rhineland, Hitler had Wagner records played to him. Without making too much of one small incident, one wonders whether he might not have been attempting to apply to his own situation the words Wagner wrote eighty years before about his own art form: 'When music and drama are in harmony true art is at once released from the world of reality, an artistic balance is established between reality and the world of ideals, physical appearances are thereby separated from reality by a wide gulf but in so doing through the language of the soul these [appearances] are brought nearer to our inner being than by any other art form.'[66]

At the beginning of the chapter the point was made that Hitler's philosophy is not in itself a sufficient explanation of the rise to power of National Socialism. At the risk of creating fresh confusion in the reader's mind, it must now be admitted that the use of the phrase 'principled opportunism' to describe the interaction between tactics and beliefs in Hitler's case, though representing an advance on the Rauschning–Heiden position, leaves many perplexing questions unanswered. How can one distinguish between occasions when Hitler's beliefs were a decisive factor in deciding a course of action and other occasions when his beliefs were nothing more than dialectical weapons to overcome opposition to his policies? There is no easy formula for resolving this riddle any more than there is an answer to the fundamental question of the relationship between his beliefs and his personal pathology; did he cling tenaciously to the notion of life as a grim struggle with the prizes going to the strong basically in order to overcome his own sense of insecurity? Could the same be said of his interest in architecture and Wagnerian opera?

The complexity of the problem is illustrated by the situation in 1937, a year which seems to have been critical in several respects for Hitler's personal development. In the autumn he declared himself ready to run grave risks, if need be, to secure *Lebensraum* for Germany; around this time he boasted that no vestiges of conventional Catholicism remained in him; and, thirdly, he expressed fears of an early death. What relationship, if any, existed between expansionism, freedom from religious guilt and intimations of mortality? Living space may by now have become little more than a convenient catch phrase to justify in terms of first principles a policy dictated largely by the military and economic realities facing Germany in the late 1930s. Is it, however, conceivable that the radicalization of policy in 1938, particularly in respect of the Jews, was only possible after he had abandoned lingering feelings of personal guilt? How important, then, was fear of death as a determinant of policy? Could this fear have some bearing on the frenzied pace of Hitler's building programme in 1938 as well as on the course of German foreign policy?

In other words, how far do the 'formative ideas' examined in this chapter really explain the Nazi phenomenon? As well as the fundamental military, economic and political reasons for the gathering pace of Nazi policy, the physical health of the Führer and his personal psychology cannot be ignored. It is to these aspects of the Hitler phenomenon that we turn in the final chapter.

5

A sick man?

Since his death in 1945 the state of Hitler's internal organs has attracted some attention among people who prefer to look for a rational explanation of the horrors of the Nazi era in the person of the Führer rather than in the state of society that made the Nazi phenomenon possible. As we have seen in an earlier chapter, ex-generals, writing to protect the good name of the army, were loath to admit that the defeat of Germany was due at least in part to their own lack of political insight at a time when Hitler might conceivably have been stopped. Instead they prefer to blame everything on one man's wilful stubbornness and woefully inadequate military expertise. Similarly, some of the ex-Nazis who ventured into print decided that the fault did not really lie with National Socialism—often depicted by such writers as a healthy recrudescence of national feeling scarcely to be wondered at in a defeated and demoralized country—but with a handful of evil advisers who exerted a malevolent influence over the easygoing and amiable Führer who much preferred petting young children and animals to the waging of aggressive warfare. Medical men, unlike soldiers and party members, have no axes to grind and no reputations to defend.[1] Nevertheless, in trying to unravel the mystery of Hitler's illnesses they also contribute to the 'personality cult', proceeding as they do on the unspoken assumption that a major reason for the disaster that befell Germany was some organic disorder incapacitating the head of state at crucial moments in his country's history.

The earliest diagnosis by a medical man in the immediate post-war period suggested that Hitler was not suffering from any serious physical disorder at all. Dr Douglas M. Kelley, the clinical psychiatrist at Nuremberg prison who interrogated Hitler's medical advisers immediately after the collapse of Germany, concluded that Hitler's trouble had been largely mental not organic. His diagnosis of hysteria remained unchallenged until 1963 when Johann Recktenwald claimed that Hitler had suffered from Parkinsonism. Three years later Hans Dietrich Röhrs, who worked in the Nazi health service, maintained that Hitler had been in sound physical condition but had been systematically poisoned by his personal physician, Theodor Morell. Since then three indefatigible researchers, Werner Maser, David Irving and John Toland, have unearthed further material (some of it unavailable in the immediate post-war period) which casts more light on the mystery.

It seems fairly safe to assume that when Hitler came to power in 1933 he was in a very reasonable state of health for a man of forty-four. He only began to worry about his health in 1935 when he started to suffer from stomach pains and flatulence. The causes of these disorders were almost certainly a combination of the effects of a vegetarian diet, a badly-ordered daily routine and the inevitable strain of high office. In 1931, deeply disturbed by the suicide of his niece Geli Raubal, Hitler turned against meat for no very obvious reason. Unfortunately, in this as in so much else, Hitler was his own diagnostician and sought no medical advice whatsoever. Consequently his diet was both inadequate in bulk—of which he often complained—and unbalanced.

Secondly, Hitler's habit of turning night into day placed a strain on his constitution in the long run. Normally he retired for the night at 3 or 4 a.m., slept through the morning and arose shortly before midday. The practice of retiring late still did not cure the insomnia from which he suffered all his life. To make matters worse, after 1937 he took virtually no exercise, though in his youth he had been a good skier and cyclist according to his military records. As his mother died of cancer, Hitler not unnaturally began to fear that he, too, suffered from that disease, a fear which must have been considerably heightened by the appearance of a growth on his vocal chords. In the event this turned out to be a harmless polyp removed by surgery in June 1935.

The stomach pains grew in intensity throughout 1936. Neither SS doctor Ernst-Robert Grawitz nor Professor Bergmann of the Berlin Charité were able to cure them. That year Hitler came into contact with Theodor Morell, a medical practitioner who was to exert the most profound influence on him. Morell, brought to the Berghof in the first instance by Hoffmann, Hitler's photographer, quickly established himself in the Führer's favour and by Christmas was officially designated personal physician to Hitler. It is undeniable that all who had dealings with this stocky, short-sighted middle-aged man of unprepossessing appearance and unhygienic habits disliked him intensely. After the war medical colleagues were quick to denounce him as a charlatan, an unfair judgement which has been widely accepted thanks to the deserved popularity of Hugh Trevor-Roper's classic account of the closing months of the war.[2] Morell's reputation has not been assisted either by his adroitness in financial affairs. Before meeting Hitler, Morell had built up a fashionable and lucrative practice on Berlin's Kurfürstendamm. After 1936 he used his privileged position to construct a vast empire based on the manufacture of patent medicines from which he netted a large fortune.[3]

After examining his new patient, Morell sent specimens to a Professor Nissle who diagnosed an infection of the intestinal tract. To treat this complaint Morell prescribed Mutaflor tablets.[4] At first the treatment was highly successful. The pains abated and a skin eczema on the leg of some years' standing was healed into the bargain. The Führer was able to eat more and partake of heavier dishes. Not unnaturally he was extravagant in his praise of the miracle worker who had kept his promise to cure the Führer 'inside a year'. However, within a few months Hitler was again troubled by epigastric pain especially severe after meals. This time Morell diagnosed meteorism, that is distension of the abdomen caused by gas produced in the intestines. To relieve the flatulence, Morell prescribed Köster's anti-gas pills which it appears Grawitz had originally recommended to Hitler. By the end of 1937 Hitler, who as late as 1934 shared the natural reluctance of all mankind to visit the physician, had turned into a hypochondriac obsessed with the feeling that time was running out for him. Convinced that he had a serious heart complaint, he avoided all exercise. For that reason he ceased to visit the so-called 'tea house' built at fabulous cost on the Kehlstein, a peak above Berchtesgaden commanding a breathtaking view of the Austrian Alps, on the grounds that the elevation and the high-speed lift installed in the rock face seriously restricted his breathing.[5]

It is at this point that Hitler's state of health becomes interesting for the historian. Because Hitler was absolutely convinced that he alone could realise the grandiose plans he had in store for Germany, it is tempting to suppose that his belief that his health was failing obliged him to accelerate the pace of his policy even before his armies were ready to march. It would be going too far to maintain that stomach pains and heart palpitations can explain the seizure of Austria and Czechoslovakia or the attack on Poland, or even that these were a factor of major importance, any more than Napoleon III's gallstones can—despite Emile Zola's observation—be seen as the major reason for the collapse of the French Empire in war. All the same, Hitler's preoccupation with his health was a factor in the situation which should not be ignored just because it cannot be precisely quantified. At the very least, signs of illness probably confirmed him in the belief that he must act in the near future and contributed their share to events which have changed the face of our world.

Not until 1941 did Hitler suffer any serious illness. Then, at the height of the attack on Russia, an official visiting Hitler's headquarters at the Wolfsschanze observed how pale, weak and tired he looked and heard him complain at dinner of shivering and fainting fits, attacks of nausea and diarrhoea and dysentry. This illness, which lasted a fortnight from the end of July to early August, may have been caused by the bad siting of the headquarters on marshy ground which attracted plagues of insects and probably infected the water supply. Morell diagnosed oedema in the calves and shin bones and treated the complaint with cardiazol and coramin injections. In the middle of August, in the course of a routine examination, an electrocardiograph revealed progressive coronary arteriosclerosis, not an unexpected condition in a man of fifty-two but potentially dangerous. Morell treated this condition with daily injections of prostrophanta and strophantin to which he added cardiozol and coramine to correct a circulatory weakness. By the end of 1941 Hitler appears to have recovered pretty well from this illness.

In the winter of 1942–3 associates began at last to notice signs of physical deterioration in Hitler. Dr Hanskarl von Hasselbach, another of Hitler's medical advisers, remarked in his post-war testimony how young Hitler had looked before 1940; between 1940 and 1943 he began to look his age; and after 1943 he suddenly started to look considerably older.[6] His eyes lost their old sparkle and became dull and protruding. He now walked with a slight stoop, the result of a slight kyphosis of the dorsal spine. His left leg and arm commenced to shake and if he had to stand for any length of time his knees also began to tremble. His voice lost its old resonance. He repeated himself more often though he remained as mentally alert as ever. He appeared noticeably more excitable than in the past, reacting more irascibly when displeased and clinging more tenaciously than ever to opinions even when they were patently ill-founded.

It is unnecessary to recount the story of Hitler's steady deterioration in health over the next two years.[7] Suffice to say that by the spring of 1945 he was rapidly approaching the point of complete collapse. A staff officer visiting him in Berlin on 25 March was appalled by the phantom facing him despite advance warning that the Führer was a quite different man from the self-confident dictator of 1939.

> The Hitler of those days was not to be compared at all to the wreck of a man to whom I reported . . . and who stretched out a weak and trembling hand. . . . Physically he was a frightful picture. He dragged himself along slowly and painfully from his living quarters to the conference room in the bunker, the upper part of his body thrust forward, his legs drawn along behind. He had lost his sense of balance, if he stopped on the way [a distance of 75–100 feet] he had either to sit down on one of the benches provided for this purpose or else hold on to the person with whom he was talking. . . . His eyes were bloodshot; despite the fact that all documents submitted to him were typed on special machines with letters three times the normal size, he still needed his glasses. Saliva often dripped from the corners of his mouth—a horrible and pathetic sight.[8]

What were the causes of Hitler's physical deterioration? It has been argued, principally by Johannes Recktenwald, that Hitler suffered from post-encephalitic Parkinsonism.[9] On the basis of Franz Jetzinger's account of Hitler's youth, Recktenwald concluded that Hitler must have contracted epidemic encephalitis from his six-year old brother Edmund who died, ostensibly of measles, in 1900. After a period of remission with no external symptoms, late Parkinsonism emerged in Hitler forty years later. Encephalitis was, Recktenwald alleges, the real cause of Hitler's poor record at Linz *Realschule* after consistently good school reports from the primary schools, and not deliberate sabotage by the boy of his father's plans to make him an official. Recktenwald thinks it significant that when quarreling with his father about his future, Hitler fell down unconscious on one occasion, in other words he described in *Mein Kampf* symptoms of his illness which a layman would be unlikely to manufacture. In support of his general diagnosis Recktenwald draws attention to what he claims are characteristic symptoms of Parkinsonism displayed by Hitler—his habitual sleeplessness, poor eyesight, proneness to uncontrollable paroxysms of rage, the stooping frame, shambling gait, fixed gaze, slightly protruding eyes, lack of saliva—he drank inordinate amounts of mineral water in the 1920s and early 1930s—and his abnormal sweating—Hitler claimed to lose four to seven pounds every time he spoke in public. The stomach pains Recktenwald thinks were caused by 'spastic vegetative neurosis', an organic complaint caused by the same brain infection which produced the encephalitis. The skin discolouration remarked upon by several observers of Hitler was, he believes, caused by 'vegetative neurosis', not encephalitis.

Much of Recktenwald's terminology and his views, particularly in respect of 'vegetative neurosis,' are not consonant with modern medical opinion. Nor can one ignore the testimony of Hitler's own doctors who had the incomparable advantage of seeing him at close quarters. In the winter of 1942–3 a neurologist, Professor Maximilian de Crinis, concluded from observation of German newsreels that Hitler was indeed suffering from Parkinsonism (paralysis agitans). But on discussing his diagnosis with Hasselbach and with Karl Brandt, a doctor who had known Hitler since 1934, de Crinis failed to convince either. Nor did Dr Ludwig Stumpfegger, who replaced Brandt in 1944, accept this diagnosis. Neither did Morell. The reports of his examination of Hitler's central nervous system reveal no evidence of Parkinsonism.[10] Certainly Morell prescribed eukoval and supavarin but simply to alleviate Hitler's stomach pains, not to treat Parkinsonism. And it might be thought significant that he did not treat his patient with belladona 606, the drug then commonly used in such cases.

Having said this, one still cannot exclude the possibility that Parkinsonism was the major cause of Hitler's physical deterioration. The fact is that Hitler displayed too many of the major symptoms associated with Parkinsonism for this diagnosis to be categorically rejected. And, significantly enough, in an interview some years after Hitler's death, Hasselbach himself admitted that he might have been mistaken.[11]

Röhr's diagnosis, first published in 1966, was much more sensational. In his opinion Hitler's deteriorating condition was directly related to the drugs prescribed by Morell. This diagnosis was subscribed to by Brandt, Hasselbach and Dr Erwin Giesing, the latter an ear, nose and throat specialist, called in to treat Hitler after the bomb plot. But all three were extremely hostile to Morell and one cannot exclude the possibility that their judgment was affected by deep resentment of Morell's monopoly of power over Hitler. After the war they unanimously denounced Morell as a charlatan who used untried drugs on the Führer. It is easy to see how Morell's secretive nature and blunt refusal to discuss 'patient A' (as he called Hitler) with medical colleagues would give rise to suspicions of a man so cordially and universally detested. Against these accusations has to be set the fact that of the thirty drugs used on Hitler, many are still in use while others have simply been replaced with the advance of medical science.[12] The important point is that in very few cases can the accusation of using fantastic secret drugs be substantiated.[13]

One drug in particular has been the subject of much controversy—the Köster anti-gas pills for the relief of flatulence. They were supposed to be taken three times a day before meals, the dosage being two to four pills. And as they contained both strychnine and strophine it was thought undesirable to exceed the daily maximum of twelve pills. However, we know that Hitler was an inveterate tablet addict, and apparently took between six and sixteen of these tablets each day. With Hitler's symptoms very much in mind, Röhrs points out that strophine poisoning can impair the eyesight through weakening the coordination of the eye muscles, turns the skin red and can cause cramp in the stomach and intestinal canal. The effect of strychnine is cumulative and can cause jaundice through damaging the liver. In the autumn of 1944 Giesing, Brandt and Hasselbach were apparently so convinced of the potential danger of these pills that they risked a major confrontation with Hitler in the hope of securing Morell's dismissal. The attempt failed. The Führer dispensed with their services and kept Morell. The latter, perhaps significantly, advised Hitler against taking Köster pills again. It is, of course, perfectly possible that in their eagerness to get rid of Morell they may have overestimated the dangers to Hitler's health from these pills.[14] Even so, one cannot exclude the possibility that the rapid changes in mood observed in Hitler in the last weeks of his life as he lurched from deep pessimism to euphoric outbursts were, in part at least, withdrawal symptoms, the inevitable result of overdependence on drugs, which brings us back to the subject of Morell's treatment of Hitler.

Morell has been severely criticized on the grounds that he concentrated on the symptoms of Hitler's complaint, that is stomach pains but failed to treat the underlying causes, that is the badly-balanced diet and irregular way of life of which Morell must have been well aware. A reasonable enough point until one remembers that Hitler was no ordinary patient to be ordered about by a mere medical practitioner. He was as opinionated about medicine as anything else. While reposing more confidence in Morell than in other doctors, he did not trust him entirely. He constantly argued with Morell and delighted to catch him out when discussing dosages—not a very difficult trick as Hitler's memory was exceptionally good and Morell's rather poor. Indeed, Hitler only took medicine if he personally approved of it, and not otherwise. Even into medicine he introduced the concept of struggle maintaining that 'when the power to fight for one's own health is no longer there, the right to life is ended in this world of struggle.'[15] Faced by such a strong-minded patient who insisted on remaining on his feet as long as possible, Morell had little alternative but to use drugs to keep him going and alleviate his condition. When Brandt discovered to his horror in 1944 how large the dosages prescribed by Morell had actually been, he remonstrated with him. Morell's simple defence was that he 'had no choice'. This is not an excuse for him. The moral weakness of a doctor afraid to speak the truth is revealed all too clearly in that damaging admission. But it is at least an explanation of his conduct which presents him in a less odious light and illustrates only too poignantly the corruption of morals which dictatorship leads to. This was no malignant charlatan spinning his devious web round a hapless dictator but a sycophantic careerist trapped in a situation beyond his control.

Kelley's diagnosis of Hitler as 'a psycho-neurotic of an obsessive and hysterical type' has much to be said in its favour.[16] True, there is no evidence that Hitler was suffering from shell shock when he was sent to Pasewalk Hospital in October 1918 following a gas attack on his salient of the front. Even if he was referred to a consultant psychiatrist, Professor Edmund Forster—and that is uncertain—this would in itself be inconclusive; so little was known about the effects of poison gas that Hitler's symptoms on admission might have misled the hospital staff. What seems certain is that the news of the revolution in Germany early in November brought on an attack of hysteria. 'Again everything went black before my eyes', he wrote six years later, describing the moving scene in the ward when the hospital chaplain informed the patients that Emperor William II had abdicated.[17] Hitler recovered quickly and was discharged on 19 November fit for active service.

During this hysterical relapse it has been alleged that Hitler experienced an hallucination which led him to believe that he had been summoned from on high to save Germany.[18] This seems unlikely. For one thing, he took no part whatsoever in the revolution, which seems a little strange in a man who had just received a categorical instruction to save his country. Secondly, the obvious propaganda value of the story, recounted on numerous occasions by Hitler and his immediate entourage, suggests a more likely explanation of the 'hallucination'.

The trembling of the left arm and leg, a symptom which first appeared after the abortive 1923 putsch, fits in very well with the hysteria diagnosis. The prison doctor at Landsberg believed that the pains in Hitler's arm were 'caused by a traumatic nervous irritation' not at all surprising in a man emotionally spent and full of black despair when arrested.[19] Significantly, the symptom disappeared once the trial was going well for Hitler, and only reappeared twenty years later in 1942–3 when Hitler began to suspect that he could not win the war whatever he did. It is true that Hitler's doctors did not observe any phobias or obsessions in him, nor did they detect a globus hystericus, that is the ball-in-the-throat sensation characteristic of a hysterical case. Nevertheless they did not exclude the possibility that the epigastric pain might have been of a hysterical origin.[20]

Finally, one other possibility must be considered–that the rapid deterioration in Hitler's condition in the last three or four years of his life was the direct result of the progressive arteriosclerosis first detected in 1941.[21] As a leading psychohistorian recently pointed out, arteriosclerosis of the brain can produce the same symptoms as Parkinsonism, that is trembling of the limbs, sleeplessness and slow physical reactions. Paranoid tendencies, particularly delusions of grandeur, might, it has been suggested recently, be attributed to this disease.[22] It would be of inestimable value for historians if a team of medical men could be prevailed upon to examine all the available evidence on Hitler and express an expert opinion on his condition. Whatever conclusion such a body arrived at, it is certain that due regard would have to be paid to the total situation in which Hitler found himself; his medical condition cannot be isolated from the general background of his last years. And it is a matter of record that for nearly three and a half years from June 1941 to December 1944 he lived for long periods at his headquarters at the Wolfsschanze with brief intervals at Winniza in the Ukraine and infrequent breaks at the Berghof. At his headquarters Hitler insisted on working and sleeping underground, taking no exercise whatsoever apart from brief afternoon walks with his Alsatian dog, Blondi. And towards the end he enjoyed only two or three hours sleep a day. In the Berlin bunker he retired in the early hours after the midnight military conference. At 6 a.m. he was up again for another conference. After breakfast he played briefly with one of Blondi's puppies, which he was trying to train, and then back to bed. Air raid sirens soon had him up and after that he remained active to the end of the day. On top of enormous physical strain Hitler faced the mental strain of a gradually worsening military situation after the fall of Stalingrad. The shame of certain defeat was especially severe for a man who had succeeded in forcing events to conform to his preconceived notions for so long. Now stark reality was breaking into his hermetically-sealed world and could not be conjured out of existence by rhetoric. To sum up: an unhealthy life style, the nerve-wracking strain of imminent defeat, the ill-effects of taking large amounts of potent drugs over a long period, progressive arteriosclerosis, and either Parkinsonism or hysteria combined together to produce a marked physical deterioration in Hitler after 1943.

For the last forty years psychiatrists have shown a keen interest in the personality of Adolf Hitler if only because the popular image of a ranting, raving and carpet-biting Führer has attracted the interest of a branch of medicine particularly concerned with the treatment of diseases of the mind. Hitler's mental state, like his physical condition, remains a matter of very considerable controversy. The old tag, *quot homines, tot sententiae*, fits the position exactly. Walter Langer, the American psychiatrist whose study of Hitler aroused much interest a few years ago, describes Hitler variously as a 'neurotic psychopath' and a 'hysterical psychopath'.[23] For Erich Erikson Hitler is a 'psychopathic paranoid' whereas the German psychiatrist Wilhelm Trauher believes him to have been schizophrenic.[24] To Erich Fromm Hitler appears to have been 'a very sick man ... on the borderline between sanity and insanity'.[25] And for Robert Waite he was a borderline personality occupying the twilight zone between neurosis and psychosis.[26]

A word of warning here. Too much importance should not be attached to these labels in trying to understand Hitler—or any other patient for that matter, as psychiatrists would be the first to admit. Labels are nothing more than rough-and-ready approximations, a kind of psychiatric shorthand to indicate a general area of mental disturbance, and are in no sense to be taken as an accurate and final assessment of a patient's mental condition.

It is not difficult to demonstrate that Hitler was a 'fanatical or neurotic psychopath'. The writer conducted a simple experiment in 1971 with the help of a psychiatrist colleague which showed this quite clearly.[27] Three standard questionnaires, the Eysenck Personality Inventory, Fould's Hysteroid-Obsessoid Questionnaire and the Hostility-Direction of Hostility Questionnaire, were answered by the writer on the basis of his knowledge of Hitler's personality. Subsequently the colleague classified these findings using the Kurt Schneider system and allocating to each of Schneider's ten categories points on the scale 0 to 10.[28] On this basis the colleague suggested that 'fanatical psychopath' was a description which could well be applied to Hitler.

But that is, of course, a very general description which does not pretend to explore the patient's mental state in depth. Certainly, many much more ingenious explanations have been offered, to which we must now turn. At this point the reader may well feel that it is sheer arrogance for a historian with no training in psychiatry to attempt any evaluation of the various opinions expressed about Hitler's health by trained psychiatrists and psychologists. This would indeed be an insuperable obstacle were their diagnoses based on first-hand knowledge of the patient. In fact, only once did Hitler submit himself to any kind of psychological testing, and that only briefly in 1944 when testing was very much in its infancy.[29] Psychiatrists who have tried to understand Hitler's personality have had to rely for their knowledge of the man on such scanty historical evidence as is available and have drawn their conclusions by analogy with cases in their immediate experience.

While a historian must obviously respect opinions based on clinical observation of patients, he need feel no inhibitions in commenting on the use—or misuse—of historical evidence. Perched precariously on the narrow ledge of historical truth, a historian can, hopefully, make some meaningful comment in the continuing debate about Hitler's mental state without necessarily committing himself wholeheartedly to a particular diagnosis. Indeed, at the present stage in the debate he would probably be exceedingly foolish to do so. Before embarking on an examination of the various theories advanced about Hitler, one should be mindful of the limits within which psychoanalytical insights are valid. Psychiatrists cannot offer any causal explanation even of a patient's behaviour. Erich Erikson expressed this most clearly when he observed of a clinical case in his charge:

> We cannot escape the conviction that the meaning of an item which may be 'located' in one of the three processes [that is, the somatic, the ego and the societal] is co-determined by its meaning to the other two. An item in one process gains relevance by giving significance to and receiving significance from items in the others . . . of the catastrophe described. . . . We know no 'cause'. Instead we find a convergence in all three processes of specific intolerances which make the catastrophe retrospectively intelligible, retrospectively probable. The plausibility thus gained does not permit us to go back and undo causes. It only permits us to understand a continuum, on which the catastrophe marked a decisive event, which now throws its shadow back on the very items which seem to have caused it.[30]

What psychiatry has to offer to the historian, therefore, is an additional explanation, a rich dimension to add to the data at our disposal but in no sense a unique causal explanation of the phenomena we are observing. Erikson's 'triple book-keeping' to understand a patient is no different from the 'multiple book-keeping' attempted in the first chapter to draw up balances of probability in ever-changing historical 'equations'.

Most psychiatrists who have written about Hitler attach central importance to the delicate relationship between father, mother and child, to which Freud gave the name oedipus complex and which reaches a climax between the third and sixth years. Our knowledge of Hitler's familial situation is extremely limited, a major difficulty which makes any serious investigation of the oedipal or pre-oedipal Hitler immensely difficult if not frankly impossible. Still, from what we do know it is safe to assume that Hitler had an overprotective mother and an insensitive and domineering father, a common enough pattern in the German-speaking world at the close of the last century. Although young Hitler probably stood in awe of his father—whose early retirement brought him into closer contact than usual with his son—it seems highly probable that he disliked him intensely.[31] Erich Erikson, who has examined the imagery used by Hitler in *Mein Kampf* to describe family life, is firmly of the opinion that whether or not Hitler's father was brutal in his relationship with his wife, Hitler believed this to be the case which, psychologically, is what counts. As for his mother, all the evidence we have indicates a deep attachment on the son's part. Her death in 1907 was a traumatic experience for the eighteen-year old youth as the family doctor vividly recalled years later.[32] Whenever Hitler spoke of her in later life it was with affection. And it is surely significant that pictures of his mother (but not of the father) were to be seen in Berlin, Munich and at the Berghof.[33]

For historians the main point of interest lies in the possible connections between a disturbed oedipal complex and that abnormal aggressiveness and lust for revenge on opponents which was so characteristic of Hitler the politician. The argument is that a sense of guilt arising out of subconscious desire for incestuous relations with his mother combined with fear of a 'castrating father' to leave Hitler with a basic feeling of inadequacy and insecurity (with strong sexual undertones) which he never overcame. If, as these psychiatrists maintain, he was indeed a sexual pervert, this would have greatly intensified the feelings of inadequacy. So, too, would the absence of a testicle, revealed by the Russian autopsy on Hitler's remains found in the garden of the chancellery in April 1945.

The practical consequences were twofold. On entering politics Hitler made strenuous efforts to repudiate all that was weak and effeminate in his own personality and to identify with a new and virile superego—the ruthless and self-confident leader of men. Secondly, it is a matter of clinical observation that patients with deep-seated feelings of inadequacy tend to project onto those around them the resentment they feel towards a parent or parents whom they hold responsible for their own plight. Applied to Hitler, this means that the violent and bitter attacks he launched on all who stood in his way, both as an adolescent and as a man, might be explained in terms of a deep sense of guilt about his own sexual inadequacy and of a desire to avenge the wrongs done to his mother by his father.

The deep love he bore towards his mother may have had more positive psychological consequences for Hitler. Instead of interpreting his political career as a negative exercise in revenge on behalf of his mother, it might be seen as an attempt to recreate that mother-child symbiosis which he never outgrew. In the all-embracing community of the army and later of the Nazi Party Hitler could insulate himself against reality in a protective maternal cocoon where, after a stormy adolescence, his infantile sense of omnipotence and invincibility could again flourish. Similarly, the mystical union he established with his audiences represented a constant renewal of this symbiosis. This is a valuable insight into Hitler's personality to which we will return later. It is not without interest that, on Hitler's own admission, contact with young people seemed to supply the comfort and reassurance his psyche craved for.[34]

The Hitler phenomenon has been interpreted very differently by Erich Fromm.[35] In his opinion Hitler was a man driven on by a malignant destructiveness who sought to destroy everything that stood in his path. Faced with what he believes to be a contradiction between Hitler's normal family life—for Fromm believes Hitler did not hate his father—and the destructive dictator of later years, Fromm looks for the answer in the pre-oedipal phase of Hitler's development. Fromm maintains that Hitler never really loved his mother but remained imprisoned in a cold narcissistic shell. His mother was never a person Hitler learnt to love tenderly, but a benign goddess to be appeased or the impersonal goddess of creation and destruction who sought to devour him.

Because Hitler never really loved his mother, it follows that he never came to terms with reality. That explains why he resented authority and why, when he failed at school, he retreated into a fantasy world where he could still believe in his own invincibility. The tragedy for mankind was that despite the setbacks of the Vienna years which would have forced many people to come to terms with reality, Hitler did not mature. On the contrary, he became more determined than ever to avenge himself on all whom he supposed had humiliated him, and also to prove to the world at large that his narcissistic image was not fantasy but reality. After the First World War through favourable historical circumstances—and not least because he possessed considerable native talent—he was able to achieve his ambitions in the end and force reality to fit into his mould for a time at least.

The historical evidence does not confirm Fromm's central thesis. As indicated above, the balance of evidence suggests very strongly that Hitler's father was an insensitive character, not a kindly authoritarian figure concerned only to ensure that his son 'did the right thing'. And in the case of Hitler's mother all the evidence points to an over-intense relationship quite undisturbed by the birth of his brother Edmund in 1894. Fromm's assertion that Hitler never returned from Vienna, where he was studying art, to Linz to visit his sick mother at the close of 1907—an omission which is seen as conclusive proof of narcissism—has been recently exploded by incontrovertible evidence that Hitler did return home and nursed his mother in the closing weeks of her life, displaying quite exemplary devotion to her.[36]

On the other hand, Fromm's belief that Hitler was 'a deeply necrophilious man' with 'a lust for destruction' is much more convincing. Hitler was undoubtedly a cold character, lacking in compassion, insensitive to the feelings of others, extremely self-centred and sadistic (that is, he craved power over others). Nor can it be denied that he was personally responsible for the euthanasia programme of 1939, which resulted in the murder of elderly and mentally sick patients, and took a lively interest in the details of it; and also for the 'liquidation' of the Polish ruling elite in 1939, the extermination of the Jews, and the scorched earth order of March 1945 in which he decreed that all industrial plant should be destroyed to prevent it falling into enemy hands.

To try to explain these deeds solely in terms of his unwavering belief in the biological struggle for existence as the key to human history or of his insistence on the cruelty of nature is not entirely satisfactory. Many shared these crude beliefs; few adhered to them so tenaciously throughout their lives. Certainly his charm, courtesy, amiability and self-control (except when it suited him politically to lose it) were genuine enough and represented another facet of his personality not to be overlooked. But Speer is surely correct in supposing that these qualities were 'only an outer skin which obviously had the function of masking his true nature and the traits dominant in him'.[37] One must conclude that an element of malevolence and self-destructiveness was present in many of Hitler's actions and moreover constituted in integral part of his personality, although whether this can be regarded as the main key to understanding his personality, as Fromm suggests, is another matter.

In recent years psychiatrists have become increasingly conscious of the crucial role family relations play in the genesis of mental illness, though probably few would go as far as David Laing in maintaining that mentally-disturbed patients are nothing more than the victims of familial pressures, and that disturbed families in effect 'elect' the weakest member to become a 'scapegoat' institutionalized on their behalf.

Recently, Helm Stierlin, a Heidelberg psychiatrist who has worked extensively on the problems of adolescence in America as well as in Germany, has advanced the view that Hitler's behaviour can be most satisfactorily explained if he is seen as a 'delegate' charged with the 'task' of satisfying the psychological needs of a parent and realizing that parent's ambitions—not the needs and ambitions of his father, too threatening a figure to inspire love in Hitler or afford him proper support in adolescence, but of his mother, the gentle and unassuming Klara Pölzl.

What were these 'tasks'? In the first place, Adolf was expected to give constant reassurance to Klara that she was a good mother, this by allowing himself to be spoilt and dependent on her. Secondly, by devoting himself to his mother Hitler was to help her overcome the guilty memory of the quasi-incestuous relationship before marriage when as a maid in her uncle's house she had intimate relations with him while his second wife was dying. Young Hitler was also expected to assist her overcome the traumatic experience of losing her first three children within a few months of each other in 1888–9. Thirdly, Klara expected Adolf to give meaning to her life which marriage with Alois had not given it, this by making a name for himself. Finally, Adolf was expected to side with his mother against her husband, in other words was to play the role of avenger *vis-à-vis* the father.

According to Stierlin, Hitler's troubles stemmed primarily from the impossible nature of these tasks rather than from a disturbed oedipal complex. An unconscious sense of guilt was generated in Hitler by the conflict between the moral imperative of delegacy and the adolescent's natural desire to live his own life, as well as by the impossibility of remaining dependent on the mother to achieve the first two 'tasks' while becoming independent of her in order to realize her secret ambitions. Observation of schizophrenic patients shows that they seek to relieve inner tension in various ways. Sometimes they sabotage their own efforts to realize parental objectives, as Stierlin believes Hitler did when he failed at school and was rejected at the Vienna art academy. Or they may denounce all who in any way frustrate the realization of their ambitions, as the adolescent Hitler seems to have been in the habit of doing. A third psychological mechanism for overcoming guilt feelings is what Stierlin calls 'heroic reconciliation', a device which when Hitler resorted to it after the First World War put him on the highroad to victory. In effect he found in serving Germany an emotional substitute for devotion to his dead mother, and a substitute which, because it could be much more easily manipulated than a person can be, enabled him to resolve his inner conflict. Out of the symbiosis between leader and motherland Germany, Hitler drew renewed strength and also an intense feeling of mission and of personal omnipotence. Through ceaseless devotion to the new cause—and not least because he possessed real talent—he succeeded in fulfilling the 'tasks' set him by his mother. By his political activity he achieved fame for her and by destroying Germany's enemies he avenged her wrongs.

Though this diagnosis is very different from Langer's and Brosse's, the practical consequences in which the historian is primarily interested are not all that different. Once again Hitler emerges as a man forced to become what he was not temperamentally cut out to be. Exploited, as all delegates are by their parents, Hitler had to carry the burden of his mother's shame and guilt feelings. In order to succeed Hitler had to suppress these feelings and cultivate a ruthless and narcissistic posture, committing himself totally to politics as a medium for imposing his version of reality on the world. Stierlin depicts him as a man imprisoned in a shame-guilt cycle: cruel deeds troubled the 'strong man'; residual feelings of guilt drove him on to greater cruelty simply to prove his own virility. While to justify himself in his own eyes he was obliged to distort reality more and more, until finally with military defeat staring him in the face, even he had to admit that no room for manoeuvre remained.

In people of this kind the development of the psyche is seriously distorted. The growth of tending loving feelings is retarded while aggressive self-assertive instincts are grossly exaggerated. The historical evidence certainly bears out the contention that Hitler lived in a stage of high tension. It is true, as indicated already, that in an intimate circle he could be an amiable and even an entertaining companion. But outside these circles he was continually on his guard suppressing all spontaneity in social relations and avoiding exposure to possible criticism. He never danced, swam or rode—unlike the Italian dictator who made great play with his physical prowess. At times, notably in 1923 when his political career came to an abrupt halt, in 1931 when his niece Geli Raubal died, in 1934 after the blood purge when Roehm and his associates were murdered on Hitler's orders, and finally in 1945, Hitler tottered on the brink of psychic collapse.

Whatever view psychiatrists take of Stierlin's sophisticated analysis—and he is the first to admit that in places it rests on very scanty evidence—there is certainly good reason for thinking that adolescence was a time of crucial importance in Hitler's development. One might explain Hitler not as a 'delegate' for his mother but simply as a casualty of adolescence much as Erich Erikson has done. Each young person, according to Erikson, experiences a 'psychosocial moratorium', that is a period in which the adolescent seeks painfully to come to terms with the outside world and discover an identity for himself, a role in which he can fulfil himself and earn thereby the esteem of his contemporaries. If he fails to overcome the crisis of adolescence, serious psychological damage will be done. This is precisely what happened to Hitler; in Erikson's words he remained 'an unbroken adolescent who had chosen a career apart from civilian happiness, middle-class tranquillity and spiritual peace'.[38]

The historical evidence confirms the view that Hitler experienced his major identity crisis between the age of eighteen and twenty. In September 1907 he failed to gain admission to the Academy of Fine Arts in Vienna. Two months later his mother died. Quite abruptly he cut himself off from his relatives, went to live permanently in Vienna, and threw himself into a bout of study, admittedly in an undisciplined fashion but probably with every hope of securing admission to the academy. His second rejection in October 1908 completely shattered the adolescent dream of a great career as an artist which his mother had allowed him to indulge in after he abandoned the *Realschule* in 1905.

Although we have practically no information about Hitler for the period between the autumn of 1908 and November 1909, all the indications are that his identity crisis worsened. Recent research has disproved Hitler's own allegations that he was penniless. All the same, as he had probably used up much of his share of his mother's estate and was completely dependent on an orphan's pension (which he claimed, though not engaged in formal education), one is justified in thinking that he must have experienced some hardship in these months. The cumulative effect of a series of disappointments must have borne in upon this lonely youth. Probably his attempts at earning a livelihood were spasmodic. Though there is no proof of it, he may have worked briefly on a building site where, as he claimed later, he soon quarreled with socialist work mates. Another pressure on him at this time was the notification for military service he received in the autumn of 1909. His aversion to the Habsburgs was already so great that he was determined not to serve in their army, and moved his lodgings three times in as many months to avoid detection. All one can say for certain about these months is that he emerged from obscurity in November 1909 when the tramp Reinhold Hanisch met him at the Meidlinger hostel for down-and-outs.

If Hanisch is to be believed—and this source must be used with extreme caution—Hitler seems to have pulled himself together at this point.[39] He wrote to his aunt Johanna for money (which was quickly forthcoming) and was persuaded by Hanisch to set up as a freelance commercial artist. With Hanisch acting as middleman (until they quarrelled and parted company in the summer of 1910) Hitler made a living for both of them and worked, often fitfully, for the next three years, staying at a respectable single man's hostel in the Meldemann Strasse. Whether he had really overcome his identity crisis is another matter. His hopes of a great artistic career had been dashed to pieces. And for the first time Hitler, the son of a first generation bourgeois family, had experienced a world he did not care for as he drifted aimlessly round the great metropolis. The experience left great scars on his psyche. He never ceased to despise that 'respectable' bourgeois world which, as he saw it, had turned its back on him when he needed its patronage most. And, secondly, he was now firmly convinced that 'dark forces' manipulating the masses were to blame for his personal failure and 'role confusion' as well as for the steady decline of Germanism in the Austrian half of the Dual Monarchy. In that sense adolescent attitudes persisted in him though superficially he had stabilized his life style.[40]

In the past the traumatic effect of the First World War on Hitler has not been sufficiently emphasized by psychiatrists probably because it was so widely believed that character development was virtually complete by the age of five or six. But, as Erich Fromm points out, while an individual may be predisposed at birth to move in a certain direction by genetic factors, intense experiences in later life can still cause significant changes in personality with the qualification that the older one is the more intense the experience has to be.[41]

The First World War seems to have had precisely that effect upon Hitler. By his own admission the years in the front line were 'the greatest and most unforgettable time of my earthly experience'.[42] That sentiment has, at some time or other, been expressed by all ex-soldiers once the immediate horror and danger of the battlefield had receded and they can look back with affection through the distorting mirror of time to the comradeship of the front line. In Hitler's case this was much more than an emotional spasm renewable annually at the regimental dinner. For him the world war was a soul-searing proof of the validity of the ideology he already believed in. Hans Frank thought the war 'by far the greatest and most decisive element in his [Hitler's] education. . . . He saw in his life as a soldier the only true vocation of man; death at the front was the only worthy deed of sacrifice in the interest of the nation; violent conflict between warring peoples was the highest and ideal form of life for states and corresponded absolutely to the plan of creation; that is war was an absolutely ineradicable and unavoidable evil of humanity.'[43]

The comment of one of Hitler's doctors in 1945 that 'this first war changed the artist or rather the artistic nature into a hard resolute man' touches the heart of the matter.[44] Hitler, who had lived an undisciplined and Bohemian life for years, conformed at once to the discipline of the army. On the battlefields of Flanders he discovered a new identity. Life could at last be lived on a heroic Wagnerian scale. Suddenly the fantasy world of adolescence became a real world where deeds of valour could be performed for the fatherland (or was it already the motherland?). He was the model soldier, cool-headed and fearless under fire, devoted to duty, and always willing as regimental runner to get the dispatches through. Not surprisingly he was also a much-decorated soldier being awarded the Iron Cross Class I in August 1918. Emotionally, Hitler enjoyed for the first time since the death of his mother the security of an ordered life within the framework of an all-embracing organization. And an organization totally dedicated to the task of destroying Germany's enemies so that the aggressive instincts more or less suppressed in Hitler in time of peace were liberated in four years of warfare and harnessed to the cause of the nation.

Yet at heart he remained an adolescent. His failure to secure promotion suggests this. That so brave and devoted a soldier never rose above the rank of corporal (to which he was promoted in November 1914) seems rather surprising. The story that he was indispensable at regimental headquarters sounds implausible; the cemeteries in wartime are full of such people. More likely, as his company commander testified later, Hitler's superior officers thought the future 'Führer' lacking in leadership qualities.[45] By all accounts he remained a rather lonely and aloof individual, a man with no close family ties who rarely went on leave and often sat in the dug-out sunk in thought, occasionally arousing himself to harangue his comrades on the cosmic significance of the war, pouring forth without restraint the eccentric and immature notions fermenting within him. A man for whom his comrades had a grudging respect but not an easy man to live with and for that reason not likely to be given command over them.

Secondly, though the first flush of idealism had long been spent in most soldiers and replaced by the cynicism bred of a savage war of attrition, Hitler never matured. To the last day of war he was the innocent abroad—incorrigibly optimistic about final victory, impervious to ominous signs and portents of war weariness and defeatism—which, characteristically, he was wont to denounce as the work of 'Jewish corrupters of the people'—and unflagging in his devotion to emperor and fatherland. For such a man the sudden shock of defeat was certain to precipitate a severe personal crisis.

Reference has been made above to the mood of black despair in November 1918. His discharge from Pasewalk hospital did not end the identity crisis. Until June (possibly September) 1919 he drifted along, as he drifted from September 1908 to December 1909, incapable of facing up to the realities of life. Without close friends and lacking a trade or profession, all that awaited him was a drab, lonely and unexciting existence back in civilian life where the high ideals of 1914 were being trampled underfoot by 'red revolutionaries.' The turning-point in this second personal crisis came not in November when according to his own account he decided to become a politician, but probably in June 1919 when Hitler was selected for 'political duties' by the army authorities. Shortly afterwards he had confirmation of his unusual talent for oratory when he was sent to a local army camp to harangue returning soldiers suspected of revolutionary sympathies. His reputation was considerable enough by September for his commanding officer to consult the corporal on political questions. It was in this new-found mood of political awareness that he was sent to observe a meeting of the small German Workers' Party. No doubt he would have walked out of the meeting after a boring address delivered by Gottfried Feder, a prominent right-wing speaker, had not a member of the audience expressed separatist views during the discussion period. This chance intervention triggered off an impassioned outburst from Hitler which deeply impressed Anton Drexler, the founder of the party, and moved the party executive to invite Hitler to join them. Doubtless Hitler would have joined some other right-wing radical group had it not been this party. In terms of his personal psychology the period of indecision was ending, and he now committed himself wholeheartedly to politics just as he had thrown himself with enthusiasm into military life. That he had found the solution to his personal problem must have been clear to him at the latest by October 1919 when he spoke briefly at the party's first public meeting. For the first time he became fully aware of his magnetic powers over a sizable audience. Oratory was the perfect medium for discharging the aggressive sentiments pent up within him since the fighting had stopped.

This time Hitler had been rescued from a personal crisis not by a chance encounter with an individual but by the prevailing mood in post-war Germany, where large sections of the middle and lower middle classes—and particularly young people—eyed the republic with sullen disapproval and blamed it for all the troubles that had befallen Germany. In this highly-charged atmosphere the anachronistic image of the front-line soldier acquired a new lease of life and a relevance unthinkable in the more homogeneous communities of Britain and France where, despite post-war problems, national unity was a social reality. The rough-and-ready virtues and vices of the battlefield, where all were bound together in the freemasonry of arms regardless of class and creed, and where all had dedicated themselves to the annihilation of the enemies of the fatherland, were directly transposed into German political life by right-wing extremists, often people with no experience of front-line conditions.[46] Nowhere were the jungle mores of the battlefield more effectively institutionalized than in the Nazi Party. The bloody street battles in Munich in the early 1920s and in countless towns throughout Germany in the early 1930s were no accidental by-product of a disordered body politic (though obviously disturbed conditions did encourage the use of violence) but a natural and inevitable consequence of that predeliction for physical violence which was displayed by the young ex-soldiers and the 'victory watchers' (in Merkl's telling phrase) who flocked into the party. In their company Hitler found emotional satisfaction and experienced once again that sense of fulfilment he had known as a soldier. The fantasy world of his adolescence and of the battlefield was perpetuated inside what in psychological terms amounted to an alternative society, a world of make-believe structured on familiar military lines, permeated by the ethos of the barrack square, deeply contemptuous of all the common decencies bourgeois society stood for and totally dedicated to the destruction of all that Weimar democracy represented.

So at the end of the book we return to the point made in the opening chapter: Hitler's political success is only properly intelligible when seen against the background of the collective trauma of the German people after the First World War. In itself this commonplace observation does not greatly advance our understanding of the Nazi period. It is precisely here that psychoanalysis and social psychology come to the rescue of the historian and offer some particularly valuable insights into the relationship between leaders and groups.

Group psychology is not, of course, a new science. It was the great German poet Schiller, writing nearly two hundred years ago, who made the observation:

Everyone seen on his own is tolerably clever and shrewd;
Seen in the mass all at once you will find him crude.

But only during and after the First World War did significant work on group psychology begin to appear, notably that of William McDougall, Gustave Le Bon and Sigmund Freud.[47] Whereas McDougall and Le Bon agreed broadly that the 'exaltation or intensification of emotion' was the essential element producing uniform responses in the members of groups, Freud explained the group situation in terms of libidinal ties. When man is in love, according to Freud, his ego identifies with and is enriched by certain properties of the object of his affections. In a group situation, on the other hand, individuals substitute one and the same object for their ego ideal and have 'consequently identified themselves with one another in the ego'.[48] In other words, the individual as a member of a group is in a regressive mental state where the ego surrenders completely to the object—a state of infatuation instead of love properly so-called. This is the explanation of the major characteristics observed in the group—the lack of emotional restraint, the diminution of personal responsibility, the lack of moderation, the sense of invincible power and the inability to distinguish between truth and falsehood. Le Bon had little to say about the role of leaders in the group situation except that they possessed a mysterious power or 'prestige'. Freud, on the other hand, compared the leader with the dreaded father in a primal horde, a being feared by his sons because he restrained them in the satisfaction of their sexual impulses and governed them as they secretly desired to be governed—by force.

More recent work on group dynamics has made it clear that it is not enough to think of a leader as a primal father or even as a successful manipulator although, naturally, this remains an important aspect of the group situation. What is new and important is the realization that a leader is also a manipulated figure, in the sense that the group has expectations of its leader which he is obliged to fulfil if he is to remain the leader.

The demands groups make on their leaders can vary. In what the psychologist Wilfred Bion calls 'basic assumption dependency groups' the members are seeking security and emotional reassurance from the leader. In 'fight-flight' groups the members are looking for someone to hate and to conquer or for someone to fear and run away from. Again, the leader's function is to supply the enemy that the group is looking for. Or, finally, in 'basic assumption and oneness groups' members are seeking to experience a sense of well-being and togetherness; in these groups the leader allows himself to be idolized so that the members can overcome an infantile fear of being deserted. But in all cases the leader is the prisoner of the group obliged to satisfy the drives and emotional needs of the particular group in order to remain the leader.

Applied to the career of Hitler this means that one cannot simply look upon the Nazi Party or the German people as passive entities, manipulated and exploited by a virtuoso playing 'on the well-tempered piano of the lower middle class heart'.[49] What these groups demanded of their leader was a categorical imperative for him. Thus, even if Hitler had been less sanguine about the chances of success in 1923, he would still have been obliged to attempt a putsch in order to appease his own followers. Similarly in 1932 if he had ever contemplated settling for less than the chancellorship, he dare not do so because the group (party) regarded that office as the irreducible minimum their leader must demand. In both instances psychological insights add a new dimension to conclusions which the historian has arrived at by a different route.

Helm Stierlin takes the argument a stage further by relating group dynamics to the familial situation.[50] Leaders have not only got to satisfy the primitive childhood fears and fantasies activating their groups. If they are leading whole peoples they are dealing not with ad hoc 'basic assumption' groups to be constructed and dismantled in the laboratory at the whim of the psychologist, but with historic communities or families. Therefore Hitler, as leader of the German people had a dual function to perform. In respect of the grievances and frustrations of individual members of German families he was the father figure expected to offer remedies and reliefs appropriate to individual situations. But in respect of the people as a whole he was expected to preserve and glorify the super ego of Germany as a historic community.

In the national context, so Stierlin argues, the 'family myth' exercised precisely the same function as in the case of individual families. For example, the myth of family harmony is a striking phenomenon often observed in the disturbed family; even the victimized members cling to the threadbare pretence that all is well when to trained observers it is patently obvious that the reverse is the case. Is it too fanciful to suggest that Hitler's constant avowals that National Socialist Germany was a people's community speaking with one voice and moving towards one national goal was basically a response to the longing of a deeply-divided people for harmony and unity.[51] Similarly, families in difficulties often choose an individual in the group as a kind of delegate whom they blame, quite illogically, for all that has gone wrong in the family situation. Might it not be that when Hitler singled out the Jews as scapegoats for all the ills troubling Germany he was simply projecting onto them the guilt complex felt by most Germans? Finally, it has been noticed that families in difficulties often cherish a vague hope that some external figure—perhaps a remote relation—will intervene and relieve them of their problems as if by magic. Might it not be that Hitler was accepted so readily by the German people because many of them were also waiting for some extraordinary figure to 'redeem' them and resolve their inner tensions?

Of particular interest to the historian—whose proper concern is with collective phenomena rather than with individual pathology—is Stierlin's argument that Hitler was not only a delegate for his mother but that he performed the same function for the German people as a whole. When Hitler transposed to Germany the love he felt for his mother it might be argued that he was at the same time satisfying the collective longing of the German people—or at any rate of a sizable section of it—for dependency on a leader, He offered them work, security and order, he restored their sense of dignity and he reaffirmed the authoritarian pattern of their family life. In return they willingly succumbed to the infallible leader and father figure whom they could follow blindly.

The same kind of argument can be applied to the other 'tasks' Hitler was given by his mother. Thus when Hitler overcame the personal trauma of his mother it was because as a delegate for the German people he was simultaneously overcoming their collective trauma over defeat. Finally, it might be argued that his attempt to avenge his mother was not purely personal; it also corresponded to the collective search for a scapegoat by a people labouring under a great sense of injustice at the wrong, as they saw it, done to them by the victorious powers in the Versailles Treaty.

These are all valuable insights adding new dimension to our understanding of the Hitler phenomenon. But it cannot be denied that this kind of argument raises many perplexing questions for the traditional historian, accustomed as he is to the sifting and evaluation of documentary evidence. Are we justified in any sense in talking about 'nations' and 'peoples' as if they were homogeneous historical entities? Do terms such as 'collective trauma' really help us to understand and clarify complex historical processes? Is it not sleight of hand to pretend that personal conflicts can be projected onto a wider national screen? Can one generalize about familial patterns or assume that Hitler's family background was 'typically' German in any meaningful sense? To pose these questions is in no way to imply that investigation of these areas would be an unprofitable exercise. On the contrary. It is precisely here that social psychology can be of real assistance to the historian, offering as it does partial answers to some of the questions posed above.

The role of familial attitudes in the genesis of National Socialism is a good example of this. As early as 1933 Wilhelm Reich, a German psychologist and active Marxist who fled from the Nazi terror, advanced his well-known thesis that the lower middle-class family was the mainstay of German authoritarianism.[52] Up to a point this phenomenon is explicable in historical terms as the result of the traditional identification of these social strata with the institutions of state power. More significantly, it reflected repressed sexuality in the home.

It is argued that the one-sided familial pattern where the father was the dominant and tyrannical figure and the mother docile and submissive to her husband seriously disturbed the normal oedipal development. The boy stood in such awe of his heavy-handed father that he was obliged to repress hatred of him, perfectly normal at that stage of development, under a veneer of submissiveness. When the boy turned to his mother for protection, her submissiveness deprived him of the support he needed. The net result was a feeling of ambivalence on the boy's part towards both parents. Children subjected to this regimen were robbed of true independence, stunted in the normal growth of the capacity to love and turned into docile followers of any Führer who chanced to come along.

Furthermore, sexual repression in the home and the guilt feelings associated with it explain, so the argument runs, the attachment of these social strata to 'pathologic emotionally tinged notions of honour as well as duty, bravery and self control',[53] their inclination to be sadistic, and their vulnerability to the mysticism and hocus-pocus of pseudo-religions like Nazism. In his classic study *Escape from Freedom*, published in 1941, Erich Fromm subscribed to much the same view, maintaining that 'for great parts of the lower middle class in Germany ... the sadomasochistic character is typical and ... it is this kind of character structure to which Nazi ideology had its strongest appeal.'[54] Hitler's personality and ideas and the structure of Nazism simply expressed 'an extreme form of the character structure we have called authoritarian'.[55]

Research conducted in recent years into the psychological foundations of Nazism has confirmed in some measure these brilliant generalizations. Just after the end of the Second World War Adorno and his co-workers, in a monumental tome based on American experience, laid the foundations for a fuller understanding of the personality 'type' most likely to be attracted by authoritarian movements.[56] Since then several important studies have appeared, especially Peter Loewenberg's analysis of the adolescent Himmler, and of the psychological motivation of National Socialist youth, and Henry

Dicks's study of selected war criminals serving long sentences in the prisons of the Federal Republic.[57]

Broadly speaking these studies confirm the view that disturbed familial backgrounds were a major factor in the growth and development of National Socialism. To take a concrete example: the sadomasochistic character referred to by Reich and Fromm ceases to be a theoretical abstraction once we have encountered patient Q in the Mitscherlichs' book.[58]

Q, born before the First World War, was a member of the Hitler Youth before 1933 and served during the war as a police officer with the SS where he was engaged in combating partisan warfare in Russia. This pathetic middle-aged man was an infantile personality incapable of maturation, who conceived of human relationships in the rigid authoritarian terms of his own childhood when he had been accustomed to receiving orders and obeying them punctiliously. Q was, in fact, a classic example of the sadomasochistic individual who recurs all too frequently in the course of modern German history, a typical representative of the *Angestelltenkultur*,[59] a man of limited intelligence ready to carry out any order without reflection and always believing himself to be in the right, a tyrant and a sadist who bullied his own wife and probably tormented his prisoners in the east but who took a masochistic satisfaction in being, as a child, the victim of an overbearing mother (on whom he was overdependent), then of his harsh SS taskmasters and finally of the Anglo-American internment authorities. Needless to say, Q found it utterly impossible to come to terms with his past and confined himself in interviews to expressions of regret at the deterioration in his personal circumstances.

Mitscherlich's patient Q was not an isolated case. Much the same picture emerges from the investigation Henry Dicks carried out into eight war criminals in the late 1960s. All of them, in Dicks's opinion, suffered from unresolved oedipal conflicts. Deficient in self-reliance, they bullied their inferiors (including women), but behaved with great deference towards their superiors. They, too, despised tender feelings and made a cult of 'manliness', being full of praise for the harsh discipline of the army. And all were paranoid in their ready assumption that every hand was turned against them. The deep psychological uncertainties in these people were revealed by the constant fluctuation between, on the one hand, a belief in the omnipotence of whatever Nazi group they had belonged to and, on the other hand, admissions of personal impotence as far as their own role was concerned. The only difference between these killers and patient Q would appear to be the absence of deep relationships with maternal figures because in nearly all cases the father was on active service during the First World War (or already deceased) so that mothers assumed an unaccustomed role. Because of their excessive severity in carrying out their task, the ego development of the children was weakened, leading to ambivalent attitudes towards both parents.

In an area where statistical information is necessarily hard to come by, the temptation to indulge in glib generalizations based on unrepresentative samples is very considerable. For this reason special mention must be made of

Peter Merkl's valuable study.[60] When due allowance has been made for the circumstances in which the 600 curricula vitae of Nazi Party members were composed—at the request of the American sociologist Theodore Abel in 1934 and through the good offices of the party—they still remain an important piece of instant history, offering a rare insight into the motivation of a respectable sample of party members as opposed to a small group of mentally-disturbed killers. Careful analysis of the data by Peter Merkl using cross-tabulation techniques and computer processing has revealed much of interest to the historian about rank-and-file members of the Nazi Party.

As suggested in chapter 1, generational differences (whether the respondents were brought up in the pre-war, war or post-war period) combined with different social backgrounds and varying responses to the traumatic 'cultural shock' of German defeat to produce not one personality type but a bewildering variety of involvement patterns and ideological motivation in individual cases.

Merkl divides Abel's sample of party members (who mostly joined the party after 1925) into three categories: the marchers (M), the fighters (F), and the proselytizers (P). The marcher-proselytizers (MP) emerge as older men unable to take an active part in punch-up politics. They were fanatical missionaries, deeply anti-semitic, devotees of Nordic-German romaticism but, interestingly enough, not particularly prone to the Hitler personality cult. The marcher-fighters (MF) 'the mindless sluggers' and 'walking wounded of a deficient childhood socialization', in Merkl's graphic phrase, were from the post-war generation.[61] Judging by their curricula vitae, these were paranoid types by any reckoning, sadomasochists who revelled in violence for its own sake. They were, on that account, a positive embarrassment after 1933 to a party striving on the surface at any rate to appear respectable. The pefect party members combining all the desirable qualities were the marcher-fighter-proselytizers (MFP). A typical MFP usually had a background of poverty at home; he went to work before he was fourteen; he lived in a town; he was socially mobile in an upward direction but frustrated and embittered by class barriers, snubs and humiliations (real or imagined) at the hands of social superiors; he was anti-semitic and militaristic in outlook; noticeably more intelligent than the MFs; and he usually brought his whole family into the party. It would be going much too far on the Abel-Merkl evidence to speak of 'modal personalities' but this is at least a step along that road.

Of particular interest is Merkl's observation that 70 per cent of those of Abel's respondents who held office in the party were paranoid types. And, further, that those who excelled at violence in the SA and SS and held most of the offices in those organizations belong in the same category. What sparse information the curricula vitae contain about childhood circumstances reveals that these members were either orphans or had been brought up in a disciplinarian household. Once again we are reminded of the importance of the childhood situation and of the consequences for political commitment of insufficient socialization at this stage.

At the end of the day we are still left with a host of intriguing questions about paranoia and leadership. Were those paranoids who achieved prominence in the party individuals who perhaps needed the stimulus of struggle to keep their personalities together? Or were they simply trying desperately to compensate for social decline (which Merkl suggests was a characteristic feature of the curricula vitae of many of them) by becoming leaders? Can one say that insufficiently socialized people are more likely than others to emerge warped and twisted by traumatic war experiences so that they are compelled to go on hating and fighting for the rest of their lives and can only tolerate the company of those who do likewise?

Merkl, not himself a trained psychologist, did not attempt to classify Abel's respondents according to 'types', on the grounds that objective assessment of the personalities involved was impossible on the information available. This does leave open the possibility that psychologists might well squeeze more out of the Abel curricula vitae. Such an exercise might profitably be extended to take in the hundreds of autobiographical accounts written in 1936 by the party's 'old guard' at the request of party headquarters and now deposited in the Federal archives in Koblenz.[62] For only by constructing as comprehensive a picture as possible of the character structure of the types who were attracted to Nazism can one really begin to appreciate that many of the prominent features of Hitler's personality—aggressiveness, paranoid hatred of opposition and total commitment to preposterous ideological concepts—were reproduced over and over again in rank-and-file members. The secret of his success, certainly in respect of the growth of National Socialism in the 1920s, was due to the coincidence of his personal pathology with the needs of a disturbed section of German society.

In these concluding pages we may appear to have travelled a long way from the psychopathology of Adolf Hitler. This is emphatically not to suggest that history can or should be turned into an appendage of the social sciences, dedicated to the study of broad trends and movements to the virtual exclusion of personality. The most cursory acquaintance with the history of Nazi Germany and of its leader shows how erroneous such an approach would be. But it is equally unproductive to pay only lip service—as many biographers of Hitler have done—to the restraints placed on men and women by the economic, social and cultural context in which historical phenomena are rooted. It is here in the interaction between personality, conceived of as a dynamic process, and the totality of historical experience that the future of historical studies lies. In so far as psychohistorians apply their psychoanalytical insights to the investigation of individual pathology, their contribution to the understanding of historical phenomena such as National Socialism is necessarily limited.

There is much truth in the comment, made by a leading German historian, that 'analytical social psychology has incomparably greater significance for the historian than individual psychology.'[63] This book has attempted, however inadequately, to see Hitler in the context of those broad social forces which moulded German history between 1871 and 1945. This does not in any way detract from his contribution to the growth of the Nazi movement or to the politics of the Third Reich. Hopefully, it will have suggested to the reader that whatever element of 'greatness' he possessed—simply and solely by virtue of the impact he made on European history—arises out of a concrete historical situation which his personality structure happened to match. The question that still remains the most challenging one for the historian of the Third Reich is what a brilliant German historian, whose untimely death diminished us all, called 'Hitler's *Ermöglichung*'.[64] If this book has contributed anything at all to the clarification of that issue it will not have been written in vain.

Notes

Abbreviations

AHR	*American Historical Review*
BA	Bundesarchiv
BA-MA	Bundesarchiv-Militärarchiv
CEH	*Central European History*
DGFP	*Documents on German Foreign Policy*
Geh.St.A	Geheimes Staatsarchiv
HZ	*Historische Zeitschrift*
IFZ	Institut für Zeitgeschichte
IMT	*International Military Tribunal*
JfW	*Jahresbuch für Wirtschaftsgeschichte*
JMH	*Journal of Modern History*
KTB des OKW	*Kriegstagebuch des Oberkommandos der Wehrmacht*
KTB der SKL	Kriegstagebuch der Seekriegsleitung
MGM	*Militärgeschichtliche Mitteilungen*
MNN	*Münchener Neuere Nachrichten*
NA	National Archives
OSS	Office of Strategic Services
VB	*Völkischer Beobachter*
VfZG	*Vierteljahreshefte für Zeitgeschichte*
ZfG	*Zeitschrift für Geschichtswissenschaft*

Preface

1 Cf. M. Bosch (ed.), *Persönlichkeit und Struktur in der Geschichte* (Düsseldorf, 1977).
2 Cf. R. Kühnl, R. Rilling, C. Sager, *Die NPD Struktur, Ideologie und Funktion einer neofaschistischen Partei* (Frankfurt a/M, 1969).

Chapter 1

1 D. Irving, *Hitler's War* (London, 1977), pp. 329–32, 390–93, 503–4.
2 For example, at a Hofbräuhaus meeting on 19 May 1920 he insisted that a young socialist be allowed to speak so that he could 'dispatch him personally'. Staatsarchiv München, PD 6698.
3 K. Heiden, *A History of National Socialism* (London, 1934), pp. 140, 146.

4 A police report in E. Deuerlein, *Der Aufstieg der NSDAP in Augenzeugen-berichten* (München, 1974), pp. 269–75.

5 Examples of highly entertaining speeches are: 3 April 1929 Munich BA, NS 26–54; and 31 August 1930 Kiel BA, NS 26–54. Pouring scorn on the republic in the latter speech he remarked: 'If today during a Reichstag session the graves in Potsdam were to open and Frederick the Great were to climb out of his grave the report to Berlin would say: Frederick the Great has risen from the dead and is marching on Berlin. Long live the king! A new amendment to the law on the defence of the republic must be drawn up. And paragraph 1 would read: kings are forbidden to leave their graves.'

6 He did, of course, tailor his speeches to appeal to more select audiences: cf. the sober impression made on Albert Speer by Hitler's address to Berlin university students in 1931. A. Speer, *Inside the Third Reich* (London, 1970) pp. 15–16; confirmed in a personal interview with Albert Speer, 24 October 1976.

7 He may have been influenced by J. R. Rossbach's lecture *Die Massenseele, Psychologische Betrachtungen über die Enstehung von Volks (Massen) Bewegungen (Revolutionen)*, circulating in Munich in 1919; cf. A. Tyrell, *Vom 'Trommler' zum 'Führer'. Der Wandel von Hitlers Selbstverständnis zwischen 1919 and 1924 und die Entwicklung der NSDAP* (München, 1975) pp. 54–6.

8 *Mein Kampf*, pp. 478–9; cf. the revealing comment in his speech to the Nationalklub on 28 February 1926: 'What is made of steel is the feeling of hatred. Because it is a human passion it can be shaken much less than an inferior evaluation based on scientific knowledge. That can alter; personal hatred endures'. BA, NS 26–60, p. 69.

9 Baldur von Schirach, *ich glaubte an Hitler* (Gütersloh, 1967), p. 49.

10 O. Strasser, *Hitler and I* (London, 1940), p. 65.

11 The mood is captured perfectly by a German-Russian aristocrat, a refugee and later party member who recalls first hearing Hitler in 1926: 'My heart pounded with curiosity and anticipation, I was awaiting the appearance of our Hitler from my seat in the crowded auditorium. A storm of jubilation rising from afar, from the street and moving into the lobby, announced the coming of the Führer. And then suddenly the auditorium went wild, as he strode resolutely in his raincoat and without a hat to the rostrum. When the speech came to an end, I could not see out of my eyes any more. There were tears in my eyes, my throat was all tight from crying. A liberating scream of the purest enthusiasm discharged the unbearable tension as the auditorium rocked with applause. I looked round discreetly, and noticed that others, too, men and women and young fellows were as deeply affected as I. They also wiped tears from their eyes. Deafened and with a sense of enormous joy I stormed into the street. At last I was no longer alone. There were people around me who felt the same as I, who were looking at each other in joyful rapture, as if they were all one family or a brotherhood or a new firm and happy community where everyone could read in the other's eyes a solemn oath of loyalty. . . . This experience I had again and again in the course of the following years and my feeling became ever stronger and deeper.' P. Merkl, *Political Violence under the Swastika: 581 Early Nazis*, pp. 105–6.

12 cf. K. Vondung, *Magie und Manipulation. Ideologischer Kult und politische Religion des Nationalsozialismus* (Göttingen, 1971); and D. Griesweile, *Propaganda der Friedlosigkeit. Eine Studie zu Hitlers Rhetorik 1920–1933* (Stuttgart, 1972). Albert Speer feels that the 'Messianic' aspect can be easily overdone and maintains that certainly after 1933 it would be an exaggeration to regard him as a Messiah figure at all: interview 24 October 1976.

13 On the death cult in Nazism cf. R. E. Herzstein, 'Goebbels et le mythe historique par le film 1942–1945,' *Revue d'historie de la deuxieme guerre mondiale* CI (1976).

14 VB 25 November 1922. Cf. Goebbels: 'We have learned that politics is no longer the art of the possible. What we want is unattainable and impossible of fulfilment according to the laws of mechanics. We know that and we act in accordance with this realization because we believe in miracles, in the impossible and in the unattainable. For us politics is the miracle of the impossible.' *Die zweite Revolution mit Widmung Adolf Hitler dem Führer* (Zwickau, 1927), p. 6.

15 Cf. the revealing analysis of Hanns Johst, a Nazi propagandist, in Vondung, *op. cit.*, pp. 204–9.

16 M. K. Kater, 'Zur Soziologie der früheren NSDAP', *VfZG* (1971–2).

17 H. A. Winkler, *Mittelstand, Demokratie und Nationalsozialismus* (Köln, 1972).

18 Merkl, *op. cit.*

19 Cf. Christian Weber, one of the inner circle who told Hitler after a rowdy meeting: 'I've

understood nothing of what you have said in your speech about politics, but I've seen that the action is where you are [bei Ihnen geht was auf] and I'm with you'. F. Wiedemann, *Der Mann der Feldherr werden wollte* (Velbert, 1964), p. 96.

20 Merkl, *op. cit.*, pp. 52–4, 142, points out that over half the respondents in the Abel sample were too young to have been in the army.

21 BA, Nachlass Krebs no. 7, 'Die Nationalsozialistische Deutsche Arbeiter Partei', pp. 3–4.

22 Hitler joined in the brawls, on occasions; cf. IFZ F-14, Ulrich Graft, 'Wie ich den Führer kennenlernte', pp. 7, 38; comment of Dr Hümmert on *MNN* report, 27 April 1921, Stadtarchiv München.

23 Important studies are R. Herberle, *From Democracy to Nazism: a Regional Case Study of Political Parties in Germany* (Baton Rouge, 1945); J. Noakes, *The Nazi Party in Lower Saxony 1921–1933* (Oxford, 1971).

24 As the basis of the party widened slightly between 1930 and 1933 the proportion of workers joining the party increased somewhat, but that did not greatly alter its middle-class complexion. Unconvincing is the thesis of Max H. Kele, *The Nazis and the Workers* (Chapel Hill, 1972), also accepted by G. Schulz, *Aufstieg des Nationalsozialismus, Krise und Revolution in Deutschland* (Frankfurt a/M and Berlin, 1975), pp. 551–2.

25 One consequence of the middle-class invasion of the party was the loss of the flattering image of youthfulness. Significantly, two thirds of Abel's respondents joining the party after 1930 were born before 1895; of those joining after 1932, 22·4 per cent were over 50 and over 50 per cent were over 40. Merkl, *op. cit.*, p. 559.

26 Describing a Hitler meeting in 1930 a contemporary observed: 'the audience was breathlessly under his spell. This man expressed their thoughts, their feelings, their hopes: a new prophet had arisen—many saw in him already another Christ who predicted the end of their sufferings and had the power to lead them into the promised land if they were only prepared to follow him.' Lilo Linke, *Restless Days*, p. 107. Cf. the revealing comment of a young man born in 1911 and active in youth movements in his teens. 'What attracted us like a magnet was precisely the fact that he [Hitler] made demands of us and promised us nothing. He demanded of every person a total commitment to his movement and therefore to Germany.' Merkl, *op. cit.*, p. 236.

27 Weigand von Miltenberg, *Adolf Hitler Wilhelm III* (Berlin, 1931), p. 11.

28 It has been argued recently by Jürgen Kocka that the persistence of pre-industrial attitudes in Germany was an important contributory cause of the Nazi triumph.

29 Cf. Horn, *Führerideologie und Parteiorganisation in der NSDAP (1919–1933)* (Düsseldorf, 1972), pp. 25–8. An interesting contemporary work is K. Hesse, *Der Feldherr Psychologos. Ein Suchen nach dem Führer der deutschen Zukunft*, published in 1922.

30 K. Hildebrand, *The Foreign Policy of the Third Reich* (London, 1973), p. 146.

31 For a penetrating analysis of this thesis as expounded by H-U Wehler in *Das deutsche Kaiserreich 1917–1918* (Göttingen, 1973), cf. T. Nipperdey, *Gesellschaft, Kultur, Theorie. Gesammelte Aufsätze zur neueren Geschichte* (Göttingen, 1976); also H-G Zmarzlik, 'Das Kaisserreich in neuer Sicht' *HZ* CCXXI, 1 (1976); cf Wehler's reply: 'Neue historische Literatur. Kritik und kritische Antikritik', *HZ* CCXXV, 1 (1977).

32 O. Fenichel, *The Psychoanalytic Theory of Neurosis* (London, 1945), p. 467.

33 T. Heuss, *Hitlers Weg* (Berlin, 1932), p. 26.

34 Cf. F. Plümer, *Die Wahrheit über Hitler und seinen Kreis* (München, 1925).

35 Cf. H. H. Hofmann, *Der Hitler Putsch. Krisenjahre deutscher Geschichte 1920–1924* (München, 1961), p. 37.

36 Tyrell, *op. cit.*

37 BA, NS-26 17, 15 July 1921.

38 *Der Hitler Prozess vor dem Volksgericht in München* (München, 1924) I, p. 163.

39 J. Gordon *Hitler and the Beerhall Putsch* (Princeton, 1972), p. 50.

40 When he stormed and raged to Lossow about red rallies taking place only over his dead body, that does not necessarily signify loss of control; this was his normal technique on encountering opposition. Fest's assertion *Hitler* (London, 1974), p. 170, that Hitler man-oeuvred himself into an 'all or nothing' situation is difficult to reconcile with Hitler's withdrawal when the odds lengthened. He gambled recklessly but did not go beyond the point of no return in 1923 any more than in 1938.

41 Gordon, *op. cit.*, p. 269.

42 Cf. an interesting defence of the putsch, probably written by Captain Weiss, editor of the *Heimatbund*, and entitled 'Die Wahrheit über den Hitler putsch' in Staatsarchiv München, St.

Anw. 3099. Kurt G. W. Ludecke, *I Knew Hitler: the Story of a Man who Escaped the Blood Purge* (London, 1938), pp. 168–70, also thought Hitler could have succeeded.

43   e.g. *VB*, 6–7 May 1923 when Hitler, commenting on the need for a dictator to come forth and save Germany, wrote: 'It is not our task to look for this person. He is either given to us by heaven or he isn't. Our task is to create the sword that the person will need when he is there. Our task is to give the dictator when he comes a people ready for him.' Cf. Hitler's interview with Max Maurenbrecher in May 1921, *Deutsche Zeitung*, 10 November 1921, when he emphasized that he was not the Führer 'able to save a fatherland sinking into chaos. He was the agitator who knew how to rally the masses. But he was not the architect who has the groundplan and elevation of the new building clearly before his eyes and can lay one stone on another with quiet confidence in his creative work. He needed a greater man behind him on whose orders he could depend.' Quoted in M. Plewinia, *Auf dem Weg zu Hitler. Der völkische Publizist Dietrich Eckart.* (Bremen, 1970) p. 85.

44   Staatsarchiv München, St. Anw. 3101: testimony of Otto Freiherr von Bachem.

45   Tyrell, *op. cit.*, p. 166.

46   A high police official observed with disgust that Hitler behaved 'like a Red Indian'. Staatsarchiv München, St. Anw. 3112.

47   W. Maser, *Die Frühgeschichte der NSDAP: Hitlers Weg bis 1924* (Frankfurt a/M and Bonn, 1965) p. 452.

48   *IMT* XII, p. 313.

49   Ludendorff maintained afterwards that Hitler had intended to speak but was unable to get through the crowds. Staatsarchiv München, St. Anw. 3101.

50   Cf. the critical comment on Ludendorff's conduct by Freiherr von Aufsess Geh. St. A, MA 103472: von Kahr to Knilling, 18 December 1923.

51   BA, NS-26 901. H. Fobkes Nachlass.

52   H. Grimm, *Warum—woher aber wohin?* (Lippoldsberg, 1954) p. 114.

53   E. Deuerlein, *Hitler eine politische Biographie* (Augsburg, 1969) p. 162.

54   Strasser, *op. cit.,* pp. 86–7. Noakes, *op. cit.,* p. 76 casts some doubt on the reliability of Strasser's account.

55   Hitler remained equivocal about Nazi participation in elections. Even when he allowed Nazis to stand in the local elections of 1926 he emphasized that the real task was: 'to forge strong weapons and the will and the energy so that when the hour comes and the red dragon rouses itself at least one section of our people will not be despondent and despairing but full of determination to offer resistance'. *VB*, 26 May 1926. Nor would he rebuke Goebbels when the latter revived the old tactics of street violence on a grand scale in Berlin in March 1927. As late as 1929 he told an audience: 'We will come to power one way or another [so oder so]; legally, or if not, then I will get there with them' and, turning, he pointed to 400 SA men behind him on the stage. An observer felt that the applause with which this remark was greeted showed that Hitler had gauged the true feelings of his audience correctly: BA, NS-26 528: F. Hirsch testimony given in 1936.

56   Cf. A. Tyrell, *Führer befiehlt . . . Selbstzeugnisse aus der Kampfzeit der* NSDAP (Düsseldorf, 1969), pp. 116–17. R. Hess to Landes and Ortsgruppenleitung, 11 December 1925.

57   Cf. A Tyrell, 'Führergedanke und Gauleiterwechsel. Die Teilung des Gaues Rheinland der NSDAP 1931', *VfZG* (1975–4); Hitler is reported as saying in 1925 that 'the most effective fighter in the NS movement is the man who wins respect for himself as leader through his own achievements.' BA, NS-26 147.

58   In Munich only the Schwabing branch was active by the autumn of 1925. In 1927 that branch lost 78 members and admitted 45. G. Pridham, *Hitler's rise to power. The Nazi movement in Bavaria 1923–1933* (London, 1973), p. 62. Difficulties in the party are referred to in Staatsarchiv München, PD 6779, police report 28 March 1927.

59   Hitler quickly recognized the potential in the new scenario; in December 1927 he addressed several thousand farmers from Lower Saxony and Schleswig-Holstein.

60   Cf. Trotsky's perceptive remark: 'I cannot help noting how obligingly the accidental helps the historical law. Broadly speaking the entire historical process is a refraction of the historical law through the accidental. In the language of biology one might say that the historical law is realised through the natural selection of accidents. On this foundation there develops that conscious human activity which subjects accidents to a process of artificial selection. . . . One can foresee a revolution or a war but it is impossible to foresee the consequences of an autumn shooting trip.' *My Life* (Gloucester, Mass. 1970), pp. 494–5, 498. By the same standard the German dictatorship was predictable whereas the personal triumph of Adolf Hitler was not.

61   Sometimes he sat silently listening to exchanges of opinion and suddenly intervened, coming down on one side or another and further discussion ceased.

62   Otto Dietrich estimated that Hitler travelled 50,000 kilometers by air, 25,000 by road and addressed in excess of ten million Germans at over 200 meetings. *With Hitler on the Road to Power* (London, 1934), p. 21.

63   That was the view of H. Hoffmann, *Hitler wie ich ibn sah. Aufzeichmungen seines Leibfotographen* (München, 1974), p. 133.

64   J. Goebbels, *Vom Kaiserhof zur Reichskanzlei. Eine historische Darstellung in Tagebuchblättern* (München, 1934), p. 104.

65   As Hitler declared on 16 June 1932: 'one cannot demand heroism of a nation if its political leaders are ready for every compromise however shabby.' M. Domarus, *Hitler Reden und Proklamationen 1933–1945* (Würzburg, 1963), 1, p. 127.

66   A. Krebs, *Tendenzen und Gestalten in der NSDAP* (Stuttgart, 1959) p. 137. Cf. Hitler to A. Dinter, 25 June 1929: 'I am 39. If fate doesn't decide otherwise I have scarcely twenty years at my disposal even in favourable circumstances.' A. Tyrell, *Führer befiehlt,* pp. 204–5.

67   Domarus, *op. cit.* i, p. 129.

68   Goebbels believed half the Gauleiters opposed Hitler. Ovens, *Mit Goebbels bis zu Ende* (Buenos Aires, 1949) i, p. 99.

69   The Nationalists preferred to stand by Papen. The Centre and the BVP with a total of ninety seats would have supported a Hitler cabinet. So might the Populists with eleven seats giving Hitler, with 196 seats, a bare majority with 297 seats.

70   Domarus, *op. cit.* i, p. 162.

71   This thought was clearly in the mind of the party official responsible for Middle Germany and Brandenburg who reported that 'In general by propaganda means we will not be able to get more than 12 to 14 millions. The others must be got by force and for that we need to be in power.' BA, NS-22 347, 11 November 1932.

72   N. Kadritzke, *Faschismus und Krise. Zum Verhältnis von Politik und Ökonomie im Nationalsozialismus* (Frankfurt and New York, 1976).

73   After 1930 the Nazis jettisoned what remained of their old economic philosophy and cashed in on the current vogue in industrial circles for *Grossraumwirtschaft*, which supplied useful economic excuses for eastward expansion. Cf. Schulz, *op. cit.,* p. 735; also H-E Volkmann, 'Politik, Wirtschaft und Aufrüstung unter dem Nationalsozialismus' in *Deutschland Hitler und die Mächte* (Düsseldorf, 1976), edited by M. Funke, pp. 286–8.

74   A general consensus in favour of a *Grossraumwirtschaft* certainly did not exist in 1933; on 1 February export-oriented industries still submitted a memorandum through the Deutscher Industrie und Handelstag in favour of a liberal trade policy to boost exports: BA, R 43 11/308a; cf. A. Sohn-Rethel, *Ökonomie und Klassenstruktur des deutschen Faschismus. Aufzeichnungen und Analysen* (Frankfurt a/M, 1973), pp. 67–8.

75   Bullock, *op. cit.,* p. 255; Fest, *op cit.,* p. 365.

76   *DGFP* C1 no. 3.

77   According to Otto Wagener, *Ergänzende Aufzeichungen 5*, Die Untergrundsbewegung gegen Hitler, IFZ, ED 60/7 2830/61, Hitler was taken aback by the news that the parties had dissolved themselves.

Chapter 2

1   W. Petwaidic, *Die autoritäre Anarchie. Streiflichter des deutschen Zusammenbruchs* (Hamburg, 1946), p. 18.

2   As K. D. Bracher points out in 'Tradition und Revolution im Nationalsozialismus' in *Hitler Deutschland und die Mächte. Materialien zur Aussenpolitik des dritten Reiches*, edited by M. Funke (Düsseldorf, 1976), p. 18, even early writers, e.g. E. Fraenckel, *The Dual State* (London and New York, 1941), were well aware of the dichotomy between monolithic state and polycratic administrative structure.

3   B. von Schirach, *Ich glaubte an Hitler* (Hamburg, 1967) p. 53.

4   *The Eden Memoirs. Facing the Dictators* (London, 1962), p. 133.

5   e.g. K. D Bracher, 'Stufen der nationalsozialistischen Machtergreifung' *VfZG* (1956) iv, p. 42.

6   H. Mommsen, *Beamtentum in Dritten Reich* (Stuttgart, 1967); cf. R. Bollmus, *Das Amt Rosenberg und seine Gegner. Zum Machtkampt im nationalsozialistischen Herrschaftssystem* (Stuttgart, 1970).

7 Referring to his practice of appointing individuals or organizations to perform the same task, he once remarked, 'that way . . . the stronger one does the job.' A. Speer, *Inside the Third Reich*, p. 210.

8 A valuable introduction to the Adjutantur by F. P. Kahlenberg in BA, NS-10 *Bestand*; cf. G. Franz-Willing, *Die Hitler Bewegung. Der Ursprung 1919–1922* (Hamburg and Berlin, 1962), pp. 126–37.

9 F. Wiedemann, *Der Mann der Feldherr werden wolte* (Velbert, 1964).

10 If Major Engels's 'diary', *Heeresadjutant bei Hitler 1938–1943. Aufzeichnungen des Major Engel,* edited by H. von Kotze (Stuttgart, 1974), can be relied upon, Hitler could be extraordinarily frank on occasions.

11 Cf. the stimulating essay by W. Michalka, 'Die nationalsozialistische Aussenpolitik im Zeichen eines "Konzeptionen-Pluralismus" Fragestellungen und Forschingsaufgaben' in Funke, *op. cit.,* pp. 46–62.

12 J. Noakes and G. Pridham, *Documents on Nazism 1919—1945* (London, 1974), pp. 508–9.

13 Cf. von Bülow's revealing memorandum drawn up in March 1933: G. Wollstein (ed.) 'Eine Denkschrift des Staatsserkretärs Bernhard von Bülow vom März 1933. Wilhelminische Konzeption der Aussenpolitik zu Beginn der nationalisozialistischen Herrschaft', *MGM* (1973) I, pp. 77–94.

14 G. Wollstein, *Vom Weimarer Revisionismus zu Hitler* (Bonn-Bad Godesberg, 1973), pp. 201–3, 293–4.

15 It was entirely characteristic of Hitler's style that he allowed Goebbels and Forster to agitate for the immediate seizure of Danzig. In the conversations with Lipski Hitler and Goering were able to present their own 'reasonable' proposals as the only alternative to the annexationist demands of reactionary Junkers and party extremists.

16 H. Zoller, *Hitler privat: Erlebnisbericht seiner Geheimsekretärin* (Düsseldorf, 1949), pp. 24–5.

17 Cf. M. Braubach, *Der Einmarsch deutscher Truppen in die entmiltarisierte Zone am Rhein in März 1936. Ein Beitrag zur Vorgeschichte des zweiten Weltkrieges* (Köln and Opladen, 1956), pp. 12–16; J. T. Emmerson, *The Rhineland Crisis 1 March 1936. A Study in Multilateral Diplomacy* (London, 1977), pp. 82–5.

18 Cf. W. Michalka, *Joachim von Ribbentrop und die deutsche Englandpolitik 1933–1940. Studien zur aussenpolitischen Konzeptionendiskussion im Dritten Reich* (Diss. Mannheim, 1976). Nor should Mussolini's influence on Hitler be overlooked. Ambassador Dodd feared that the Italian dictator would stimulate Hitler's adventurous instincts 'and more specially [act] as a spur and support to those rash influential personalities about Hitler'. *Foreign Relations of the United States 1936* II, 19 November 1936, p. 561.

19 Cf. H-H Abendroth, 'Hitlers Entscheidung' and W. Schieder 'Spanischer Bürgerkrieg und Vierjahresplan. Zur Struktur nationalsozialistischer Aussenpolitik', in W. Schieder and C. Dipper (ed.), *Der spanischer Bürgerkrieg in der internationalen Politik (1936–1939),* (München, 1976).

20 Domarus, *op. cit.,* I, p. 606.

21 Cf. M. Geyer, 'Militär Rüstung und Aussenpolitik Aspekte militärischer Revisionspolitik in der Zwischenkriegszeit', in Funke, *op. cit.,* pp. 239–68.

22 Fest, *op. cit.,* p. 574.

23 *DGFP,* D 11 no. 221.

24 Although Goering expressed his concern at the prospect of war to Wiedemann on 28 May 1938 after Hitler's address, he congratulated the Führer on his genius. Wiedemann, *op. cit.,* pp. 127–8; W. Bross, *Gespräche mit Hermann Goering wahrend des Nürnberger Prozesses* (Flensburg and Hamburg, 1950), p. 182 for Weizsäcker's appreciation of Goering.

25 Quoted in W. L. Shirer, *The Rise and Fall of the Third Reich. A History of Nazi Germany* (London, 1964), p. 619.

26 Especially T. Mason, *Arbeiterklasse und Volksgemeinschaft. Dokumente und Materialien zur deutschen Arbeiterpolitik 1936–1939* (Düsseldorf, 1975); 'Innere Krise und Angriffskrieg 1938/9' in F. Forstmeier and H-E Volkmann, *Wirtschaft und Rüstung am Vorabend des zweiten Weltkriegs* (Düsseldorf, 1975).

27 Domarus, *op. cit.,* II, p. 1054.

28 *DGFP,* D VII no. 192.

29 These thoughts occurred to the military quite early on; cf. memorandum of General Fromm, head of the Allgemeines Heeresamt dated 1 August 1936, BA-MA, RH 15 AHA 1790/36 Ia, discussed by E. M. Robertson in *Hitler's Pre-war Policy and Military Plans 1933/9* (London,

1963), p. 84; but cf. Geyer, *op. cit.*, p. 265, note 127.

30 G. Hallgarten and J. Radkau, *Deutsche Industrie und Politik von Bismarck bis heute* (Frankfurt a/M-Köln, 1974), p. 342.

31 *DBFP*, series III VI, p. 659.

32 'The war must be waged soon on account of the armament of the others', 10 March 1939. H. Groscurth, *Tagebücher eines Abwehroffiziers 1938–1940* (Stuttgart, 1970), p. 167; 'the time is more favourable now than in 2–3 years. . . . we face the hard alternative of striking now or of being annihilated with certainty sooner or later', 22 August 1939. Domarus, *op. cit.,* II, p. 1235; on 18 March 1940, justifying his decision to attack Poland, Hitler told Mussolini: 'There was no doubt . . . that the conditions of the struggle would in two years' time at best not have become more favourable for Germany'. M. Muggeridge (ed.), *Ciano's Diplomatic Papers* (London, 1948), p. 361.

33 E. von Weizsäcker, *Erinnerungen* (Munich and Leipzig, 1950), p. 208.

34 T. Taylor (ed.), *Hitler's Secret Book* (New York, 1961), p. 119.

35 Some attempts have been made to correct this. Cf. John D. Heyl, 'Hitler's Economic Thought: a Reappraisal', *CEH* (1973) I; Bernice Carroll, *Design for Total War Arms and Economics in the Third Reich* (The Hague, 1968), p. 140, who argues that Hitler's expansionist programme was derived directly from his economic analysis.

36 Hitler was not alone in his veneration for the business man; cf. Hallgarten and Radkau, *op. cit.*, pp. 270–79; cf. the fulsome praise of big business in P. Wiel, *Krieg und Wirtschaft, Kriegswirtschaft, Wehrwirtschaft* (Berlin, 1938), p. 70: 'Even the best administrative organization can never gain the experience of those who go into business on their own account. Business and bureaucratic organization stand in relationship to each other like front line and rear echelon. The constant danger at the front arouses all the instincts of aggressiveness and self-assurance.'

37 The Deutscher Industrie und Handelstag representing export-oriented industry favoured a liberal commercial policy to boost exports, the stimulation of private industry and minimal dependence on public investment. Memorandum of 1 February 1933, BA, R43 II/538 308a. The Deutscher Landwirtschaftsrat, on the other hand, demanded a protected and controlled agrarian sector at the expense of the needs of industry. Memorandum of 23 February 1933.

38 e.g. A. Schweitzer, *Big Business in the Third Reich* (Bloomington, 1964); T. Mason, 'The Primacy of Politics—Politics and Economics in National Socialist Germany' in S. J. Woolf (ed.) *The Nature of Fascism* (London, 1968). But Hallgarten and Radkau, *op. cit.*, pp. 296, 315–20 maintain that the major combines retained substantial power and intervened effectively in the minutiae of economic policy.

39 Cf. Geyer, *op. cit.*, pp. 261–2.

40 T. Mason, *Arbeiterklasse und Volksgemeinschaft Einleitung*, pp. 1–16. The same point is made by A. Speer, *Inside the Third Reich*, p. 214.

41 BA, R43 1470 Bl.265/6, ministry of the interior, 5 November 1934.

42 A. Speer, *Inside the Third Reich*, p. 158; cf. *Spandauer Tagebuch*, p. 225.

43 As Mason, *op. cit.,* points out, p. 9, Hitler's loss of faith is apparent in *Hitler's Secret Book*, p. 13: 'The struggle for daily bread stands at the forefront of all vital necessities. To be sure brilliant leaders can hold great goals before a people's eyes so that it can be further diverted from material things in order to serve higher spiritual ideals. . . . A people can quite well endure a certain limitation of material goals as long as it is given compensation in the form of active ideals. But if those ideals are not to result in the ruin of a people, they must never exist unilaterally at the expense of material nourishment.'

44 *DGFP*, D I no. 19.

45 A. Milward, 'Der Einfluss ökonomischer und nicht-ökonomischer Faktoren auf die Strategie des Blitzkriegs' in F. Forstmeier und H-E Volkmann, *Wirtschaft und Rüstung an Vorabend des Zweiten Weltkrieges* (Düsseldorf, 1975).

46 T. Mason, *Arbeiterklasse und Volksgemeinschaft*, pp. 102–3, 158–9. Cf. J. Düllfer, 'Der Beginn des Krieges 1939: Hitler, die innere Krise und das Mächtesystem' in *Gesellschaft und Geschichte* (1976), pp. 465–7.

47 T. Mason, 'Women in Germany 1925–1940: Family Welfare and Work' part 2, *History Workshop* (1976) II.

48 E. Calic, *Unmasked. Two Confidential Interviews with Hitler in 1931* (London, 1971), p. 40.

49 K. Pätzold, *Faschismus Rassenwahn Judenverfolgung. Eine Studie zur politischen Strategie und Taktik des faschistischen deutschen Imperialismus* (Berlin, 1975), pp. 265–71.

50 Quoted in H. Buchheim, M. Broszat, H-A Jacobsen, *Anatomy of the SS State* (London, 1968),

p. 35. At the same meeting after Reichsärtztefführer Wagner had spoken about the problem of heredity, Hitler told him that in a future war he intended to permit euthanasia. A Platten-Hallermund, *Die Tötung Geisteskranke in Deutschland* (Frankfurt, 1948), p. 30.

51   Quoted in L. Kochan, *Pogrom 10 November 1938* (London, 1957), p. 51.

52   On 10 November Goebbels informed Frank that Hitler would order Goering to create a 'Jew-free' economy: *IMT* XIII, p. 131. The same day Hitler gave Goering detailed instructions to that effect: *IMT* IX, p. 313.

53   The exact figure was agreed by Hitler, Goebbels and Goering on 10 November.

54   Though the industrial combines had hoped to benefit from this, their 'friend' Goering saw to it that the state was the chief beneficiary. For instance, when Hitler ordered massive arms increases in October 1938, Goering agreed that the seizure of Jewish assets would ease the precarious foreign exchange position. Goering spelt this out to the *Reichsverteidigungsrat* on 18 November 1938. 3575 PS *IMT* XXXII.

55   'But the problem would soon be solved. On this point his mind was irrevocably made up. . . . One day the Jews would disappear from Europe.' Hitler to Pirow, 24 November 1938, *DGFP*, D IV no. 271; 'We are going to destroy the Jews. They are not going to get away with what they did on 9 November 1918. The day of reckoning has come.' Hitler to Chvalkovsky, 21 January 1939, *DGFP*, D IV no. 158.

56   Domarus, *op. cit.*, II, p. 1057.

57   As Hitler remarked to Colin Ross, 12 March 1940, *DGFP*, D VIII no. 671.

58   The reasons for Hitler's interest in the plan are obscure but anti-semites had been attracted by the possibilities of Madagascar for many years. For example, *VB*, 29 June 1926, contains an article by an unnamed Englishman on the subject and the editorial comment (presumably by Rosenberg) that as 'a final solution' Madagascar had more to offer then Palestine. I am indebted to Geoffrey Stoakes of the College of Ripon and York St John's for this information.

59   P. Schmidt. *Statist auf diplomatischer Bühne 1923—1945: Erlebnisse eines Chefdolmetschers im Auswärtigen Amt mit den Staatsmännern Europas* (Bonn, 1950), p. 495; *DGFP*, D X no. 345.

60   A. Hillgruber, *Staatsmänner und Diplomaten bei Hitler* (München, 1969) p. 310. In 'Die Endlösung und das deutsche Ostimperium als Kernstück des rassenideologischen Programmes des Nationalsozialismus', *VfZG* (1972) II, Hillgruber maintains that Hitler decided on extermination in July at the height of his success in Russia, not in the autumn as U. D. Adam argues in *Judenpolitik im Dritten Reich* (Düsseldorf, 1972), p. 312–13.

61   G. Reitlinger, *Die Endlösung. Hitlers Versuch der Endlösung der Juden Europas* (Berlin, 1960), p. 94; cf. Rosenberg's comment to Frank, 14 October 1941: 'The intention is to send all anti-social elements in Reich territory to the sparsely settled eastern territories.' W. Prag and W. Jacobmeyer, *Das Diensttagebuch des deutschen Generalgouverneurs in Polen 1939–1945* (Stuttgart, 1975), p. 413.

62   L. P. Lochner (ed.), *The Goebbels Diaries* (London, 1948), p. 103; cf. pp. 48, 296–70.

63   As Himmler observed: 'The extermination of the Jews brings pain with it but it is a good thing if the million Jews are annihilated at once for there will be a thousand years of peace, joy and well-being.' A. Besgen, *Der stille Befehl* (München, 1960), p. 20.

64   Domarus, *op cit.*, II, p. 2085.

Chapter 3

1   A. Speer, *Inside the Third Reich*, p. 232. The same was true of architectural and artistic experts to whose judgment Hitler invariably bowed, p. 79.

2   E. Hansfstaengl, *Zwischen Weissem und Braunem Haus* (München, 1970), p. 46.

3   Even when it was apparent by November 1943 that this could not be done Messerschmitt was still reassuring Hitler. D. Irving, *The rise and fall of the Luftwaffe* (London, 1976), p. 257.

4   This was later confirmed by practical experience; *ibid.*, p. 283.

5   Speer, *op cit.*, p. 366. Hitler did allow the Heinkel firm to work on a new jet fighter prototype in the autumn of 1944. H. Jung, *Die Ardennen Offensive 1944/5* (Stuttgart, 1971), p. 71–2. But the He 162, like the Me 262, arrived too late to affect the outcome of the war.

6   H. Heiber, *Hitlers Lagebesprechungen. Die Protokollfragmente seiner militärischen Konferenzen 1942–1945* (Stuttgart, 1962), p. 171.

7   *ibid.*, p. 584.

8   Jung, *op. cit.*, appendix 4, p. 277.
9   *Brassey's Naval Annual* (1948), Führer Naval Conferences, p. 398, 29 June 1944.
10 *KTB des OKW* IV, 2, p. 1647.
11 Jung, *op. cit.*, extract from the diary of General Werner Kreipe, chief of airforce general staff, 19 September 1944, p. 219.
12 The sober-minded Dönitz seldom went to the Führer's headquarters because he felt that he would lose his independence of mind in Hitler's presence. *IMT* XIII, pp. 243–4.
13 F. Hossbach, *Zwischen Wehrmacht und Hitler 1934–1938* (Wolfsbüttel, 1949), p. 45.
14 H-A Jacobsen and W. Jochmann, *Ausgewählte Dokumente zur Geschichte des National-sozialismus 1933–1945* (Bielefeld, 1961), doc. 23, November 1939, p. 2.
15 H-E Volkmann, 'Autarkie, Grossraumwirtschaft und Aggression. Zur ökonomischer Motivation der Besetzung Luxemburgs, Belgiens und der Niederlande 1940', *MGM* (1976) I.
16 G. Wagner (ed.), *Lagevorträge des Oberbefehlshabers der Kriegsmarine vor Hitler 1939–1945* (München, 1972), p. 37. Hitler to Raeder 23 October 1939.
17 Army general staff headquarters were at Zossen, a town 35 kilometers southeast of Berlin.
18 B. Liddell Hart, *A History of the Second World War* (London, 1970), p. 66. Cf. Jodl's comment to Hitler: 'We are taking a sneaky path here in military terms and the god of battle had better not catch us on it.' BA-MA, *Jodl Nachlass* N 69/8 Capt. Meckel's essay, p. 7.
19 On the other hand, Admiral Dönitz, commander of the German submarine force, maintained later that Britain could only have been brought to her knees by a German victory in the Battle of the Atlantic. Diverting scarce submarines to the Mediterranean simply made victory where it really counted even less likely. *KTB des OKW* I, pp. 230–1E.
20 D. Irving, *Hitler's War* (London, 1977), p. 143.
21 W. Dlugoborski and C. Madajczyk, 'Ausbeutungssystem in den besetzten Gebieten Polens und der UdSSR', pp. 375–416 and H-E Volkmann, 'NS-Aussenhandel im "geschlossenen" Kriegswirtschaftsraum', pp. 93–133 in F. Forstmeier and H-E. Volkmann, *Kriegswirtschaft und Rüstung, 1939–1945* (Düsseldorf, 1977).
22 That Hitler was well aware of the failure of a continental economy which excluded Russia is suggested by his comment to Todt and Keitel, 20 June 1941, that autarkical measures had gone too far and that in future Germany should 'secure by conquest all the areas of particular economic-strategic interest'. *IMT* XXVII, pp. 120–21.
23 B. A. Leach, *German Strategy against Russia 1939–1944* (Oxford, 1973), pp. 87–99.
24 Quoted in A. Bullock, *Hitler: Study in Tyranny* (London, 1972), p. 652. But it is clear from Leach, *op. cit.*, pp. 156, 158–9 that Hitler also had reservations about the outcome of the operation.
25 M. von Creveld, *Hitler's Strategy 1940–1941. The Balkan Clue* (Cambridge, 1973), pp. 170–76.
26 An imposing array of Russian generals thought Hitler right—Rokossovsky, Zhukov and Sokolovsky. L. Bezymenski, *Sonderakte Barbarossa* (Stuttgart, 1968) pp. 299–300; cf. Timoshenko's admission that Hitler's strategy was correct. Irving, *Hitler's War*, p. 348.
27 'On the whole the expectation is being expressed that the recognition that neither enemy formation can annihilate the other will lead to a compromise peace.' F. Halder, *Kriegstagebuch 1939—1942* (Stuttgart, 1962–4), 19 November 1941, p. 295. Speaking to Scavenius, the Danish foreign minister, on 27 November 1941 Hitler said that if the German people was not strong enough to sacrifice itself it ought to be destroyed by a stronger power. A. Hillgruber, *Staatsmänner und Diplomaten bei Hitler 1939–1941* (Frankfurt, 1967), I, doc. 91.
28 BA-MA, *KTB der SKL*, 28 October 1941.
29 G. Blumentritt, *The Fatal Decisions* (London, 1956), p. 67 thought him right. That is the view of the latest researcher, K. Rheinhardt, *Die Wende vor Moskau. Das Scheitern der Strategie Hitlers im Winter 1941/2* (Stuttgart, 1972). For the contrary view cf. G. E. Glau, *The German Campaign in Russia Planning and Operations* (Washington, 1955).
30 F. Halder, *Hitler als Feldherr* (München, 1949), p. 45.
31 *KTB des OKW* IV, p. 1503; Jodl said it was clear to Hitler that victory was impossible after 1941–2.
32 Domarus, *op cit.* II, p. 1935.
33 Hillgruber, *op. cit.* I, doc. 27.
34 Irving, *op. cit.*, p. 346.
35 *KTB des OKW* I, p. 107E.
36 R. G. Waite, *Adolf Hitler: the Psychopathic God* (New York, 1977), pp. 408–9, points out

that a borderline personality in a crisis situation seeks reassurance by provoking a greater crisis.

37   Not, however, a decisive blow. He informed Goebbels that when the campaign season was over in October he would go into winter quarters. L. Lochner (ed.) *The Goebbels Diary* (London, 1948), p. 92.

38   Of course, the heroic resistance of working-class elements, led by Communists and Socialists, of committed Christians and of those middle-class and aristocratic circles involved in the July 1944 Bomb Plot shows that there were many honourable exceptions.

39   W. Maser, *Hitler* (London, 1973), p. 303; cf. Irving, *op. cit.*, pp. 293–4, 501.

40   Irving, *op. cit.*, pp. 376–7.

41   *ibid.*, p. 413, 424.

42   Keitel maintained that Hitler recognized the danger but thought the risk acceptable as long as the Don was not frozen. BA-MA, Keitel Nachlass Bd. 7, p. 20.

43   L. S. Hill (ed.), *Die Weizsäcker Papiere 1933–1950* (Propyläen Verlag, n.d.), p. 303.

44   Irving, *op cit.*, p. 457.

45   *ibid.*, pp. 457–9.

46   H. von Kotz (ed.) *Heeresadjutant bei Hitler 1938–1943. Aufzeichnungen des Major Engel* (Stuttgart, 1974), p. 140.

47   Irving, *op. cit.*, p. 446 maintains that he was misled into thinking that Stalingrad was virtually in German hands through a message from the chief of staff of Army Group B.

48   Cf. Albert Speer who believes that, when Hitler was compelled after 1941 by the tight military schedule to turn incessantly from one problem to another without time to mull things over, the secret of his success in the old days, he became mentally fatigued and incapable of effective decision-making. Interview 24 October 1976; cf. *Inside the Third Reich*, pp. 293–4.

49   Heiber, *op. cit.*, pp. 614–16, 620.

50   Speaking to divisional commanders in July 1944 he remarked that 'no one will make a separate peace with me.' G. Buchheit, *Hitler also Feldherr Die Zerstörung einer Legende* (Rastatt, 1958), p. 463.

51   BA-MA, N69/8 Nachlass Alfred Jodl. Essay of Capt. Meckel, p. 19.

52   Speer, *op. cit.*, p. 473.

53   *ibid.*, p. 463.

54   *KTB des OKW* IV, 2, p. 1689.

55   *ibid.*, p. 1694.

56   *Nazi Conspiracy and Aggression* (Washington, 1946) VI, p. 562.

57   K. Koller, *Der letzte Monat. Die Tagebuchaufzeichnungen des ehemaligen Chefs des Generalstabes der deutschen Luftwaffe* (Mannheim, 1949), p. 61.

58   Waite, *op. cit.*, pp. 415–32 advances the interesting theory that Eva Braun shot Hitler.

59   J. M. McRandle, *The Track of the Wolf. Essays in National Socialism and its Leader Adolf Hitler* (Evanston, 1965), pp. 148–50.

60   *Der Hitler Prozess vor dem Volksgericht in München* I, p. 184.

61   K. A. von Müller, *In Wandel einer Welt: Erinnerungen 1919–1932* (München, 1966), p. 163.

62   Quoted in Fest, *op. cit.*, p. 187.

63   E. Hanfstaengl. *Zwischen Weissem und Braunem Haus* (München, 1970), p. 6. A police report of his capture in Geh. St. A, Ministry of Interior 13696.

64   J. Goebbels, *Vom Kaiserhof zur Reichskanzlei: Eine historische Darstellung in Tagebuchblättern* (München, 1934), p. 220; Oven, *op. cit.* II, p. 109.

65   Domarus, *op. cit.* II, p. 1316.

66   *ibid.*, p. 1427.

67   *ibid.*, p. 1984.

68   *ibid.*, p. 2146. He did, however, go on to say: 'That I am alive I thank Providence.'

69   A. Zoller. *Hitler privat: Erlebnisbericht seiner Geheimsekretärin* (Düsseldorf, 1949), p. 229.

70   *ibid.*, p. 230.

71   W. Maser, *Hitlers Briefe und Notizen. Sein Weltbild in handschriflichen Dokuments* (Düsseldorf, 1973), p. 375.

Chapter 4

1   H. Rauschning, *Hitler Speaks* (London, 1939); K. Heiden, *A History of National Socialism* (London, 1934).

2   In his preface to N. Cameron and R. H. Steven (ed.), *Hitler's Table Talk 1941–1944* (London, 1953).

3   E. Jäckel, *Hitlers Weltanschauung. Entwurf einer Herrschaft* (Tübingen, 1969).

4   E. Deuerlein, *Hitler. Eine politische Biographie* (Augsburg, 1969), p. 162.

5   As Gauleiter Krebs maintained in 1931: 'The [party] was not born of perceptive insights but of the irrational force of instinct which revolted against the collapse of 1918 and having espied the forces responsible for it fought against them': BA Nachlass Krebs, no. 7. 'Die nationalsozialistische Deutsche Arbeiterpartei', p. 33; cf. the perceptive analysis in T. Heuss, *Hitlers Weg*, pp. 24–5.

6   IFZ, Hitler's speech to officer cadets at the Berghof, 22 June 1944.

7   *ibid.*

8   e.g. K. Pätzold, *Faschismus, Rassenwahn, Judenverfolgung. Eine Studie zur politischen Strategie und Taktik des faschistischen deutschen Imperialismus 1933–1935* (Berlin, 1975).

9   e.g. D. Schoenbaum, *Hitler's Social Revolution: Class and Status in Nazi Germany 1933–1939* (New York, 1967); R. Dahrendorf, *Society and Democracy in Germany* (New York, 1967).

10 For a careful evaluation of this source cf. T. Schieder, *Hermann Rauschnings Gespräche mit Hitler als Geschichtsquelle* (Oplanden, 1972).

11 Rauschning, *op. cit.*, p. 49.

12 *Ibid.*, p. 50.

13 *ibid.*, pp. 229–30.

14 *ibid.*, p. 273.

15 *IMT* XXXVIII, doc. 221–L p. 92.

16 *Ursachen und Folgen vom deutschen Zusammenbruch 1918 und 1945 bis zur staatlichen Neuordnung Deutschlands in der Gegenwart* (Berlin, no date) XXI, p. 511.

17 P. von zur Mühlen, *Rassenideologien. Geschichte und Hintergründe* (Berlin, Bonn, 1977) p. 237.

18 Cf. W. Daim, *Der Mann der Hitler die Ideen gab* (Munich, 1958).

19 F. Bradley Smith, *Adolf Hitler: his Family Childhood and Youth* (Stanford, 1967), p. 125.

20 Hitler's comment 29 November 1921, BA NS-26 17a, that he became a convinced anti-semite 'within a year' of arriving in Vienna should not be taken too literally; R. Binion, who thinks the Pasewalk experience was the decisive moment in the evolution of Hitler's anti-semitism, admits that when he left Vienna his anti-semitism was 'absolute but repressed'. *Hitler Among the Germans* (New York, 1977), p. 20.

21 The following summary of his anti-semitic views is based very largely on a speech on 13 August 1920, BA, NS-26 46.

22 He remarked to Otto Wagener (probably in 1931) that he doubted whether a Jewish state could ever be founded because parasites by their very nature had to live on other peoples. IFZ Otto Wagener Tagebuch ED 60/2 XII, p. 701.

23 *ibid.*, XI, p. 690.

24 BA NS-26 2 'Der völkischer Gedanke und die Partei', p. 4.

25 The revolting crudity of his anti-semitism is strikingly illustrated in a reply in 1922 to Josef Hell, IFZ ZS 640 Folio 6: 'If I am ever really in power the destruction of the Jews will be my first and most important job. As soon as I have the power, I shall have gallows after gallows erected, for example in Munich on the Marienplatz—as many of them as the traffic allows. Then the Jews will be hanged one after another and they will stay hanging until they stink. They will stay hanging as long as hygienically possible. As soon as they are untied, then the next group will follow and that will continue until the last Jew in Munich is exterminated. Exactly the same procedure will be followed in other cities until Germany is cleansed of the last Jew.' Cf. the remarks of Esser at a party meeting, 22 December 1922 that 500,000 Jews would be held as hostages and 'ruthlessly dispatched as foreign soldiers entered Germany'. H. S. Gordon, *Hitler and the Beer Hall Putsch*, p. 265.

26 R. G. Waite, *Adolf Hitler the Psychopathic God* (New York, 1977); W. Langer, *The Mind of Adolf Hitler* (London, 1972).

27 Cf. G. Mendel, *La révolte contre la père* (Paris, 1968), chapters 4–6.

28 R. G. Waite, 'Adolf Hitler's Anti-Semitism: a study in History and Psychoanalysis' in B. J. Wolman (ed.), *The Psychoanalytic Interpretation of History* (London, 1971).

29 H. B. Gisevius, *Adolf Hitler. Versuch einer Deutung* (München, 1963), pp. 383–4.

30 R. Binion, 'Hitler's Concept of Lebensraum: the Psychological Basis' in *History of Childhood Quarterly* (1973).

31 *ibid.*, p. 189.
32 *ibid.*, p. 190. But in *Hitler among the Germans*, p. xii Binion maintains that mutually exclusive solutions to a problem can be advanced by people seeking to relieve a traumatic experience.
33 H. Frank, *Im Angesicht des Galgens* (München-Gräfelding, 1953), pp. 320–21; cf. Brosse, *op. cit.*, pp. 23–35.
34 *Geh St A*, Ges. B1/1184 no. 126, 20 July 1928. Reichskommisar für Überwachung der öffentlichen Sicherheit und Ordnung reported that 'it has been noticeable for a long time now that in his speeches Hitler is clearly abandoning pure anti-semitism.'
35 I am indebted to Geoffrey Stoakes of the College of Ripon and York, St John's, whose doctoral dissertation (University of Sheffield) on the evolution of Hitler's foreign policy concepts is soon to be published, for the following comments.
36 BA, R43 1/2681. Bericht nach Hitlers persönlichen Ausführungen Ende December 1922, p. 4.
37 BA, NS-26 56, 18 October 1928 at Oldenburg.
38 It is, however, worth noting that during the Czech crisis Hitler was being supplied by Wiedemann with tendentious material on population trends to justify further expansion. BA, NS-10 386 Schmalfuss to Wiedemann.
39 M. Broszat, 'Soziale Motivation und Führer-Bindung des Nationalsozialismus', *VfZG* XVIII (1970), p. 408.
40 For Hitler's woolly thinking on the subject cf. *Hitler's Table Talk* 25 August 1941, 6 August 1942. This inherent contradiction in German plans is recognized by W. Dlugoborski and C. Madaczyk, 'Ausbeutungssysteme in den Besetzten Gebieten Polens und der UdSSR', p. 385 in F. Forstmeier and H-E Volkmann (eds.), *Kriegswirtschaft und Rüstung 1939–1945* (Düsseldorf, 1977).
41 A. Hillgruber, *Hitlers Strategie. Politik und Kriegführung 1940 bis 1941* (Frankfurt a/M, 1965).
42 G. Moltmann, 'Weltherrschaftsideen Hitlers' in O. Brunner and D. Gerhard, *Europa und Übersee. Festschrift für Egmont Zechlin* (Hamburg, 1961).
43 This is one of several important conclusions Geoffrey Stokes has arrived at.
44 J. Thiess, *Architekt der Weltherrschaft. Die 'Endziele' Hitler's* (Düsseldorf, 1976).
45 It should be pointed out that though Hitler did order increases in U boat construction in 1938 he never expected to defeat Britain with a total of 130 U boats. The aim was the modest one of deterring Britain from intervening in Europe; cf. J. Dülffer, *Weimar, Hitler und die Marine. Reichspolitik und Flottenbau 1920–1939* (Düsseldorf, 1973), pp. 548–9.
46 F. Heer, *Der Glaube des Adolf Hitler. Anatomie einer politischen Religiosität* (Munich and Esslingen, 1968), e.g. pp. 85–112.
47 G. M. Gilbert, *Nuremberg Diary* (New York, 1947), p. 351.
48 *Der Bolschewismus von Moses bis Lenin* (München, 1924).
49 *Mein Kampf*, pp. 65, 562.
50 Domarus, *op. cit.* I, p. 570.
51 *ibid.*, I, p. 745.
52 H. Picker, *Hitler's Tischgespräche im Führerhauptquartier* (Stuttgart, 1965), p. 149.
53 Or as he expressed it to leaders of the armaments industry in July 1944: 'Perhaps I am not one of those pious church people, that I am certainly not: but I am a pious person in my deepest being i.e. I believe that whoever fights in this world and never capitulates according to the laws of nature, which a god has created, but who picks himself up again and again and always goes onwards, such a person will not be left in the lurch by the Lawgiver but will receive the blessing of providence in the end:' H. von Kotze and H. Krausnick, *Es spricht der Führer. 7 exemplarische Reden* (Gütersloh, 1966), p. 397.
54 Domarus, *op. cit.*, p. 893.
55 W. Maser, *Adolf Hitler* (London, 1974), p. 175.
56 Speer had a counterpart in the USSR—Aleksandr Viktorovich Shchusev (1873–1949). This architect made his name before the October Revolution as a builder of churches in a medieval style. After the revolution he designed the Lenin Mausoleum. In the 1930s while Speer was replanning Berlin, Shchusev was replanning Moscow adopting the same neo-classical style for much of his work. After the Second World War he was engaged on reconstruction work up to his death. I am indebted to Dr Nikolai Dejevsky for this information.
57 J. Brosse, *Hitler avant Hitler*, p. 133.
58 H. Hoffman, *Hitler was my friend* (London, 1955), p. 184.
59 A. Speer, *Spandauer Tagebücher* (Propyläen, 1975), p. 31.

60   *VB*, 10 January 1939 cf. BA, NS-28 speech on 10 February, 1939.
61   Frank, *op cit.*, p. 320.
62   Waite, *Adolf Hitler the Psychopathic God*, p. 99.
63   Speer, *op cit.*, p. 136.
64   Picker, *op. cit.*, p. 168.
65   *ibid.*, p. 242.
66   Quoted in W. Schüler, *Der Bayreuther Kreis. Wagnerkult und Kulturreform im Geiste völkischer Weltanschauung* (Münster, 1971), p. 197.

Chapter 5

1   But cf. H-D Röhrs, *Hitlers Krankheit. Tatsachen und Legenden* (Neckargemünd, 1966), pp. 114–15.
2   H. Trevor-Roper, *The Last Days of Hitler* (London, 1952).
3   Details in the Morell papers NA, Record Group T-253. David Irving denies that Morell made a large fortune. The most he will concede is that in the event of victory Morell would have made a great deal of money. IFZ D. Irving, 'Hitler and his medicine men' MS part I, pp. 38–9.
4   A strain of coli communis bacillus with the property of colonizing the intestinal tract.
5   The building on the Kehlstein is often confused with the real tea-house within half-an-hour's walk of the Berghof which Hitler continued to visit. This together with the Berghof was totally destroyed after the war.
6   NA, OI/CIR/2, 15 October 1945.
7   This was been recounted in detail in W. Maser, *Hitler* (London, 1973), chapter 8.
8   R. E. Schramm, *Kriegstagebuch des Oberkommandos der Wehrmacht* (Frankfurt a/M, 1961) IV, 2, p. 1701.
9   J. Recktenwald, *Woran hat Adolf Hitler gelitten? Eine neuropsychiatrische Deutung* (München, 1963). This view is shared by W. Backhaus, *Sind die Deutschen verrückt?* (Bergisch Gladbach, 1968); and John H. Walters, 'Hitler's Encephalitis: a Footnote to History', *Journal of Operational Psychiatry* (1975) VI.
10   In fairness it should be noted that in 1953 Hasselbach admitted that paralysis agitans was a possibility. IFZ, ZS 242, p. 6.
11   NA, OI/CIR/4, 29 November 1945. Neurological data (based on examinations in the summer of 1944), pp. 6–9.
12   An 'almost complete' list of the drugs in NA, OI/CIR/4, pp. 11–5. cf. Ernst Günther Schenck report on the drugs prepared in 1969. BA, Kl. Erw. 525.
13   Schenck is critical of only three drugs—ultraseptyl, penicillin-hamma, and mutaflor.
14   Schenck writes in his report, p. 23, that according to the Gehes Codex a patient would have to take over 120 pills daily before he exceeded the prescribed limit. And the possibility of chronic poisoning due to cumulative strychnine effects can be discounted in his opinion.
15   *Mein Kampf*, p. 257.
16   D. M. Kelley, *22 Cells in Nuremberg. A Psychiatrist Examines the Nazi Criminals* (New York, 1947), p. 235.
17   *Mein Kampf*, p. 204.
18   R. Binion, 'Hitler's Concept of *Lebensraum*: the Psychological Basis', *History of Childhood Quarterly*, pp. 189, 203–4.
19   Staatsarchiv München, St Anw. 3099, certificate of Dr Brinsteiner, 19 December 1923.
20   NA, OI/CIR/4, p. 10.
21   *ibid.*, annex VII for ECGs of 14 August 1941, 11 May 1943 and 24 September 1944.
22   R. G. Waite, *Adolf Hitler. The Psychopathic God* (New York, 1977), p. 353. Professor John Pemberton thinks this most unlikely.
23   W. Langer, *The Mind of Adolf Hitler* (London, 1972), p. 17.
24   E. Erikson, 'The Legend of Hitler's Childhood' in *Childhood and Society* (New York, 1950), pp. 329–30; W. Trauher, *Hitler Steiner Schreiber. Ein Beitrag zur Phänomenologie des kranken Geistes* (Emmendingen, 1966), p. II.
25   E. Fromm, *The Anatomy of Human Destructiveness* (New York, 1973), p. 432.
26   Waite, *op. cit.*, p. 356.
27   Dr Gerald Wallen at that time in the Department of Psychiatry at Sheffield University.
28   The personality categories and Dr Wallen's score were—hyperthymic 3, depressive 0; insecure (sensitive and obsessional) 0; fanatic 10; attention-seeking 4; labile 2; explosive 8;

affectionless 7; weak-willed 0; asthentic 0.
29   I am indebted to John Toland for this information from an interview with Dr Giesing C-58 II/T3/SI/24. The half-hour test was conducted by Dr Giesing on 1 October 1944.
30   *Childhood and Society*, pp. 37–8.
31   Alois seems to have beaten his son fairly regularly: NA, Hitler Source Book, pp. 924–30, testimony of William Patrick Hitler; University of Pennsylvania Berchtesgaden interrogations 46 M-13, testimony of Angela Hammitzsch (a half-sister); J. Toland, *Adolf Hitler* (New York, 1976), pp. 12–13.
32   E. Bloch, 'My patient Hitler', *Colliers Magazine* (1941).
33   To show his affection for his mother he intended after the war to erect a tall bell tower in Linz the base of which was to be a mausoleum for the bodies of his parents: NA, Brandt interrogation, p. 10.
34   IFZ Wagener Tagebuch ED 60/2, pp. 525–33 where Hitler discussed the reasons why he felt 'strengthened, refreshed and more alive in the company of young people. It is as if one received from them invisible strength.' And later: 'I have always said that I receive the strength for further work from the gleaming eyes of the young SA,'
35   E. Fromm, *The Anatomy of Human Destructiveness* (New York, 1973).
36   Binion, *op. cit.*, pp. 196–8.
37   In the foreword to J. Brosse, *Hitler avant Hitler. Essai d'interpretation psychoanalique* (Paris, 1972), pp. 378–9.
38   Erikson, *op. cit.*, p. 337. Cf. A and M. Mitscherlich, *Die Unfähigkeit zu trauern* (München, 1967), chapter 4.
39   Hanisch's account in BA, NS-26 41; cf. Maser, *op. cit.*, pp. 47–9; Toland, *op. cit.*, p. 42.
40   Albert Speer testified to the persistence of adolescent attitudes in Hitler. *Inside the Third Reich* (London, 1970), p. 42.
41   Fromm, *op cit.*, p. 370.
42   *Mein Kampf*, p. 163.
43   H. Frank, *Im Angesicht des Galgens. Deutung Hitlers und seiner Zeit auf Grund eigener Erlebnisse und Erkenntnisse* (Neuhaus bei Schliersee, 1955), p. 230.
44   Kelley, *op cit.*, p. 207; cf. Brosse, *op. cit.*, pp. 264–8.
45   F. Wiedemann, *Der Mann der Feldherr werden wollte* (Velbert, 1964), p. 26.
46   It has been observed that these young men, whether front-line soldiers or not, acquired from military service only the habit of external obedience and a willingness to die bravely. What they lacked was the sense of moral restraint as well as the intellectual stamina of the old Prussian professional soldier. They remained amateurs imbued with the civil war mentality in which brother kills brother fanatically and ferociously and gives no quarter: cf. A. Krebs, *Tendenzen und Gestalten der NSDAP* (Stuttgart, 1969), p. 209.
47   W. McDougall, *The Group Mind* (London, 1920); G. Le Bon, *The crowd: a Study of the Popular Mind* (London, 1921); S. Freud, *Group Psychology and the Analysis of the Ego* (London, 1948).
48   Freud, *op cit.*, p. 80.
49   H. Schacht, *Account Settled* (London, 1949), p. 206.
50   *Adolf Hitler: a Family Perspective* (Psychology Press, 1976).
51   Cf. Le Bon's comment *op. cit.*, p. 117 on the magical power of words to move a group of people: 'Reason and argument are incapable of combating certain words and formulas. They are uttered with solemnity in the presence of groups and as soon as they have been pronounced, an expression of respect is visible on every countenance and all heads are bowed. By many they are considered as natural forces, as supernatural powers.'
52   W. Reich, *The Mass Psychology of Fascism* (Frome and London, 1970).
53   *ibid.*, pp. 54–5.
54   E. Fromm, *Escape from Freedom* (New York, 1941), pp. 163–4.
55   *ibid.*, p. 221.
56   T. W. Adorno etc., *The Authoritarian Personality* (New York, 1950).
57   P. Loewenberg, 'The Unsuccessful Adolescence of Heinrich Himmler' *AHR* (1971) LXXVI; 'The Psychological Origins of the Nazi Youth Cohort', *AHR* (1971) LXXVI; Henry V. Dicks, *Licensed Mass Murder. A Sociopsychological Study of Some SS Killers* (London, 1972).
58   A. and M. Mitscherlich, *Die Unfähigkeit zu trauern* (München, 1967).
59   'the cultural outlook of the employee'.
60   P. Merkl, *Political Violence under the Swastika. 581 Early Nazis* (Princeton, 1975). Cf. T. Abel, *The Nazi Movement: why Hitler Came to Power* (New York, 1966).

61 *ibid.*, p. 772–3.
62 BA, NS-26 513, Kampferlebnisse der alten Garde der NSDAP. Use has been made of part of this collection by Henry V. Dicks, *op. cit.,* pp. 74–86.
63 H-U Wehler, 'Zum Verhältnis von Geschichtswissenschaft und Psychoanalyse' *HZ* (1969) p. 208.
64 E. Deuerlein, *Hitler Eine politische Biographie* (Augsburg, 1969): 'a historical situation did not exactly create him but made him possible,' p. 62.

Bibliography

Unpublished primary material

BUNDESARCHIV KOBLENZ:
NS 26 Hauptarchiv der NSDAP: 2, 4, 11, 12, 16, 17a, 46, 51–62, 79, 106.
NS 10 Adjutantur: 29, 35, 36, 37, 89, 115, 199, 253, 386.
Kl.Erw. 525 David Irving collection.
Nachlass Krebs.

BUNDESARCHIV-MILITÄRARCHIV FREIBURG:
Nachlässe Jodl, Keitel, Zeitzler.
KTB der SKL.

BAYERISCHES STAATSARCHIV MÜNCHEN:
Akten der Staatsanwaltschaft: 3099, 3101, 3112.
Polizeidirektion München: PD 6698, 6708.

BAYERISCHES GEHEIMES STAATSARCHIV MÜNCHEN:
MA 103472, 103473 (Hitler Putsch); 103476.
MA 102138 Kreisregierungen reports Oberbayern 1930–32.

STADTARCHIV MÜNCHEN:
Local newspaper cuttings 1921–33.

INSTITUT FÜR ZEITGESCHICHTE MÜNCHEN:
Otto Wagener Aufzeichnungen, 35 Notebooks with ergänzende
   Aufzeichnungen.
Zeugenschriften: ZS 194, 242, 313, 680, 1479, 2235, 2239.
Völkischer Beobachter selected years.

NATIONAL ARCHIVES WASHINGTON:
Interrogation reports of Hitler's doctors 01/CIR/2, 01/CIR/4.
OSS Hitler Source Book.

UNIVERSITY OF PENNSYLVANIA LIBRARY, PHILADELPHIA:
Interrogation reports of George Allen 46 M-7 to 26.

Printed primary sources

N. H. BAYNES (ed.), *The Speeches of Adolf Hitler. August 1922–August 1939*
   (London, 1942), 2 vols.

W. BOELCKE (ed.), *Deutschlands Rüstung im Zweiten Weltkrieg. Hitlers Konferenzen mit Albert Speer 1942–1945* (Frankfurt a/M, 1969). The stenographic reports of Speer's conferences with Hitler.

E. BOEPPLE (ed.), *Adolf Hitlers Reden* (München, 1934).

E. DEUERLEIN (ed.), *Der Hitler Putsch. Bayrische Dokumenten zum 8/9 November 1923* (Stuttgart, 1963). A major documentary collection on the 1923 putsch but with little commentary.

M. DOMARUS (ed.), *Hitlers Reden und Proklamationen 1932–1945* (Würzburg, 1962–3), 2 vols.

D. EICHHOLTZ and W. SCHUMAN (eds.), *Anatomie des Krieges. Neue Dokumente über die Rolle des deutschen Monopolkapitals bei der Vorbereitung und Durchführung des zweiten Weltkrieges* (Berlin, 1969).

'Führer conference on naval affairs 1939–1945', *Brassey's Naval Annual* (New York, 1948), pp. 25–496.

F. GENOUD (ed.), *The Testament of Adolf Hitler. The Hitler-Bormann Documents February–April 1945* (London, 1960).

H. J. GORDON (ed.), *The Hitler Trial before the Peoples' Court in Munich* (New York, 1977), 3 vols. The first translation in English and the first to include the secret sessions.

H. HEIBER (ed.), *Hitlers Lagebesprechungen. Die Protokollfragmente seiner militärischen Konferenzen 1942–1945* (Stuttgart, 1962). Only 900 pages of the stenographic reports have survived but sufficient to convey a vivid impression of the cut and thrust of argument at the daily war conferences.

A. HILLGRUBER (ed.), *Staatsmänner und Diplomaten bei Hitler. Vertrauliche Aufzeichnungen über die Unterredungen mit Vertretern des Auslandes 1939–1941* (Frankfurt a/M, 1967–70), 2 vols.

R. HOCHHUTH (ed.), *Joseph Goebbels Tagebücher 1945. Die letzten Aufzeichungen* (Hamburg, 1977). Apparently genuine fragments of the Goebbels diary for April 1945.

W. HUBATSCH (ed.), *Hitlers Weisungen für die Kriegsführung 1939–1945. Dokumente des Oberkommandos der Wehrmacht* (Frankfurt a/M, 1962). Hitler's directives for the conduct of the war.

H-A JACOBSEN (ed.) *Kriegstagebuch des Oberkommandos der Wehrmacht (Wehrmacht-führungsstab) 1940–1941* (Frankfurt a/M, 1961–5), 4 vols. The war diary of the OKW.

H-A JACOBSEN and W. JOCHMANN (eds.), *Ausgewählte Dokumente zur Geschichte des Nationalsozialismus 1933—1945* (Bielefeld, 1961).

H-A JACOBSEN (ed.), *Generaloberst Halder: Kriegstagebuch. Tägliche Aufzeichnungen des Chefs des Generalstabes des Heeres 1939–1942* (Stuttgart, 1962–4), 3 vols. The diary of the chief of army general staff 1938–42.

LOUIS P. LOCHNER (ed.), *The Goebbels Diaries 1942–3* (London, 1948).

R. MANHEIM (ed.), *Mein Kampf* (Boston, 1943). One of several translations.

W. MASER (ed.), *Hitlers Briefe und Notizen. Sein Weltbild in handschriftlichen Dokumenten* (Düsseldorf, 1973).

Nazi Conspiracy and Aggression (Washington, 1946–8), 10 vols. An important documentary collection supplementing the IMT collection.

J. NOAKES and G. PRIDHAM (eds.), *Documents on Nazism 1919–1945* (London, 1974).

R. SCHUMAN and A. HILLGRUBER (eds.), *Hitlers Tischgespräche im Führerhauptquartier 1941–1942* (Stuttgart, 1963). The most reliable version.

Trial of the Major War Criminals before the International Military Tribunal (Nuremberg, 1947–9) *42 vols.*

A. TYRELL (ed.). *Führer befiehlt ... Selbstzeugnisse aus der Kampfzeit der NSDAP. Dokumentation und Analyse* (Düsseldorf, 1969).

G. WAGNER (ed.), *Lagevorträge des Oberbefehlhabers der Kriegsmarine vor Hitler 1935–1945* (München, 1972). Raeder's reports to Hitler and his comments.

G. L. WEINBERG (ed.), *Hitlers Secret Book* (New York, 1962).

Memoirs

Of the very many reminiscences that have appeared the following are the most informative:

W. BROS, *Gespräche mit Hermann Goering während des Nürnberger Prozesses (Flensburg, 1950).*

H. FRANK, *Im Angesicht des Galgens. Deutung Hitlers und seiner Zeit auf Grund eigener Erlebnisse und Erkenntnisse* (Neuhaus b. Schliersee, 1955).

J. GOEBBELS, *Vom Kaiserhof zur Reichskanzlei. Eine historische Darstellung in Tagebuchblättern vom 1 January 1932–1 May 1933* (München, 1940).

E. HANFSTAENGL, *Zwischen Weissem und Braunem Haus* (München, 1970).

A. KREBS, *Tendenzen und Gestalten in der NSDAP. Erinnerungen an die Frühzeit der Partei* (Stuttgart, 1959).

B. VON SCHIRACH, *Ich glaubte an Hitler* (Hamburg, 1967).

P. SCHMIDT, *Statist auf diplomatischer Bühne 1923–1945. Erlebnisse eines Chefdolmetschers im Auswärtigen Amt mit den Staatsmännern Euopas* (Bonn, 1950).

A. SPEER, *Inside the Third Reich* (London, 1970).

A. SPEER, *Spandau: the Secret Diaries* (London, 1976).

F. WIEDEMANN, *Der Mann der Feldherr werden wollte. Erlebnisse und Erfahrungen des Vorgesetzten Hitlers im I Weltkrieg und seines späteren persönlichen Adjutanten* (Velbert, 1966).

H. ZOLLER, *Hitler privat. Erlebnisbericht seiner Geheimsekretärin* (Düsseldorf, 1949).

Secondary sources

This does not pretend to be an exhaustive list of all the books consulted. It seemed much more sensible to indiate only works which I found particularly helpful and also to arrange them by chapter for the convenience of the reader.

Works of general importance
A. BULLOCK, *Hitler: a study in tyranny* (London, 1963).
E. DEUERLEIN, *Hitler. Eine politische Biographie* (Augsburg, 1969).
J. FEST, *Hitler* (London, 1974).
J. TOLAND, *Adolf Hitler* (New York, 1976).

G. SCHULZ, *Aufstieg des Nationalsozialismus. Krise und Revolution in Deutschland* (Frankfurt a/M, Berlin, 1973).

W. LAQUEUER (ed.), *Fascism. A Reader's Guide. Analysis, Interpretations, Bibliography* (California, 1976).

Chapter 1

On Hitler's oratory an excellent introductory essay is H. VON KOTZE and H. KRAUSNICK (eds.), *Es spricht der Führer. Sieben exemplarische Reden* (Gütersloh, 1966). Four important books on the pseudo-religious basis of Nazism are H-J. GAMM, *Der braune Kult. Das dritte Reich und seine Ersatzreligion.* (Hamburg, 1962); D. GRIESWELLE, *Propaganda der Friedlosigkeit. Eine Studie in Hitlers Rhetorik, 1920—1933* (Stuttgart, 1972); G. G. MOSSE, *The Nationalization of the Masses. Political Symbolism and Mass Movements in Germany from the Napoleonic Wars through the Third Reich* (New York, 1975); K. VONDUNG, *Magie und Manipulation. Ideologischer Kult und politische Religion des Nationalsozialismus* (Göttingen, 1971).

For the beginning of Hitler's political career see W. MASER, *Die Frühgeschichte der NSDAP: Hitlers Weg bis 1924* (Bonn, Frankfurt, 1965) and G. FRANZ-WILLING, *Die Hitlerbewegung: Der Ursprung 1919–1922* (Hamburg, Berlin, 1962). Excellent on the Munich background is H. AUERBACH, 'Hitlers politische Lehrjahre und die Münchener Gesellschaft 1919–1923' *VfZG* (1977).

On the Putsch see H-H HOFMANN, *Der Hitler Putsch. Krisenjahre deutscher Geschichte 1920–1924* (München, 1961) and J. GORDON, *Hitler and the Beer Hall Putsch* (Princeton, 1972). A seminal work analysing Hitler's changing role in the 1920s is A. TYRELL, *Vom 'Trommler' zum 'Führer'. Der Wandel von Hitlers Selbstverstandnis zwischen 1919 und 1924 und die Entwicklung der NSDAP* (München, 1975).

The function of charisma in the Nazi Party has been examined by J. NYOMARKAY, *Charisma and Factionalism in the Nazi Party* (Minneapolis, 1967).

Of the studies on the growth of the Nazi Party in various regions J. NOAKES, *The Nazi party in Lower Saxony 1921–1933* (Oxford, 1971) is quite excellent. For the early 1930s when the Nazis became a mass party see W. S. ALLEN, *The Nazi Seizure of Power: the Experience of a Single German Town from 1930–1935* (London, 1966). Indispensable for this period are K. D. BRACHER, *Die Auflösung der Weimarer Republik* (4th edn., Villingen 1964) and K. D. BRACHER, *Die nationalsozialistische Machtergreifung. Studien zur Errichtung des totalitären Herrschaftssystems in Deutschland 1933/34* (2nd edn., Köln Opladen, 1962).

Chapter 2

The administrative history of the Third Reich has attracted much attention in recent years. The main works are R. BOLLMUS, *Das Amt Rosenberg und seine Gegner. Studien zum Machtkampf im nationalsozialistischen Herrschaftssystem* (Stuttgart, 1970); M. BROSZAT, *Der Staat Hitlers. Grundlegung und Entwicklung seiner inneren Verfassung* (München, 1969); P. DIEHL-THIELE, *Partei und Staat im Dritten Reich. Untersuchungen zum*

Verhältnis von NSDAP und allgemeiner innerer Staatsverwaltung (München, 1969); E. N. PETERSON, *The Limits of Hitler's Power* (Princeton, 1969). On the *Gauleiters* see P. HÜTTENBERGER, *Die Gauleiter. Studien zum Wandel des Machtgefüges in der NSDAP* (Stuttgart, 1969).

Two substantial works on the history of the Nazi Party are: W. HORN, *Führerideologie und Parteiorganisation in der NSDAP (1919–1933)* (Düsseldorf, 1972) and D. ORLOW, *The History of the Nazi Party 1933–1945* (Pittsburg, 1973), 2 vols.

Foreign policy has been written about more than any other aspect of the Third Reich. Books useful in attempting to determine the extent of Hitler's influence are A. HILLGRUBER, *Deutschlands Rolle in der Vorgeschichte der beiden Weltkriege* (Göttingen, 1967) and *Kontinuität und Diskontinuität in der deutschen Aussenpolitik von Bismarck bis Hitler* (Düsseldorf, 1971); K. HILDEBRAND, *Deutsche Aussenpolitik 1933–1945. Kalkül oder Dogma?* (Stuttgart, 1971). For the influence of party organizations on foreign policy see H-A JACOBSEN, *Nationalsozialistische Aussenpolitik 1933–1938* (Frankfurt, Berlin, 1968). The role of military planning is discussed in E. M. ROBERTSON, *Hitler's Pre-war Policy and Military Plans 1933–1939* (London, 1963) and G. MEINCK, *Hitler und die deutsche Aufrüstung 1933–1937* (Wiesbaden, 1959). For 1933–4 see G. WOLLSTEIN, *Vom Weimarer Revisionismus zu Hitler* (Bonn, 1973). On Austria D. ROSS, *Hitler und Dollfuss. Die Deutsche Österreichpolitik 1933–1934* (Hamburg, 1966). For the Anglo-German Naval Convention and naval policy generally see J. DÜLFFER'S excellent *Weimar Hitler und die Marine. Reichspolitik und Flottenbau 1920–1939* (Düsseldorf, 1973). The Spanish connection is examined in W. SCHIEDER and C. DIPPER, *Der spanische Bürgerkrieg in der internationalen Politik (1936–1939)* (München, 1976). For the origins of the axis see J. PETERSEN, *Hitler-Mussolini. Die Entstehung der Achse Berlin-Rom 1933–1936* (Tübingen, 1973). R. M. SMELSER examines the role of improvization in German policy in *The Sudeten Problem 1933–1938. Volkstumpolitik and the Formulation of Nazi Foreign Policy* (Middletown, 1975). An indispensable symposium for the 1930s is M. FUNKE (ed.), *Hitler Deutschland und die Mächte. Materialien zur Aussenpolitik des Dritten Reiches* (Düsseldorf, 1976).

The economic history of the Third Reich has become a growth area in recent years. A useful survey is D. PETZINA, *Die Deutsche Wirtschaft in der Zwischenkriegszeit* (Wiesbaden, 1977). Also good is G. HALLGARTEN and J. Radkau, *Deutsche Industrie und Politik von Bismarck bis heute* (Frankfurt a/M, 1974). Two important symposia are F. FORSTMEIER and H-E VOLKMANN (eds.), *Wirtschaft und Rüstung am Vorabend des Zweiten Weltkrieges* (Düsseldorf, 1975) and *Kriegswirtschaft und Rüstung 1939–1945* (Düsseldorf, 1977). Important monographs are B. CARROLL, *Total War: Arms and Economics in the Third Reich* (Hague, Paris, 1968); D. EICHHOLTZ, *Geschichte der deutschen Kriegswirtschaft 1939–1945* (Berlin, 1969) vol. I; A. MILWARD, *The German Economy at War* (London, 1965); and A. SCHWEITZER, *Big Business in the Third Reich* (London, 1964). On the reaction of the working class to the regime, T. MASON, *Arbeiterklasse und Volksgemeinschaft Dokumente und Materialen zur deutschen Arbeiterpolitik 1936–1939* (Opladen, 1975) is a major pioneering work.

Nothing definitive has been written about the role of industry in the Third

Reich. H. A. Turner, *Faschismus und Kapitalismus in Deutschland. Studien zum Verhältnis zwischen Nationalsozialismus and Wirtschaft* (Göttingen, 1972) argues that Hitler deceived industry. For the view that industry knew very well what it was doing cf. R. Kühnl and G. Hardach (eds.), *Die Zerstörung der Weimarer Republik* (Köln, 1977); with a rather different emphasis N. Kadritzke, *Faschismus und Krise. Zum Verhältnis von Politik und Ökonomie im Nationalsozialismus* (Frankfurt a/M, 1976). A most useful survey of the problem in E. Hennig. *Bürgerliche Gesellschaft und Faschismus in Deutschland. Ein Forschungsbericht* (Frankfurt a/M, 1977).

A considerable literature exists on the treatment of the Jews by the Nazis. The best accounts in the older literature are G. Reitlinger, *Die Endlösung. Hitlers Versuch der Ausrottung der Juden Europas 1939–1945* (Berlin, 1956) and R. Hilberg, *The Destruction of the European Jews* (Chicago, 1961). A first-rate analysis is U. D. Adam, *Judenpolitik im Dritten Reich* (Düsseldorf, 1972), a view largely accepted by M. Broszat, 'Hitler und die Genesis der Endlösung' *VfZG* (1977) IV. A DDR symposium is K. Drobisch, R. Goguel, W. Müller, *Juden unterm Hakenkreuz Verfolgung und Ausrottung* (Frankfurt, 1973). The early persecution is studied in K. Pätzold, *Faschismus Rassenwahn Judenverfolgung. Eine Studie zur politischen Strategie und Taktik des faschistischen deutschen Imperialismus 1933–1935* (Berlin, 1975). On the economic aspect of the persecution H. Genschel, *Die Verdrängung der Juden aus der Wirtschaft im Dritten Reich* (Göttingen).

Chapter 3
The most recent general account is D. Irving, *Hitler's War* (London, 1977) bringing some new material. A useful general essay in P. Schramm, *Hitler the Man and the Military Leader* (London, 1972).

Hitler's relations with the army are discussed in R. J. O'Neill *The German Army and the Nazi Party 1933–1939* (London, 1966); M. Messerschmidt, *Die Wehrmacht im NS-Staat* (Hamburg, 1969); and K-J Müller, *Das Heer und Hitler. Armee und nationalsozialistisches Regime 1933–1940* (Stuttgart, 1969). Valuable is W. Warlimont, *Inside Hitler's Headquarters* (London, 1964).

For the navy M. Salewski, *Die deutsche Seekriegsleitung 1939–1945* (Frankfurt a/M, 1970–73), 3 vols is based on the KTB der SKL. Useful for the air force is D. Irving, *The Rise and fall of the Luftwaffe* (London, 1974) based on the Milch papers.

On the planning of the western campaign, H-A Jacobsen, *Fall Gelb. Der Kampf um den deutschen Operationsplan zur Westoffensive* (Wiesbaden, 1957). The attempt to invade Britain is examined in K. Klee, *Das Unternehmen Seelöwe* (Göttingen, 1958). An important study is A. Hillgruber, *Hitlers Strategie Politik and Kriegführung 1940–1941* (Frankfurt a/M, 1963) for the analysis of Hitler's plans and the 'two-stage' theory.

For the Mediterranean theatre of war see W. Baum and E. Weichold, *Der Krieg der Achsenmächte im Mittelmeerraum. Die 'Strategie' der Diktatoren* (Göttingen, 1973). The planning of Barbarossa is the theme of B. Leach, *German Strategy against Russia 1939–1941* (Oxford, 1973), a fine book. On German strategy 1941–2 quite excellent is K. Reinhardt, *Die Wende vor*

Moskau. Das Scheitern der Strategie Hitlers im Winter 1941/2 (Stuttgart, 1972). On Stalingrad M. Kehrig, *Stalingrad Analyse und Dokumentation einer Schlacht* (Stuttgart, 1974). The Ardennes campaign is studied in H. Jung, *Die Ardennes Offensive 1944/45* (Stuttgart, 1971) and P. Elstob, *Hitler's Last Offensive* (London, 1970). H. Trevor-Roper, *The Last Days of Hitler* (London, 1947) still cannot be bettered.

Chapter 4
(References to works on psychohistory have been collected together in the final chapter).

Hitler's philosophy of life has been analysed by E. Jäckel, *Hitlers Weltanschauung. Grundriss einer Herrschaft* (Tübingen, 1969). On the ideological background G. L. Mosse, *The Crisis of German Ideology. Intellectual Origins of the Third Reich* (London, 1966). Good on racialism and Social Darwinism is P. von zur Mühlen, *Rassenideologien. Geschichte und Hintergründe* (Berlin, 1977). The latest work on Schönerer is A. G. Whiteside, *The Socialism of Fools. Georg Ritter von Schönerer und Austrian PanGermanism* (California, 1975). For the Pan-Germans in the Reich see A. Kruck, *Geschichte des Alldeutschen Verbandes 1890–1939* (Wiesbaden, 1954), the standard work.

On the modernization controversy D. Schoenbaum, *Hitler's Social Revolution. Class and Status in Nazi Germany 1933–1939* (New York, 1966) and H. A. Turner, 'Fascism and Modernization', *World Politics* XXIV (1972) are both in favour.

On the background to anti-semitism P. G. Pulzer, *The Rise of Political Anti-semitism in Germany and Austria* (New York, 1964). For Rosenberg's influence on Hitler see R. Cecil, *The Myth of the Master Race: Alfred Rosenberg and Nazi Ideology* (London, 1972).

The *Lebensraum* question is discussed in an excellent study by J. E. Farquharson, *The Plough and the Swastika: the NSDAP and Agriculture in Germany 1928–1945* (London, 1976). An important article is M. Broszat, 'Soziale Motivation und Führer-Bindung der NS Bewegung', *VfZG* (1970).

Basic to the discussion of whether Hitler had world ambitions is A. Hillgruber, *Hitlers Strategie. Politik und Kriegführung 1940–1941* (Frankfurt a/M, 1965). Hillgruber's thesis is developed by K. Hildebrand, *Vom Reich zum Weltreich. Hitler NSDAP und koloniale Frage 1919–1945* (München, 1969). Stimulating if rather overdone is J. Thiess, *Architekt der Weltherrschaft. Die 'Endziele' Hitlers* (Düsseldorf, 1976).

On Hitler's religious views F. Heer, *Der Glaube des Adolf Hitler. Anatomie einer politischen Religiosität* (München, Esslingen, 1968) stresses the Catholic-Austrian elements.

For Hitler's architectural interests A. Speer, *Inside the Third Reich* is indispensable. Also B. Miller Lane, *Architecture and Politics in Germany 1919–1945* (Cambridge, Mass. 1968); R. R. Taylor, *The Word in Stone: the Role of Architecture in the National Socialist Ideology* (Berkeley, Los Angeles, London, 1974) and J. Thiess, *op. cit.*

On the Wagner connection in general W. Schüler, *Der Bayreuther Kreis Wagnerkult und Kulturreform im Geiste völkischer Weltanschauung* (Münster, 1971).

Chapter 5
On Hitler's health there is no definitive work. The most detailed and carefully documented analysis is D. IRVING, 'Hitler and his Medicine Men', IFZ MS which appeared as a series of articles in *Stern* in 1969. W. MASER, *Hitler* (London, 1973) has a chapter on the subject. For varying diagnoses of his condition see D. M. KELLEY, *22 Cells in Nuremberg: a Psychiatrist Examines the Nazi Criminals* (New York, 1947); J. RECKTENWALD, *Woran hat Adolf Hitler gelitten? Eine neuropsychiatrische Deutung* (München, 1963); H-D RÖHRS, *Hitlers Krankheit Tatsachen und Legenden* (Neckargemünd, 1966).

The speculative literature on Hitler's mental state continues to grow. The most important works are: J. BROSSE, *Hitler avant Hitler. Essai d'interpretation psychoanalique* (Paris, 1972); E. FROMM, *The Anatomy of Human Destructiveness* (New York, 1973); W. LANGER, *The Mind of Adolf Hitler: the Secret Wartime Report* (New York, 1972); J. M. McRANDLE, *The Track of the Wolf: essays on National Socialism and its Leader Adolf Hitler* (Evanston, 1965); H. Stierlin, *Adolf Hitler: a Family Perspective* (New York, 1976); R. G. L. WAITE, *Adolf Hitler the Psychopathic God* (New York, 1977).

The best account of Hitler's early years is BRADLEY F. SMITH, *Adolf Hitler: his Family, Childhood and Youth* (Palo Alto, Calif., 1967). Accounts to be used with care are A. KUBIZEK, *The Young Hitler I Knew* (Boston, 1955) and F. JETZINGER, *Hitler's Youth* (London, 1958).

One of the best introductions to psychohistory is B. WOLMAN (ed.), *The Psychoanalytical Interpretation of History* (New York 1971). Also the June 1975 number of the *Journal of Modern History* devoted exclusively to the present state of research.

Books which are helpful in relating Hitler's personal pathology to the collective pathology of the German people include R. BINION, *Hitler among the Germans* (New York, 1976); E. FROMM, *Escape from Freedom* (New York, 1966); A. and M. MITSCHERLICH, *Die Unfähigkeit zu trauern* (München, 1967); W. REICH, *The Mass Psychology of Fascism* (Frome, London, 1973).

Special mention must be made of P. MERKL, *Political Violence under the Swastika: 581 early Nazis* (Princeton, 1975) which shows what use can be made of the computer in investigating Nazi attitudes. Much of the material used by Merkl was first published by T. ABEL, *Why Hitler Came into Power: an Answer based on the Original Life Stories of Six Hundred of His Followers* (New York, 1938).

INDEX